HOUSING, TENANCY AND PLANNING LAW Made Simple

The Made Simple Series
has been created
especially for self-education
but can equally well
be used as
an aid to group study.
However complex the subject,
the reader is taken
step by step,
clearly and methodically,
through the course. Each volume
has been prepared by experts,
taking account of
modern educational requirements,
to ensure the most
effective way of
acquiring knowledge.

In the same series

Accounting	French
Acting and Stagecraft	Geology
Additional Mathematics	German
Administration in Business	Housing, Tenancy and Planning
Advertising	Law
Anthropology	Human Anatomy
Applied Economics	Human Biology
Applied Mathematics	Italian
Applied Mechanics	Journalism
Art Appreciation	Latin
Art of Speaking	Law
Art of Writing	Management
Biology	Marketing
Book-keeping	Mathematics
British Constitution	Modern Biology
Business and Administrative	Modern Electronics
Organisation	Modern European History
Business Economics	New Mathematics
Business Statistics and Accounting	Office Practice
Calculus	Organic Chemistry
Chemistry	Personnel Management
Childcare	Philosophy
Commerce	Photography
Company Law	Physical Geography
Computer Programming	Physics
Computers and Microprocessors	Practical Typewriting
Cookery	Psychiatry
Cost and Management Accounting	Psychology
Data Processing	Rapid Reading
Dressmaking	Retailing
Economic History	Russian
Economic and Social Geography	Salesmanship
Economics	Secretarial Practice
Effective Communication	Social Services
Electricity	Sociology
Electronic Computers	Spanish
Electronics	Statistics
English	Transport and Distribution
English Literature	Twentieth-Century British History
Export	Typing
Financial Management	Woodwork

HOUSING, TENANCY AND PLANNING LAW Made Simple

A. J. Lomnicki, DrIur, LLM

Made Simple Books
HEINEMANN: London

Printed and bound in Great Britain
by Richard Clay (The Chaucer Press), Ltd., Bungay, Suffolk
for the publishers William Heinemann Ltd.,
10 Upper Grosvenor Street, London W1X 9PA

SBN 434 98481 7 casebound
SBN 434 98487 6 paperbound

Preface

This book deals in three parts with the most vital legal subjects pertaining to the use of land—namely, the law of housing, of landlord and tenant, and of town and country planning. It is designed to meet the needs of students preparing for professional examinations, or reading for degrees in estate management, planning, architecture or allied disciplines. It is also intended as a quick reference guide for those already in professional practice and as a 'refresher' in view of the substantial recent changes in the law. Further, it is hoped that anyone who is interested in restrictions in the use of land may find this book an interesting and useful exposition.

It is not an easy task to present these subjects in a simple manner. One judge (Lord Justice Harman in the case of Davy v. Leeds Corporation, 1964, deciding the problem of compensation for land compulsorily acquired) has stated: 'To reach a conclusion in this matter involved the Court in wading through a monstrous legislative morass, staggering from stone to stone and ignoring the marsh gas exhaling from the forest of schedules lining the way on each side!' Nevertheless, great care has been taken to make this book readable and understandable even for a reader without a legal background and to avoid legal jargon as far as possible.

I am indebted to my colleagues at the Polytechnic of the South Bank for their advice and counsel, to my daughter, Eva Lomnicka, MA, LLB, of the Middle Temple, Barrister, lecturer in laws at King's College, London, who read the manuscript and made numerous suggestions, and to Robert Postema, publisher of Made Simple Books, for his help and advice in the presentation of the text. I am, of course, fully responsible for any shortcomings which the book may still contain.

I have endeavoured to state the law as it was on January 1, 1981. Thus important changes in housing, landlord and tenant and planning law introduced by the Housing Act, 1980, and by the Local Government, Planning and Land Act, 1980, as well as by statutory instruments issued up to the end of 1980, have been included.

One important statutory instrument concerning town and country planning law has been amended. On February 27, 1981, the Parliamentary Under-Secretary of the Department of the Environment issued two statutory instruments reducing planning control over minor developments by amending the General Development Order 1977. These statutory instruments are outlined in Appendix 1.

A. J. LOMNICKI
Polytechnic of the South Bank
London

Contents

PART 2. LANDLORD AND TENANT LAW

PART 3. TOWN AND COUNTRY PLANNING

PART 1
HOUSING LAW AND RELATED ORGANISATIONS

1

THE SCOPE OF HOUSING LAW AND ADMINISTERING AUTHORITIES

1.1 The Scope of Housing Law

Housing law (in the system of English administrative law) has a somewhat narrower meaning than the layman may suppose. In general terms, housing law deals with housing conditions and the duties of local authorities in the housing field. However, this definition requires some qualifications. Thus Building Regulations are considered to be a part of public health law and not housing law, as they are issued under s. 4 of the *Public Health Act, 1961*. Similarly, landlord and tenant law—protecting tenants against excessive rent or abitrary eviction—is not considered a part of housing law as such, and for this reason will be dealt with in Part 2 of this book.

Housing legislation is progressive, ever changing and developing and not free from political colour. The principal Act still in force is the *Housing Act, 1957*. This has been amended on several occasions by the *Housing Acts, 1961, 1964, 1969*, by the *Housing (Amendment) Act, 1973*, by the very important *Housing Act, 1974*, by the *Housing (Homeless Persons) Act, 1977*, and by the *Housing Act, 1980*. Nevertheless, the *Housing Act, 1957*, remains the principal Act.

These Acts have been supplemented by two separate Acts dealing mostly with financial matters—namely, the *Housing (Financial Provisions) Act, 1958*, and the *Housing Finance Act, 1972*—although the Housing Acts mentioned above also deal with financial matters.

A brief note about the new towns legislation is also included. The *New Towns Act, 1965*, consolidated the earlier Acts and is now the principal Act.

1.2 Administering Authorities

The general supervision of local housing authorities is in the hands of the Secretary of State for the Environment, acting through the Minister of Housing and Local Government.

Local authorities were reorganised by the *Local Government Act, 1972*, which came into operation on April 1, 1974. Under this Act, England (apart from Greater London) is divided into six metropolitan and 39 non-metropolitan counties. The metropolitan counties are: Greater Manchester, Merseyside, South Yorkshire, Tyne and Wear, West Midland and West Yorkshire. The metropolitan and non-metropolitan counties are divided into 332 districts (s. 1 of the *Local Government Act, 1972*, and Schedule 1). Wales is divided into eight counties and 37 districts (Schedule 4 to the *Local Government Act, 1972*).

Housing authorities are the district councils, but in London the responsibility is divided between the Greater London Council and the London boroughs.

3

The London boroughs are responsible for the whole range of housing; the Greater London Council may exercise powers under Part V of the *Housing Act, 1957*, i.e. the provision of housing accommodation. County councils outside London also have limited powers in regard to the provision of houses.

2

INDIVIDUAL HOUSES

Note: All references in this chapter are to the *Housing Act, 1957*, unless otherwise stated.

2.1 Powers of Local Authorities in Respect of Houses Unfit for Human Habitation

S. 3 imposes on every local authority a duty to inspect their district in order
to ascertain whether all houses within its area are fit for human habitation.
In addition, it is the duty of the Medical Officer of Health to make
official representation if any house is found to be unfit for human habitation.
In practice, local authorities take advantage of any source of information to
learn about unfit houses within their area. In addition to the powers outlined
below in respect of houses unfit for human habitation, the local authorities
may take the actions described not only if the house is unfit for human
habitation, but also if it is in 'substantial disrepair' and may be repaired at
reasonable expense (s. 9A introduced by the *Housing Act, 1969*).

Unfitness for human habitation is defined in s. 4 (as amended by the *Housing
Act, 1969*) and in ss. 5 and 18. S. 4 provides that in determining whether a
house is unfit for human habitation regard shall be had to its condition with
regard to the following, and only the following, matters:

repair;
stability;
freedom from damp;
internal arrangement;
natural lighting;
ventilation;
water supply;
drainage and sanitary convenience;
facilities for preparation and cooking of food and for the disposal of waste
water.

Only the above aspects should be taken into account, but defects in any
of these matters do not render the house automatically unfit. They only do
so if the house is so defective that it is not reasonably suitable for occupation
in that condition.

It is a matter of degree whether any defect enumerated in s. 4 makes the
house really unfit. In one case (*Summer v. Salford Corporation*, 1943) even a
defective window (the sash cord of the window was broken) was accepted as
rendering the house unfit. In this case the judge said: 'Since the only window
in one of the two bedrooms in the house could not be opened or could only
be opened with the risk of injury to the person opening it, the home was not
in all respects reasonably fit for human habitation.'

5

In addition, s. 5 states that it is now unlawful to erect back-to-back houses, but those erected before 1909 were lawfully erected and are still in use.

Under s. 18 basement rooms (i.e. rooms whose floor surface is more than three feet below the level of the adjoining street) are deemed to be unfit for human habitation unless the average height of the room is at least 7 feet; in addition, the local authority may prescribe regulations for securing proper ventilation and lighting of such rooms and protection against dampness, effluvia or exhalation.

The person who is responsible for the state of the house and with whom the local authority deals, is the person 'having control of the house'. This means the person receiving the rack rent, or who would receive it if the house were let. (Rack rent is a rent not less than two thirds of the rateable value of the house.) Thus the owner-occupier or landlord is the person having control, but not the freeholder of long leases where only a nominal ground rent is paid. Here it is the leaseholder who is in control of the house.

If the local authority finds that a house is unfit for human habitation it has to consider, in the first instance, whether the house 'is capable of being rendered fit for human habitation at a reasonable expense' or not. If it is, the procedure is simple. The local authority serves on the person having control of the house a **repair notice**, specifying the work which must be done within a reasonable time (not less than 21 days) and stating that after these repairs are done, the house will be fit for human habitation. Another notice may be served only if new defects arise in the house.

No penalty is provided for non non-compliance with the repair notice, but the local authority may do the work themselves and it is an offence to prevent them from carrying out such works. The expenses incurred may be recovered as a simple debt; the local authority may, however, agree to accept the expenses in instalments within up to 30 years. The debt is a charge on the premises, registered in the local land charges register, and the local authority has all the powers of a mortgagee (i.e. they may obtain possession of the house and sell the property to recover the debt).

If the local authority considers that a house cannot be rendered fit for human habitation at reasonable cost, they must invite the person having control, the freeholder (if different) and mortgagees (if any) to discuss the problem. Any person who receives this invitation may, within 21 days, submit an undertaking to carry out the work necessary to render the house fit. The local authority may accept such an undertaking and give the person concerned a specified period in which he has to fulfil it.

If no undertaking is forthcoming, or the offer has not been carried out, the local authority may do one of three things:

(*a*) It may issue a **demolition order**, requiring the vacation of the house within a specified period (not being less than 21 days) and the demolition of the house within a further six weeks. These periods may be extended. If the house is not demolished within the specified period the local authority must demolish it, sell material which has any value and sue for the balance of the cost of demolition.

(*b*) It may issue a **closing order**. Such an order may be issued in one of the following circumstances:

if a demolition would remove the support of adjoining houses; thus a terrace house is usually subject to a closing, and not a demolition, order;

if the house is unfit for human habitation, but may be used for another purpose (e.g. storage), then it may be closed as far as human habitation is concerned;

if the house is only in part unfit for human habitation, then the closing order may be applied to the unfit part (e.g. basement);

if the building is of special historical or architectural interest.

(*c*) Lastly, the local authority may **compulsorily purchase** the house.

There is a right of appeal by the aggrieved person to the County Court within 21 days. The appeal may be made against all orders affecting the rights of the appellant, such as a repair notice, a demand for the recovery of the expenses incurred by the local authority in executing work, a demolition order, a closing order, etc. The County Court has a very wide discretion in deciding the appeal. It can substitute a closing order for a demolition order, a repair notice for the demolition order, etc. The Court may extend the specified period in which the house should be demolished, but when in one case the Court substituted seven years for the six weeks allowed by the local authority, the Court of Appeal decided that this was an unreasonable exercise of the discretion (*Pocklington v. Melksham U.D.C.*, 1964).

Once a demolition or closing order has been made, any tenant of the house is no longer protected by the Rent Act, but s. 39 of the *Land Compensation Act, 1973*, imposes a duty on the local authority to secure suitable alternative accommodation.

2.2 Houses in Multiple Occupation

The *Housing Acts 1961, 1964* and *1969* confer a number of powers on local authorities with respect to houses in multiple occupation. This term means a house occupied by persons who do not form a single household (s. 58 of the 1969 Act).

These powers may be summarised as follows:

(*a*) *Registration*

S. 22 of the 1961 Act empowers local authorities to submit to the Secretary of State a scheme of registration of houses in multiple occupation occupied by more than two households or more than four individuals. Once such a scheme has been introduced, the authority may refuse to register a house on certain grounds or require that certain works should be carried out. Summary criminal penalties are prescribed for infringements of registration schemes.

(*b*) *Code of Management*

S. 13 of the 1961 Act authorises the Secretary of State to make Regulations prescribing a code of management for any house in multiple occupation, and such a Code has been prepared in Regulations issued in 1962 (Housing (Management of Houses in Multiple Occupation) Regulations, S.I. 1962/668). A local authority may issue an order which applies this Management Code to any house in multiple occupation which is found in an unsatisfactory condition. There is a right of appeal to a Magistrates' Court against the order.

Apart from this, the local authority may prescribe the maximum number of persons who may be housed in multiple occupation and may order the carrying out of specified works to improve the lodging house.

(c) Control Orders (*Part IV of the 1964 Act*)

Where the living conditions in a house of multiple occupation are so bad that immediate action is necessary, the authority may make a control order, installing themselves in immediate control of the house. While a control order is in force, the authority has all the rights of the dispossessed owner and must carry out the necessary works. An appeal against a control order lies to the County Court. The maximum duration of such an order is five years.

2.3   Abatement of Overcrowding (Part IV of the 1957 Act)

A dwelling-house is deemed to be overcrowded when the number of persons sleeping there either:

(*a*) Is such that any two persons, being 10 or more years old of opposite sexes, and not being persons living together as husband and wife, must sleep in the same room; or

(*b*) Is in excess of the number permitted by either Table 2.1 or 2.2 (infants under one year of age are ignored: children between one and 10 years are counted as half a person).

Table 2.1

Where a house consists of:	*The permitted number of persons is:*
one room	two
two rooms	three
three rooms	five
four rooms	seven and a half
five rooms	ten
with an additional two persons for each room over five.	

Table 2.2

Where a room in a house has a floor area of:	*The permitted number of persons is:*
110 sq. feet or more	two
90–110 sq. feet	one and a half
70–90 sq. feet	one
50–70 sq. feet	half
under 50 sq. feet	nil

An occupier or landlord who causes or permits a dwelling-house to be over-crowded is guilty of an offence. The offence is not committed, however, in the following circumstances:

If the overcrowding arose solely through children being born or attaining the age of one, or 10, as the case may be.

If the overcrowding was created only by a temporary visit.

If the local authority was asked for permission to cause overcrowding and the permission has been granted.

3

SPECIAL AREAS

3.1 Clearance Areas

Part III of the *Housing Act, 1957*, allows the local authority to declare an area to be a 'clearance area'. A clearance area (s. 42(1)) is one in which the most satisfactory method of dealing with it is by the demolition of all buildings. A clearance area may contain any number of houses as long as there are more than one.

Before the local authority may pass the resolution creating a clearance area it must be satisfied on all of the following respects:

(*a*) That all the houses are either: unfit for human habitation; or by reason of their bad arrangement or the narrowness or bad arrangement of the streets, dangerous or injurious to the health of the inhabitants, and that any other building in the area—i.e. not dwelling houses—fulfil the second condition mentioned above.

(*b*) That the most satisfactory method of dealing with the condition of the area is the demolition of all the buildings in it.

(*c*) That the local authority is able to provide other accommodation for displaced persons.

(*d*) That the local authority has sufficient resources to carry out the plan.

Immediately after the passing of the resolution a copy of it has to be submitted to the Secretary of State for his information. The copy must be accompanied by a statement of the number of persons involved.

Before 1974 there were two possible ways of dealing with a clearance area once it had been declared: either by a 'clearance order', or by purchase by the local authority. The 1974 Act abolished 'clearance orders', so that now the only way of dealing with a clearance area is by purchase of all buildings. The purchase may be effected either by agreement or compulsorily.

If any of the houses are capable of being raised to a standard which is adequate 'for the time being' (which usually means only weather- and wind-proof) the authority may retain them for temporary use. Such retention may, to the chagrin of the previous owners, last for some years.

The displaced persons are to be provided with alternative accommodation and, under the *Land Compensation Act, 1973*, they are entitled to the 'home loss payment' (see page 205).

Under the *Housing Act, 1974*, there were three types of other special areas— 'Housing Action Areas', 'General Improvement Areas' and 'Priority Neighbourhoods'—but the *Housing Act, 1980*, abolished Priority Neighbourhoods.

3.2 Housing Action Areas

Under s. 36 of the *Housing Act, 1974*, if the local authority considers that the living conditions in an area are unsatisfactory and should be dealt with within five years to secure both the improvement of the housing accommodation in the area as a whole and the proper and effective management and use of the accommodation, then the local authority may declare the area to be a Housing Action Area.

Proper publicity should be given to this declaration and persons interested may make inquiries and representations concerning any action to be taken in such an area. The creation of a Housing Action Area is registered in the local land charges register and all owners and occupiers within this area are notified accordingly.

A Housing Action Area should be dealt with within five years but this period may be extended for an additional two years by the Secretary of State.

The most important legal consequences of such a declaration are:

(a) A much more generous percentage of the cost of improvement may be granted by the local authority (see Chapter 4).

(b) The local authority may give assistance to the owners of the land towards carrying out works for the purpose of improving the amenities of the area (s. 45—'environmental improvement').

(c) The local authority may be authorised to purchase compulsorily land in the Housing Action Area (s. 43).

(d) If the landlord serves a notice to quit on a tenant or wants to dispose of the dwelling, he has to inform the local authority, who may take action as they think appropriate (s. 47).

3.3 General Improvement Areas

The concept of General Improvement Areas was created originally by the *Housing Act, 1957* (called by that Act 'Redevelopment Areas'), amended by the *Housing Act, 1969* (which renamed these areas 'General Improvement Areas'), and eventually amended and consolidated by the *Housing Act, 1974* (ss. 50, 51 and Schedule 5).

If the local authority considers that living conditions should be improved by exercising its powers under the Housing Acts, the local authority may declare an area a 'General Improvement Area'.

Procedure for creating a General Improvement Area is prescribed by Schedule 5 to the *Housing Act, 1974*. The local authority passes a 'preliminary resolution' which is submitted to the Secretary of State. The Secretary of State may veto the scheme, but if he does not intervene the local authority may confirm the scheme and publish the designation in two local newspapers and take steps to ensure that the resolution is brought to the attention of persons residing in the designated area.

The main practical effect of this designation is that more generous grants are available for the improvements of houses in General Improvement Areas (see Chapter 4).

4

IMPROVEMENT, CONVERSION AND REPAIR OF HOUSES

4.1 Types of Grants

The *Housing Act, 1974*, consolidated and extended the provisions about grants for improvement, conversion and repair of houses. This has been done in realisation of Government policy (formulated comprehensively for the first time in 1969) that the slender resources for housing purposes would be put to better use in the improvement of existing houses than in providing new buildings.

Four kinds of grants are payable by local authorities:

(a) *Intermediate Grants (ss. 65–8)*

This is a grant in respect of works required for the improvement of a dwelling by the provision of 'standard amenities'.

(b) *Special Grants (ss. 69–70)*

This grant is in respect of works required for the improvement of houses in multiple occupation by the provision of 'standard amenities'.

(c) *Improvement Grants (s. 61)*

This grant is for the provision of more dwellings by the conversion of houses or other buildings or for the improvement of dwellings to a higher standard than that of providing only standard amenities. 'Improvement' also includes adaptation of houses to make them suitable for the requirements of disabled persons.

(d) *Repair Grants (ss. 71–2)*

This is a grant for works of repair or replacement relating to a dwelling in Housing Action or General Improvement Areas, not being work associated with the three previous grants.

4.2 Common Provisions

There is a number of provisions common to all grants, which may be summarised as follows (ss. 56–60):

(a) There is a general rule (subject to exceptions with the permission of the Secretary of State) that no grant may be given in respect of houses erected after October 2, 1961.

(b) The applicant should be a freeholder, a leaseholder with not less than five years of the unexpired lease, or a protected or secured tenant (see Chapters 17 and 20).

(c) If, for reasons beyond the applicant's control (e.g. inflation), the amount of the grant appears to be insufficient, the local authority may increase the amount when the works are being performed.

11

(*d*) 'Standard amenities' are: fixed bath or showers with hot and cold water, wash-handbasin with hot and cold water, sink with hot and cold water and water-closet. Part II of Schedule 6 contains detailed provisions which the amenities must comply with.

(*e*) All grants amount to an 'appropriate percentage' of the costs; the general rule is that they amount to 50 per cent of costs, but in General Improvement Areas they amount to 60 per cent and in Housing Action Areas to 75 per cent. Moreover, if the applicant in the Housing Action Area is in difficult financial circumstances, the local authority may increase the percentage to 90. The appropriate percentage may be changed by an order issued by the Secretary of State.

(*f*) An application for any grant must be accompanied by the 'certificate of future occupation'. This means either a 'certificate of owner occupation' or a 'certificate of availability for letting'. The first certificate means that the applicant intends to live in the house for five years; the second that the house will be available for letting as a residence (e.g. not as a holiday letting) for the next five years. If the intention is not carried out, the applicant may be compelled to repay the grant received. This provision is directed against those development companies who improve or convert a house with the help of a grant, only to sell it immediately at an enormous profit. The *Housing Act, 1980*, extended the class of persons who may occupy the house without breach of the certificate, by including members of the applicant's family or his successors on death.

4.3 Intermediate Grants

The payment of an intermediate grant is not within the discretion of the local authority; the authority has to pay it if it is satisfied, after the work covered by the grant has been completed, that:

(*a*) The house will be provided with all the standard amenities for the exclusive use of the occupants.

(*b*) The house will be in good repair (disregarding the state of internal decorative repair), having regard to its age, character and the locality in which it is situated.

(*c*) It will conform with such requirements with respect to thermal insulation as may be specified by the Secretary of State.

(*d*) It will be in all other respects fit for human habitation (within the meaning of the *Housing Act, 1957*—see Chapter 2) unless the local authority considers that in all the circumstances this condition should be dispensed with.

(*e*) It probably will be available for use as a dwelling for a period of 15 years (or other period specified by the Secretary of State).

The 'eligible expense' (i.e. maximum amount of the cost) is assessed separately for each amenity; the total grant (including necessary structural works, if any) is limited to £1200. In addition, the grant may include a further sum up to £1500 for necessary works of repair or replacement. All these sums may be increased by the Secretary of State.

4.4 Special Grants

This grant, in respect of houses in multiple occupation, is discretionary. It is for the improvement of houses in multiple occupation by the provision of standard amenities. The grant resembles an intermediate grant, but provides for higher standard in that there must be a separate bathroom and an external w.c. is not permitted. The amount of the grant is calculated in a similar way to the intermediate grant.

4.5 Improvement Grants

An improvement grant is discretionary. It may be given subject to the following conditions:

(*a*) That the house will be provided with all the standard amenities for the exclusive use of its occupants.

(*b*) That it will be in good repair (disregarding the state of internal decorative repair) having regard to its age, character and the locality in which it is situated.

(*c*) That it will conform with such requirements with respect to construction and physical condition and the provision of services and amenities as may be specified by the Secretary of State (they used to be called by the profession the 'twelve points standard', but after the Secretary of State's 1974 Circular 160/74, para. 11, these requirements have been reduced to ten points). This means that the dwelling house must after improvement or conversion:

(1) be substantially free from damp;
(2) have adequate lighting and ventilation in each habitable room;
(3) have adequate and safe provision throughout for artificial lighting and have sufficient electric socket outlets for the safe and proper functioning of domestic appliances;
(4) be provided with adequate drainage facilities;
(5) be in a stable structural condition;
(6) have a satisfactory internal arrangement;
(7) have satisfactory facilities for preparing and cooking food;
(8) be provided with adequate facilities for heating;
(9) have proper provision for the storage of fuel (where necessary) and for the storage of refuse;
(10) conform with the specifications applicable to the thermal insulation of roof spaces laid down in Part F of the Building Regulations in force at the date of grant approval.

(*d*) That it is likely to provide satisfactory housing accommodation for a period of 30 years; this period, however, may be shortened by the local authority but not below 10 years.

There is a rateable value limit for houses which may be subject to improvement grants. This limit is specified by the Secretary of State (Improvement Grants (Rateable Value Limits) Order 1977, S.I. 1977/1213) as £500 in London, or £350 elsewhere. There is also a limit of eligible expense: £5000 for a house of up to two storeys; for houses of three or more storeys the limit is £5800. These limits may be increased by the Secretary of State but do not apply to grants in a Housing Action Area or for houses adapted for disabled persons.

4.6 Repair Grants

A repair grant is within the discretion of the local authority. It may be paid if the following conditions are satisfied:

(*a*) The dwelling-house is situated in a Housing Action or General Improvement Area.

(*b*) On the completion of the relevant works the dwelling will attain the relevant standard of repair. This means good repair (disregarding the state of internal decorative repair), having reagard to its age, character and the locality in which it is situated.

Generally speaking, the eligible expenses should not exceed the sum of £1200 or such larger sum as may be determined by the Secretary of State.

4.7   Compulsory Improvement of Dwellings (ss. 85–104)

Part VIII of the *Housing Act, 1974*, introduced this new idea which is applicable, generally speaking, only to Housing Action and General Improvement Areas. However, even outside these Areas, if the house is leased, the compulsory improvement of the dwelling in question may be ordered by the local authority if the tenant makes a formal request. The compulsory improvement of a dwelling may be ordered if it is without some of the standard amenities and is capable of being repaired or improved to the full standard at reasonable expense.

The procedure in arranging the compulsory improvement is as follows. The local authority first issues a **provisional notice** in order to discuss with the owner the necessary works and other arrangements (e.g. alternative accommodation for the duration of works). The owner may undertake to improve the dwelling, but if no undertaking is forthcoming or the undertaking is not kept, the local authority may serve an **improvement notice**; this notice, with some exceptions, may not be served if the house is owner-occupied. Thus the compulsory improvement of dwellings has its most important application to houses let to tenants.

Appeals against improvement notices may be lodged with the County Court. There are seven grounds on which the appeal may be based—e.g. that it is not practicable to comply with the notice, that the house is already provided with the standard amenities, etc.

If the enforcement of the notice is necessary, the local authority may itself carry out the works, recovering expenses from the person being in default.

S. 100 allows the local authority to grant loans to the persons carrying out improvement works.

5

PROVISION OF HOUSING ACCOMMODATION BY LOCAL AUTHORITIES

(Part V of the *Housing Act, 1957*, and Part I of the *Housing Act, 1980*.

5.1 Powers of Local Authorities

Both district and county councils (and in London the London boroughs and the Greater London Council) may provide accommodation by acquiring houses, by erecting houses on land which the authority owns, by conversion and by altering, enlarging, repairing or improving houses acquired by local authorities. These powers may be exercised outside the authority's area. The authority may provide shops, recreation grounds and other amenities to serve its housing estates, may sell furniture to council house tenants (for cash or on hire-purchase), and may provide laundry facilities and facilities for obtaining meals and refreshments.

The general management and control rests with the authority. The rent of council dwellings must be a 'reasonable' rent, i.e. a rent considered by the local authority concerned to be reasonable. This creates a lack of uniformity in the country. Labour councils are inclined to establish rent at lower levels than Conservative councils, which adhere to the principle of a 'fair rent' by analogy with the private sector. The *Housing Finance Act, 1972*, imposes a duty on local authorities to grant rebates to a tenant who cannot afford to pay his rent. The scale of income to qualify is such that very few persons in full-time employment are entitled to this rebate, although recent Regulations (Rent Rebate and Rent Allowance Schemes (England and Wales) Regulations 1980, S.I. 1980/780) have increased the maximum rebates and allowances.

5.2 The Right to Acquire the Freehold or Long Lease in the Public Sector

The *Housing Act, 1980*, gave 'secure tenants' the right:

(*a*) To acquire the freehold of the dwelling occupied by the tenant if it is a house.

(*b*) To be granted a long tenancy if the dwelling is a flat. (A long tenancy is a tenancy for at least 125 years for a rent not exceeding £10 p.a.—Schedule 2, para. 11.)

The rules governing these two rights are complex, but in outline they may be summarised as follows:

Secure tenancies are defined by s. 28 of the Act. Generally speaking, they are tenancies granted by a local authority, the Commission for the New Towns, a development corporation, the Housing Corporation or a housing trust (unless the trust is a charity within the meaning of the *Charities Act, 1960*, in which case a tenant of such secure tenancy has no right to acquire the dwelling).

The purchasing tenant is entitled to obtain a mortgage amounting to the full price of the house and cost of acquisition; the mortgage, however, is subject to a limit, which will be defined by Regulations in connection with the tenant's income. If the value of the dwelling is not agreed between the parties, any question in this connection is determined by the District Valuer.

The tenant acquiring the house is entitled to a discount, which may amount to 33 per cent of the price if he has been a tenant of the dwelling for a period not exceeding four years. If he has been in occupation for a longer period, the discount amounts to 33 per cent plus 1 per cent for each complete year by which that period exceeds three years, but the discount cannot exceed 50 per cent of the price.

If (as it is usually the case) the tenant acquires the dwelling with a discount, the conveyance shall contain a covenant binding the tenant and his successors in title, that if within a period of five years he disposes of the dwelling, he shall repay the amount of the discount obtained, but this repayment is reduced by 20 per cent for each year of occupation after purchase. Thus after five years the tenant may dispose of the dwelling without any repayment.

This right to dispose of dwellings let in the public sector is politically controversial and it is doubtful if it would survive a change of Government in its present form.

6

HOUSING ASSOCIATIONS, HOUSING TRUSTS AND THE HOUSING CORPORATION

6.1 Housing Associations and Housing Trusts

A **housing association** is defined in s. 189 of the *Housing Act, 1957*, as 'a society, body of trustees or company established for the purpose of constructing, improving or managing or facilitating or encouraging the construction or improvement of houses, being a society which does not trade for profit'.

A **housing trust** means a corporation or body of persons which:

(*a*) Is required to devote the whole of its funds to the provision of houses for persons the majority of whom are in fact members of the working classes, or

(*b*) Is required to devote the whole or substantially the whole of its funds to charitable purposes set out in (*a*) above (s. 86 of the *Rent Act, 1977*).

These bodies represent attempts to encourage the provision, on a corporate basis, of houses outside the framework of council houses. However, in spite of every encouragement by Government, their impact on the housing problem has been—so far—rather limited.

6.2 The Housing Corporation: Powers and Functions

S. 1 of the *Housing Act, 1964*, created a Housing Corporation with the general power of helping housing associations. It is a body corporate, consisting of up to nine members. The main function of the Housing Corporation is to help housing associations financially, the money being supplied by Parliament. The Corporation may also acquire land and sell it or lease it to a housing association.

The 1974 Act extended the functions of the Housing Corporation. It created a register of housing associations, which is kept by the Corporation. Generally speaking, only registered housing associations are eligible to obtain grants or loans from the Corporation, and only registered associations are, to some extent, exempted from the provisions of the *Rent Act, 1977* (the exemption applies only to security of tenure; limitation of rent provisions are identical to dwellings in the private sector).

The 1980 Act enlarges the powers of the Housing Corporation. Thus the Act allows registered housing associations to dispose of their dwellings with the consent of the Housing Corporation (which may be given either generally or for individual sales).

SS. 120 and 121 of that Act gives the Housing Corporation extensive control over the finances of housing associations.

7

NEW TOWNS

7.1 Statutory Provisions of New Towns

The *New Towns Act, 1965*, consolidated the earlier Acts of 1946 and 1958. It has been subsequently amended by the *New Towns Acts, 1969, 1977*, and also the *New Towns (Amendment) Act, 1976*.

In the post-war period the arguments in favour of New Towns were obvious. The large cities were too large and there was a need for improved housing conditions. Thus between 1947 and 1979, 28 New Towns were created in Great Britain. It seems, however, that in the foreseeable future no New Towns will be started, due both to economic factors and the marked reluctance of people to move into new and unfamiliar surroundings.

7.2 Development Corporations and the Commission for New Towns

The area of a New Town is determined by the Secretary of State for the Environment, and the Order creating a New Town is issued after the Secretary has considered objections and a report prepared by an Inspector who has conducted a public inquiry. The site of a New Town may include the area of an existing town or other centres of population and does not affect the areas or boundaries of local government.

After a New Town has been designated, the Secretary of State appoints a **Development Corporation** to carry out building and other operations necessary for the purposes of the New Town. The Development Corporation's task is 'to acquire, manage and dispose of land and other property, to carry out building and other operations, to provide the necessary services and to do anything necessary or expedient for the purposes of the New Town'.

After the Development Corporation for the town has done its work, the land becomes vested in a central body, the **Commission for New Towns**. The Commission has general powers of management of the town in much the same way as local authorities. So far four New Towns have been taken over by the Commission (Crawley, Hemel Hempstead, Hatfield and Welwyn Garden City). The *New Towns (Amendment) Act, 1976*, arranged for the transfer to district councils of the ownership of dwelling houses within New Towns.

The 1980 Local Government, Planning and Land Act in Part XVI ('Urban Development') allows the Secretary of State for the Environment to designate any area of land as an 'urban development area' with an 'urban development corporation' for that area. The Corporation might be made the planning and housing authority for the area with the power to acquire or dispose of land within that area.

PART 2
LANDLORD AND TENANT LAW

8

HISTORICAL BACKGROUND

8.1 Leases in Feudal Society

One effect of the Norman conquest of Great Britain in the eleventh century was to introduce into England a body of administrators who were familiar with the highly organised feudal society existing on the Continent. Although feudalism existed in a crude form in England, the Norman conquest contributed to the development of the system in England to such an extent that England became the most thoroughly feudal of all European states.

William the Conqueror fully implemented the feudal idea that the land belonged to the Crown and that the King's subjects might only own an interest, an 'estate' in land (for example, a 'fee simple', nowadays called 'freehold', or a life interest).

The term of years, 'leasehold', has a long history and underwent considerable changes in the course of time. Up to the fifteenth century a 'term of years' was considered only as creating a contractual relationship between the landlord and the tenant: therefore the tenant had no right to retain the land against the rightful claims of third parties. His only claim was against the landlord for breach of contract, enabling him to obtain damages from the landlord only if the contract was actually broken. The Chancellor sometimes intervened and, using his discretionary powers, could order 'specific performance' of the contract, instead of damages for its breach, but this matter belongs to the realm of Equity and not the Common Law.

Eventually, however, leases gave not only a personal right to sue the landlord, but also a right in the land itself. Therefore by 1481 a tenant had acquired the right, for the duration of the lease, to recover the land against third parties.

8.2 Legislation of 1925 to Simplify Property Law

As a consequence of the idea that the land belongs to the Crown and its subjects only have 'estates', the complexity of these estates which existed either in law or in Equity (under trusts)—as life interests, varieties of fee tail, fees simple and terms of years—made it a difficult and complicated task to convey real property. A number of Acts passed in 1925 greatly simplified this branch of the law. It was recognised that the fewer estates and interests that could exist in land, the simpler would be conveyancing and the less precarious the position of the purchaser.

For this reason s. 1 of the *Law of Property Act, 1925*, reduced the number of legal estates that can exist in land to only two, namely:

(*a*) An estate in fee simple absolute in possession (**freeholds**).
(*b*) A term of years absolute (**leaseholds**).

The advisability of retaining in some form those other estates which existed before 1925 was realised, and such estates may still exist, but only as equitable estates under a trust (which means that there must be a legal owner of one of the estates (*a*) or (*b*) above, but holding the land not for his own benefit, but for the benefit of another person who may enjoy the land, for example, for life only).

Apart from the two legal estates mentioned above (which entail possession of land), there are five ways of creating other legal interests or charges in or over the land that do not involve possession of the land (such as easements, rent charges, charges by way of legal mortgages, etc.).

9

CONCEPT OF LEASES

9.1 Definition of Lease

A leasehold ('tenancy') arises when one party, known as the **landlord**, confers on other party, known as the **tenant**, the right of exclusive possession of land for a period which is either subject to a definite limit, or can be made subject to a definite limit by either party.

Apart from tenancies which may exist by virtue of statute or by virtue of the doctrine of estoppel (see below), a tenancy is created by agreement between the landlord and tenant.

An example of a tenancy created by a statute is the **statutory tenancy** under the *Rent Act, 1977*. Here a tenancy subsists not because the parties agree (as such a tenancy often exists against the wish of the landlord, who would like to evict the tenant), but because statute (the *Rent Act, 1977*) protects the tenant against eviction by granting him security of tenure, even if the contractual tenancy has come to the end. Another example is the new tenancy created by the Court under the *Landlord and Tenant Act, 1954*, after the contractual tenancy of business premises had expired. Also, the *Leasehold Reform Act, 1967*, allows the tenant of a long lease (under certain conditions) to obtain an extension of the contractual tenancy for an additional 50 years even against the wishes of the landlord.

It is also worth noting that some tenancies may be accepted by the Court as in existence by applying the doctrine of **estoppel**. Thus if a person grants a lease without authority (e.g. a son of the freeholder acting without his father's authority) and afterwards becomes the owner of a superior estate in the same land (thus becoming authorised to grant the lease), he cannot deny the existence of the lease granted by him at the time when he was not entitled to do so.

However, apart from these exceptional circumstances, the usual way in which a lease is created is by **agreement**. But because the agreement (if conforming with the requirements explained in the next chapter) creates a legal estate— namely, a leasehold—it creates more than a contractual relationship. Thus a lease, once created, has a dual meaning: on the one hand it is a contract, creating a number of rights and duties binding the contractual parties *in personam;* on the other hand it gives the tenant an estate in land, which creates rights and duties *in rem* independent of the contract. A right *in personam* is enforceable only against specified parties (i.e. the original landlord and tenant); a right *in rem* is enforceable against anybody. Therefore the tenant can enforce the right to the land in question not only against the original landlord with whom he made the contract, but, generally speaking, also against third parties, including the landlord's successor in title (see Section 11.2).

9.2 Leases and Licences Distinguished

It is of paramount importance to distinguish between a lease and a licence

23

although in some instances the line between the two concepts is blurred. The distinction is vital since, generally speaking, only leases are within the scope of social legislation protecting tenants (however, some occupational licences may be protected under Part VII of the *Rent Act, 1977*, as 'restricted contracts', as decided by Lord Denning in the case *Luganda v. Service Hotels Ltd*, 1969— see Chapter 17). Furthermore, the implied obligations of parties in leases (Chapter 11) do not apply to licences.

A **licence** permits the licensee to do some act on the licensor's land that does not create an estate or interest in the land. It simply allows the licensee to act in a manner which, but for the licence, would amount to a trespass. If the licence is possessory, giving possession of the land to the licensee, its affinity to a lease is clear.

There are three main categories of licences;

(*a*) Gratuitous or bare licence.
(*b*) Licence coupled with the grant of an interest.
(*c*) Contractual licence.

(Licence may also arise by applying the doctrine of estoppel or by a constructive trust, but these exceptional situations have no direct bearing on the problems discussed here.)

A **bare licence** is a licence granted without any valuable consideration and as such is not a contract and is therefore revocable at any time. Nevertheless, a licensor must give reasonable notice of the revocation and in some circumstances a licensee may be entitled to damages if no reasonable notice has been given (*Facchini v. Bryson*, 1952).

An example of a **licence coupled with the grant of an interest** is an implied licence to enter land in order to enjoy an existing servitude—for example, a right to fish in an other person's pond. Such a licence to enter the land is irrevocable, as revocation would amount to a derogation from the grant of the interest.

A **contractual licence** is a licence created by a valid contract and so with valid consideration (usually payment of money). Examples of such licences are those whereby guests are accepted by hotels or boarding houses or those whereby paying spectators are permitted to attend spectacles. Whether they are revocable is a debatable matter. The leading case is *Hurst v. Picture Theatres Ltd* (1915) where the plaintiff, ejected mistakenly from a cinema during a performance (in breach of contract, as he had a valid ticket), sued in assault and succeeded. The Court accepted as a matter of construction of the contract that the licence was irrevocable during the duration of the performance. Thus it appears that the revocability of a contractual licence depends on the intention of the contracting parties (i.e. by the application of the general rules governing contracts). Therefore the revocation of a contractual licence contrary to its terms is a breach of contract and so gives the right to damages.

Sometimes it is not easy to distinguish between a lease and a contractual licence. A **lease** must always give exclusive possession to the tenant; if there is no exclusive possession, it cannot be a lease. At one time it was thought that the right to exclusvie possession was the decisive factor showing that the transaction created a lease. Now, however, it is possible for a licence to give the right to exclusive possession. In deciding whether a grant amounts to a lease or only to a licence, regard must be had to the substance rather than to the form of the agreement. In the case *Cobb v. Lane* (1952), Lord Denning said: 'The question in all these cases is one of the intention: did the circumstances and conduct of the parties show that all that was intended was that the occupier should have a personal privilege with no interest in land?'

Thus the agreement that 'bombed out' people should occupy a cottage rent-free for the duration of the war was accepted as a licence in *Booker v. Palmer* (1942).

Nowadays many landlords, in attempting to avoid the protection afforded by the Rent Acts, try to shape their agreements as licences. The Courts, of course, are wary of accepting such agreements as genuine licences, but face formidable difficulties in distinguishing such 'licences' from leases. This is shown by three recent cases: *Walsh v. Griffith* (1977), *Somma v. Hazlehurst* (1978) and *Demuren v. Seal Estates Ltd* (1979). All three are very similar: two persons took a flat (in the second case a room) as 'licensees'. In the first case the Court considered that the relevant contract (called 'licence') was a lease, treating the provisions indicating a 'licence' as a sham. In the second case the Court of Appeal stated: 'There is no reason why an ordinary landlord should not be able to grant a licence to occupy an ordinary house exclusively. If that is what both he and the licensee intended and if they can frame any written agreement in such a way as to demonstrate that it is not really an agreement for a lease masquerading as a licence, the Court will not prevent them from achieving that object.'

This statement, however, should be treated with great reservations, as is shown by the third case, when the Court of Appeal established that a similar contract called a 'licence' was in effect a lease. These three cases do not overrule one another; different conclusions were reached by accepting minute distinctions of facts. It seems, however, that only in very clear and unambiguous circumstances will the Court be prepared to accept such agreements as licences. A recent case, *O'Malley v. Seymour* (1979) (where the facts were similar to the three cases cited above, but where there was only one 'licensee'), shows clearly that the Court is inclined to regard a 'contract of licence' to use a dwelling as a sham and consequently to grant security of tenure to the 'licensee'.

An employee who occupies premises owned by his employer may be either a **service tenant** or a **service licensee**. Of course, the agreement may make the position of the employee clear. But if doubt arises he will be a licensee if he is required to occupy the premises for the better performance of his duty. This means that the need for residence must arise from the nature of the servant's duties (e.g. caretaker). But if the employee lives in the premises belonging to the employer only as a matter of convenience to all parties, he will be a tenant.

9.3 Varieties of Leases

Before discussing leases within the meaning of the *Law of Property Act, 1925*, it is necessary to describe two types of 'tenancies' which are not proper leases, in spite of their names: these are 'tenancies at sufferance' and 'tenancies at will'.

A **tenancy at sufferance** arises when a person who has held land by a lawful title continues in possession after his title expires without either the agreement or disagreement of the person entitled to the property. Such a tenant has no legal estate in the land and may be sued at any time for possession and for damages for 'use and occupation' of land. He must not be sued for rent (which cannot be due from his as he is not a real tenant); suing for rent may be (and usually is) interpreted as accepting him as a proper tenant.

A **tenancy at will** is a tenancy under which the 'tenant' is in possession of the land with the permission of the landlord and which is determinable at the will of either party. It is not a proper lease as the minimum duration is not certain. Tenancies at will are not favoured by the Courts and in modern times are not frequent. Examples of such tenancies are entry on land pending the completion of a contract to purchase, or a lawful tenant holding over after the expiration of lease with the consent of the landlord but without creating a new tenancy.

The two above examples not being leases, they are not protected by the Rent Acts.

Proper, legal tenancies within the meaning of the *Law of Property Act, 1925*, are of two kinds: 'periodic tenancies' (periodic yearly tenancies are called 'tenancies from year to year') or tenancies for years (called also 'fixed-term tenancies').

Periodic tenancies are included in the definition of a 'term of years absolute' in the *Law of Property Act, 1925*. Such a tenancy may be a weekly tenancy, monthly tenancy or a tenancy for any other period chosen by the parties. Payment of rent usually corresponds with the period of lease, although there may be, for example, a quarterly tenancy with the rent payable monthly. A periodic tenancy may be created by express agreement or by implication if a person being in possession of the land with the consent of the landlord pays rent with reference to a period of time. Acceptance of rent by the landlord is evidence that a periodic tenancy has been created.

Periodic tenancies continue until determined by a notice to quit. This, subject to any stipulation to the contrary and to statutory exceptions (social legislation protecting tenants—see Chapters 17–24), should be given so as to expire at the end of the period of the tenancy and must be of a length equal to the period of the tenancy. Thus a weekly tenancy requires a week's notice, a monthly tenancy a month's notice, etc., but the longest period required is six months; thus yearly and longer period tenancies require only six months' notice.

A **tenancy for years** (fixed-term tenancy) is a tenancy for any period (for example, a fortnight or 99 years), the commencement and duration of which are certain. A tenancy for years ends at the expiration of the term without the necessity of giving any notice (but this, of course, is also subject to protection of tenants under the social legislation).

9.4   The Legal Problem of Squatters

The legal problem of squatters deserves some attention, as occupation of vacant premises by squatters is nowadays a not uncommon occurrence. Desperate, homeless persons resort to self-help and occupy empty houses, creating a problem for the owners.

A squatter is a person who, without any colour of right, enters an unoccupied house or land, intending to stay there as long as he can (*McPhail v. Persons, Names Unknown*, 1973; *Bristol Corporation v. Persons, Names Unknown*, 1974).

A squatter has no legal possession of the land, unless the owner acquiesces to his presence. He is simply a trespasser and as such may be evicted by the owner, who may use such force as is reasonably necessary to effect eviction. Although the law thus enables the owner to take the remedy into his own hands, this is not a course to be encouraged because of the disturbance which may follow. The owner should rather go to Court and obtain an order that the owner 'do recover' the land and the summons may be addressed to the persons occupying the premises even if their names are unknown. The order of the Court may be enforced immediately and the Court cannot give any relief to the squatters, leaving it to the generosity of the owner to allow adequate time for the squatters to move out.

The *Criminal Law Act, 1977*, in ss. 6–13 deals with offences relating to entering and remaining on property. S. 6 makes it an offence for a person to use or threaten violence for the purpose of securing entry into any premises. S. 7 makes it an offence for a person to enter and remain on premises as a trespasser once he has been requested to leave. Obstruction of Court officers executing process for possession against unauthorised occupiers is also now an offence.

The fate of evicted squatters has been considerably improved by the *Housing (Homeless Persons) Act, 1977*, which imposes on the local authorities an extensive duty to provide council housing accommodation or to ensure that other suitable accommodation is provided for genuinely homeless persons.

Under s. 4 of the *Limitation Act, 1939*, no action shall be brought by any person to recover any land after the expiration of 12 years from the date on which the right of action accrued to him; thus if a squatter is tolerated for such a long period the landowner loses his right to evict him.

10

CREATION OF LEASES

10.1 Introduction

A lease, unless created by statute or estoppel, comes into existence as a result of an agreement between the parties. A lease may be created by agreement in one of two ways.

First, the agreement may of itself create a lease in favour of the tenant and convey the estate to him. Such an agreement vests the estate in the tenant immediately, although the commencement of the lease may be postponed to a future date. The agreement must generally speaking (with the exceptions explained below) be made by deed. Rather confusingly this agreement creating the lease is also called a 'lease' and it depends purely on the context whether the word 'lease' denotes the *estate* created or the *agreement* creating the estate.

Secondly, the parties may bind themselves, one to grant, and the other to accept the estate in the future. Such an agreement does not create the estate immediately, but only imposes on the parties an obligation to implement the lease in the future. If the agreement for the lease is one of which a specific performance will be granted by a Court (and this is usually the case), the parties are for most purposes in the same position as if the lease had actually been granted. For this reason it is accepted that such an agreement for a lease is also a way in which a lease can be created. This is because such an agreement must be followed either by a deed creating the estate (this is usually only the case in long—e.g. 99-year—leases), or by allowing the tenant to take possession of the land and paying rent (which, by implication, creates a legal lease), or by a Court order granting a specific performance (if either party refuses to implement the lease, thus committing a breach of contract for lease).

10.2 Legal Requirements for a Valid Lease

The general principle is that all leases must be created by a document under seal (i.e. by deed) in order to create a legal estate for the benefit of the tenant (s. 54 of the *Law of Property Act, 1925*). Possession of the land (i.e. beginning of the lease) may be postponed, but no longer than 21 years (s. 149(3) of the *Law of Property Act, 1925*).

There is one exception to this rule that a deed is required, contained in s. 54 of that Act. A lease may be created without any formality if the following three conditions are fulfilled:

(*a*) It must be for a period not exceeding three years; periodic leases, if the period does not exceed three years, fulfil this condition.

(*b*) It must take effect in immediate possession (i.e. immediately after concluding the agreement). This condition is obviously imposed in order to avoid troublesome disputes over whether an oral contract has been concluded or not; but even if the tenant does not take possession of the subject of the lease immediately, when he moves in later with the consent of the landlord and pays rent which is accepted, then a periodic tenancy is created by implication of law, the period depending on how often he pays rent.

(*c*) It must be at the best rent reasonably obtainable, without taking a 'fine' (an initial capital payment or premium). This condition has been imposed to protect possible creditors of the landlord.

A lease for a term exceeding three years, or not fulfilling the other conditions mentioned above, must be under seal (unless a periodic tenancy is created in the way described under (*b*) above). But even if it is not under seal, it may nevertheless be construed as an agreement for a lease (see Section 10.3) by applying the doctrine of *Walsh v. Lonsdale* (page 32).

10.3 Leases Created by Agreements for a Lease—Formal Requirements

An agreement for a lease is a contract to create a legal estate in the future. In order to be effective it must comply with all the usual conditions for a valid contract (i.e. there must be an intention to create legal obligations, the parties must have full capacity to contract and the contract must not be tainted by illegality or other factors vitiating the contract). The concluded contract must contain all the essential terms of the lease, namely:

(*a*) The identification of the parties.
(*b*) The clear identification of the premises.
(*c*) The commencement and duration of the lease.
(*d*) The rent or other consideration to be paid.

The contract may contain other terms of the lease, but where there is no valid agreement on terms, the law implies the terms discussed in Chapter 11.

In addition, there is a requirement in respect of the form of such agreements, introduced originally by the *Statute of Frauds, 1677*, and now contained in s. 40(1) of the *Law of Property Act, 1925*, which reads: 'No action may be brought upon any contract for sale or other disposition of land or any interest in land, unless the agreement upon which such action is brought, or some memorandum or note thereof, is in writing and signed by the party to be charged, or by some other person thereunto by him lawfully authorised.'

This section applies to an agreement for a lease, as a lease is an 'interest in land'. As the existence of many leases depends on agreement for a lease and as it is therefore important that such agreements should be enforceable, the full effect of this section should be well understood.

The effect of non-compliance with s. 40(1) does not make the agreement completely void, but merely unenforceable by action in the courts if the defendant expressly pleads the lack of formality as a reason for avoiding liability.

The 'note' or 'memorandum' need not be in any particular form or contained in a single document in order to satisfy the requirements of the Statute. It may be prepared at any time after the contract has been concluded, provided it is done before the Court action has started. Several documents (even if none of them contains all the necessary terms of the contract) satisfy the requirements of s. 40(1) if they refer to one another in an unequivocal manner and if taken together they cover all the necessary terms of the future lease. (However, the time-honoured expression 'subject to contract' inserted in a letter puts such a letter clearly outside the requirements of s. 40(1) of the *Law of Property Act, 1925*.) It is of interest to note that even a letter expressing refusal to comply with an oral agreement may be accepted as sufficient memorandum proving that the contract has been concluded, if it contains the necessary terms of the oral contract (*Bailey v. Sweeting*, 1861).

For the purposes of s. 40(1), if the name or even only the initials of the party to be charged appear on any part of the document this is an adequate signature. The requirement is that it must be inserted with the intention to confirm the accuracy of the document.

As the document needs to be signed only by the person 'to be charged' it is possible for an agreement to be enforceable against the party who signed the document by the party who did not, but not vice versa.

10.4   Doctrine of Part Performance

The strict application of the requirement that there must be at least a note or memorandum may cause injustice to the party who, believing in the validity of an oral agreement, incurs some expenses.

Rawlison v. Ames (1925) is a good example of such a situation. The defendant agreed to take a lease of a flat from the plaintiff for 21 years. The letters which passed between the parties were insufficient to satisfy the requirements of the *Statute of Frauds* (now s. 40(1) of the *Law of Property Act, 1925*). The flat was part of a house owned by the plaintiff, which was in the course of conversion and redecoration. At the defendant's request and in many cases under her direct supervision, alterations were made in the original plan for conversion. The flat was not ready by the date on which the defendant required it and she refused to take the lease. An action by the plaintiff for specific performance succeeded.

The doctrine of part performance means that although there is no memorandum of an agreement for a lease (or for any other disposition of land) such as to satisfy the requirements of s. 40(1), yet if the agreement is partially performed, parol evidence of it may be given in an action for specific performance (s. 40(2) of the *Law of Property Act, 1925*). For this purpose the act of part performance relied upon must be unequivocally referable to some agreement about the land and be consistent with that alleged. Thus in the case *Rawlison v. Ames* it was obvious that the landlord's action (conversion, in accordance with the wish of the future tenant) referred clearly to some agreement about the premises.

The limitations of the doctrine of part performance are well illustrated by the case *Madison v. Alderson* (1887). The plaintiff relied on promises by her employer that if she continued to work as his housekeeper (without wages) for the rest of the employer's life, he would leave her a life interest in his house. The appellant continued to work in that capacity until the employer's death, but the Court refused to grant specific performance on that agreement, as there was no evidence of a contract *concerning the master's land*, as alleged by the plaintiff. The plaintiff's action was really referable to the contract of employment, not a contract relating to land.

In a more recent case, however (*Steadman v. Steadman*, 1974), the House of Lords considerably extended the scope of the doctrine. The facts of the case were as follows: the parties were married in 1962. In 1963 a house was bought and conveyed to the husband and wife jointly. After their divorce in 1968, there was a dispute between them about arrears of maintenance due from the husband and about the ownership of the house. In 1972 (outside the Magistrates' Court dealing with the dispute) they agreed orally that the wife would transfer her interest in the house to the husband for £1500 and that the arrears of maintenance (some £194) would be remitted for £100 which the husband undertook to repay within a month. The husband paid the £100 in time, but when he asked his ex-wife to execute the conveyance of her interest in the house, she refused to do so and asked for £2000 instead of £1500 as agreed. The Court held that the oral agreement was a contract for the disposition of an interest in land, within s. 40 of the *Law of Property Act, 1925*, and that the husband's payment of £100 was, in the circumstances, unequivocally referable to an agreement between the parties and, therefore, a sufficient part performance, even though the act of part performance was not *referable* to the terms relating to the disposition of an interest in land, but was *consistent* with the alleged agreement.

The following acts have been accepted as sufficient part performance:

(*a*) Entry into possession and expenditure of money on improvements in pursuance of an agreement, or even entry into possession alone.

(*b*) Expenditure of money on alterations by a tenant already in possession where the expenditure is not obligatory under the existing lease (but, of course, it must be done with the landlord's approval).

(*c*) Payment of rent at an increased rate by a tenant in possession.

However, the mere retention of possession by itself after the contractual lease has terminated is not sufficient part performance of an extended lease.

If an enforceable agreement for a lease is broken, the injured party always has a right to damages, as in the case of a breach of any other contract. However, this remedy cannot be obtained by a party who cannot produce a written memorandum in compliance with s. 40(1) of the *Law of Property Act, 1925*, but only relies on the doctrine of part performance. This doctrine, although recognised by s. 40(2), is an equitable doctrine and therefore only the equitable remedy of specific performance is available. If a party is able to base his claim on agreement complying with s. 40(1) he may claim damages or specific performance.

Specific performance is a discretionary remedy. Although it is discretionary, it is usually granted in respect of breach of a contract for a lease, as, generally speaking, damages are not considered an adequate remedy. Specific performance will not be granted, however, if for any reason it would be inequitable to do so. Thus, for example, specific performance will not be granted if the agreement is uncertain in any material respect or if its enforcement would involve undue hardship to the other party.

Leases for a period exceeding three years, which require a deed for their validity, pose a problem if they are in writing but not by deed. Here we are faced with a clear case of a variance between the Common Law and Equity. The Common Law requires a deed for the validity of such a lease; Equity is ready to treat such a lease as an agreement for a lease and, if appropriate, to grant a specific performance of such an agreement. In this situation Equity prevails, and the ruling stems from 'the Rule in *Walsh v. Lonsdale* (1882)'. In this case it was decided that a tenant who held under an agreement for a lease of which specific performance would be decreed, occupied the same position vis-à-vis the landlord as regards mutual rights and liabilities as he would occupy if a formal lease under seal had been executed.

But it cannot be said that an agreement for a lease is as good as the lease itself. The doctrine of *Walsh v. Lonsdale* is excluded if the agreement is one of which Equity will not grant specific performance, which is a discretionary remedy. Thus in *Coatsworth v. Johnson* (1885) the plaintiff entered into possession under an agreement that the defendant would grant him a lease for 21 years. Before the rent was due or had been paid, the defendant gave him notice to quit and evicted him on the grounds that he was in breach of a repair covenant contained in the agreement and intended to be inserted in the lease. He was not protected by Equity, as he did not come 'with clean hands', as one of the Equity maxims required.

11

COVENANTS

11.1 General

Strictly speaking, covenants are obligations effected by deed by one or other party to the leasehold. However, since many leases are now created informally in everyday life, any obligation of a landlord or tenant is called a **covenant**. Some covenants—for example, in respect of maintenance of the premises let, assignment and subleases—are discussed in separate chapters; others are dealt with here.

Covenants are either express or implied. **Express** covenants are those which have been agreed between the parties and are clearly expressed. **Implied** covenants are those which are implied by law in the absence of express agreement.

Implied covenants are implied by law only if an express covenant does not cover the matter, because, generally speaking, contracting parties are allowed to regulate their obligations as they wish. There are, however, some covenants created by statute out of which the parties cannot contract, or out of which they can contract only with the permission ('leave') of the Court. This means that these covenants are imposed even against the wish of the parties. Such covenants (e.g. in respect of liability for repair of the premises) will be discussed later.

11.2 Implied Covenants

Some implied covenants impose obligations on the landlord, some on the tenant.

The most important covenants on the side of the landlord are those for **quiet enjoyment** and against **derogation from grant**. The landlord covenants that he is entitled to grant some tenancy and that the tenant will enjoy quiet possession without interruption by the landlord or by the lawful act of anyone claiming through him or under him. This means that any successor in title of the landlord is bound by the lease. However, the covenant in its implied form does not impose liability on the landlord for acts of persons claiming by 'paramount title' (i.e. a title prevailing over the landlord's title). Thus under the implied covenant an undertenant for a term longer than the residue of the head term has no remedy against his immediate landlord if the undertenant is evicted by the head landlord at the expiration of the head term. Hence the covenant in this form is not entirely satisfactory for the tenant. In a properly drawn-up agreement this covenant is expressly extended so as to apply to the acts of persons claiming even by a paramount title.

An example of the application of the covenant for quiet enjoyment is the case of *Markham v. Paget* (1908): the plaintiff was the tenant and the defendant the landlord of Styffynwood Hall. A mine nearby had been let earlier by the defendant to a third person. This mine was in use after the lease of the Hall and subsidence caused by the working of the mine resulted in damage to the

Hall. It was held that the defendant was bound by an implied covenant to give the plaintiff quiet enjoyment of the Hall and that this covenant had been broken by the defendant when the third person (claiming through the defendant) caused the subsidence.

The covenant protects against substantial interference with the ordinary enjoyment of the premises (e.g. when the landlord omits to repair a culvert on adjoining land with the result that water damages some of the buildings). But it does not protect from an unlawful act of a stranger, as it is the tenant's responsibility to defend himself against trespassers. Threats by letter or by shouting and banging on the door amount to a breach as tending to deprive the tenant of the full benefit of the right of possession (*Kenny v. Preen*, 1963). This may also be a harassment of the occupier, which is a criminal offence under the *Protection from Eviction Act, 1977* (see Chapter 21).

The second covenant is against 'derogation from the grant'. This means that the landlord must not do anything which is inconsistent with the purpose for which the premises were let. The landlord, 'having given a thing with one hand, is not to take away the means of enjoying it with the other'.

In the case *Aldin v. Latimer, Clark, Muirhead & Co*, (1894) the premises had been leased for the purpose (known to the landlord) of timber storage and it was held a derogation from his grant for the landlord to obstruct the flow of air necessary for drying the timber by building on adjoining land. It was not a breach of covenant for quiet enjoyment, as it was not interference with *ordinary* enjoyment of the premises, but it was a derogation from the grant, which protects the tenant's *special* use of the premises.

But a landlord who let business premises was held in a Canadian case not to have derogated from his grant when he let nearby premises to a competitor (*Clarke Gamble of Canada v. Grand Park Plaza*, 1967). Moreover, where it was found that all that the tenant suffered was interference with amenities, relief was not given (*Kelly v. Battershell*, 1949). But the landlord may not use his adjoining land so as to interfere, by reason of vibration, with the stability of the premises let (*Grosvenor Hotel Co. v. Hamilton*, 1894).

In the absence of an express provision there is no implied covenant by the landlord that the premises let are fit for any particular purpose, but in certain circumstances statute imposes on the landlord obligations in respect of maintaining the premises let. The whole problem of maintaining premises during the tenancy will be discussed in Chapter 12.

The following covenants are implied by the tenant: to pay rent, to pay rates and taxes; to use the premises 'in a tenant-like manner'; 'not to disclaim the landlord's title'; and to deliver the possession at the termination of the lease.

Problems of rent and the use of premises are dealt with later, as they require more detailed exposition.

If nothing is said in the contract, rates should be paid by the tenant. There are no taxes at present due from the land. If, however, the rent is described as 'inclusive', this means that the rates are the landlord's responsibility.

'Not to disclaim the landlord's title' means that if the tenant by word or action denies the landlord's title and this fact is clearly established, the covenant is broken and the lease is terminated. An example of disclaiming is the delivery of possession of the premises to a third person to enable him to claim an adverse title. In our regulated society this covenant is at present of rather theoretical significance, but in the past, when titles to land were often doubtful, it was important.

The kind of disclaimer described above should be distinguished from the disclaiming of the lease by a trustee in bankruptcy if the tenant becomes bankrupt. In such case, a leasehold forming part of bankrupt's property vests in the trustee. He may disclaim leases which are a liability for and not an asset to the bankrupt's estate. A landlord injured by the operation of a disclaimer may prove in the bankruptcy the amount of his loss.

11.3 Express Covenants

Contracting parties may insert all sorts of express covenants in the lease, but there are some which are more commonly included such as:

(*a*) To pay rent in the manner agreed.
(*b*) To pay rates (and taxes if appropriate) in the manner agreed.
(*c*) To repair (see Chapter 12).
(*d*) Not to alter the premises (Chapter 13).
(*e*) Not to assign the lease or sublet (Chapter 13).
(*f*) To allow or forbid a particular trade.
(*g*) To pass on notices received.
(*h*) To surrender the subject of the lease at the end of term (Chapter 12).
(*i*) An absolute covenant for quiet enjoyment.

Covenants mentioned under (*c*), (*d*), (*e*) and (*h*) are discussed in the chapters following; others are explained below.

(*a*) Rent

Rent is part of the consideration which the tenant furnishes to the landlord for the landlord's allowing the tenant to occupy the leased premises. The rest of the consideration consists of the obligation to comply with the tenant's covenants and possibly the payment of a 'fine' or premium, i.e. a sum at the beginning of the tenancy. Rent should be regarded as of twofold significance: first it is a part of the consideration due for the grant of possession of the premises; and secondly it is an acknowledgement made by the tenant that he possesses the land under the lease with the consent of the landlord and that therefore his possession is not 'adverse'. Therefore as long as rent is paid, prescription does not run against the landlord. For this reason rent is a necessary condition of a lease.

Thus in the case of *Lynes v. Snaith* (1899) the owner of a cottage permitted a woman to live in it rent-free in circumstances in which the Divisional Court found, she was a tenant at will. A tenancy at will, for the purpose of the Limitation Act was deemed to terminate after one year. In the above case, after 13 years of occupation by the woman the owner died. It was held that the successor to the owner lost his right to sue for possession, as his claim was barred by the Act.

As the consideration need not be adequate, if somebody wants to grant a lease rent-free he should reserve a nominal, or 'peppercorn', rent.

Rent may be monetary or consist of chattels or services.

In the absence of express provision, rent is payable at the end of each year, or at the end of each period of a shorter, periodical tenancy. Usually, however, there is an express agreement stipulating payment of rent in advance at times stated.

It is provided by the *Landlord and Tenant Act, 1962*, that a rent book must be prepared and handed to the tenant in all tenancies of dwelling-houses if the rent is payable weekly.

It is useful to be acquainted with some nomenclature of rent:

(*a*) **Ground rent** is a low rent, reserved when the land is let for a long period for building purposes and the premium is high, covering virtually the price of the building.

(*b*) **Peppercorn rent** is a symbolic rent to prevent the *Limitation Act, 1939*, operating against the landlord.

(*c*) **Rack rent** is a rent representing the rentable value of the property. The *Housing Act, 1957*, considers 'rack rent' a rent amounting to more than two thirds of the rateable value of the subject of the lease.

(*d*) **Best rent** is the highest rack rent which can reasonably be obtained.

(*e*) **Head rent** is the rent paid by a head tenant who sublets the property to a subtenant.

In agricultural tenancies it is often stipulated that the rent is payable on 'quarter days', i.e. Lady Day (March 25), Midsummer (June 24), Michaelmas (December 29) and Christmas (December 25).

(*b*) *Rates and Taxes*

The express covenant to pay rates and taxes (the latter now obsolete) is identical with the implied covenant. The time, place and manner of payment may be described in detail by express stipulation.

(*c*) *Particular Trade*

Leases of business premises often contain a covenant that only a particular trade may be carried out in the leased premises, or the covenant may be formulated in a negative form, forbidding some types of trade. This is often done if the landlord is also the landlord of adjoining premises where a particular trade is already carried on. Leases of dwelling-houses frequently contain a covenant 'to use the house as a private dwelling only'.

(*d*) *'To Pass Notices Received'*

A landlord may be affected by a variety of statutory notices, which may be delivered at the leased premises and be binding on him. Such notices—e.g. a compulsory purchase order—are of extreme importance. It is desirable, therefore, to include a covenant that the tenant forward any such notices immediately to the landlord.

(*e*) *Absolute Covenant for Quiet Enjoyment*

As has been mentioned, the implied covenant for quiet enjoyment is rather unsatisfactory. It is obviously insufficient protection for the tenant and, therefore, it is often covenanted that the landlord promises quiet enjoyment in absolute terms, being responsible for interference by anybody with the exclusion of a mere stranger (trespasser).

12

REPAIRS

12.1 Implied Covenant to Repair under Common Law

The respective liabilities of the landlord and the tenant to repair the premises which are let depend chiefly upon the terms of the letting. In almost every case, in practice there is an express covenant which governs the matter.

However, cases do often arise where the terms of the letting do not define responsibility for repair, and before dealing with express covenants to repair it is useful to discuss briefly those cases where there is no express covenant.

The landlord, not being in possession of the property, is under no implied obligation to repair the premises. Exceptions to this rule are: at Common Law the obligation of the landlord in the case of furnished houses to let them in a habitable state; in addition, the *Housing Acts 1957, 1961*, and *1974* and the *Defective Premises Act, 1972*, impose some obligations on the landlord (see below).

The tenant also has no obligation to repair the premises; he is generally considered only under an implied duty to use the premises in a 'tenant-like' manner and deliver them up to the landlord at the termination of the tenancy in the same state as when let, fair wear and tear excepted.

The tenant's obligations have been described by Lord Denning in the following words (*Warren v. Keen*, 1953): 'Apart from express contract, a tenant owes a duty to the landlord to keep the premises in a husband-like or, what is the same thing, in a tenant-like manner. It can, I think, best be shown by some illustrations: the tenant must take proper care of the premises. He must, if he is going away for the winter, turn off the water and empty the boiler; he must clean the chimneys when necessary, and also the windows; he must mend the electric light when it fuses. In short he must do little jobs about the place which a reasonable tenant would do. In addition, he must not, of course, damage the house wilfully or negligently; and he must see that his family and guests do not damage it, and if they do so, he must repair it. But apart from such things, if the house falls into disrepair through fair wear and tear or lapse of time, or for any reason not caused by him, the tenant is not liable to repair it.'

12.2 Responsibility for Waste

In addition to any contractual (whether implied or expressed) obligation with regard to maintaining the premises or repairing them, any occupier of land, having a lesser estate than freehold (and this means also a leaseholder), may also be liable for waste. Waste may be defined as **any act which alters the nature of the land**. If the act causes unlawful damage to land and building whereby the value of the property is depreciated to the detriment of the person who is entitled to immediate reversion or remainder, the tenant is liable. This is a tortious liability, independent of any express or implied covenant, and is imposed on any limited owner, not only the tenant holding the land under lease.

The old Common Law interpretation and punishment for waste was most severe and any alteration in the character of the property, even if it was an improvement, was held to be waste. Thus in the case *Cole v. Forth* (1672) a conversion of a manual mill into a horse-driven mill and pulling down a brewhouse and erecting a cottage, whereby the rent was raised from £120 to £200 was held a waste, although a 'meliorating' waste.

Waste may be of two kinds, either voluntary or permissive. **Voluntary waste** is an offence of commission, and consists of doing damage to the premises. Examples of voluntary waste are: pulling down a house, altering its structure, destroying or removing the landlord's fixtures, converting meadow land into arable, cutting trees, despositing rubbish, etc.

Permissive waste is an offence of omission or negligence—that is, permitting something causing damage to the premises to happen, which the tenant is bound by the law to prevent. Examples of permissive waste are: allowing a building to fall for want of necessary repairs, allowing the fence round a park to decay so that deer in the park are dispersed, or allowing a breach in a sea wall to increase so that the land is flooded.

As the Common Law attitude to waste was extremely troublesome for a limited owner in that he was not allowed to use the land to his best abilities, an estate was often granted without 'impeachment for waste', which meant that the limited owner was not liable for any waste whatsoever. To prevent an unconscientious abuse of the power given to tenants in such cases, the Court of Chancery began to intervene and to grant injunctions to restrain limited owners from committing extreme acts of damage. Such gross damage is called **equitable waste**. Pulling down or dismantling a mansion house and cutting down ornamental trees are examples of equitable waste.

The whole doctrine of waste is seldom invoked nowadays as far as leases are concerned, because the tenant is clearly under a much stricter responsibility to use the premises in tenant-like manner.

12.3 Landlord's Responsibility for Repair under the Housing Acts

Apart from the above responsibilities of the tenant under the implied covenant and under the doctrine of waste, which are both of Common Law origin, Statutes impose on the landlord some obligations to repair in respect of some tenancies.

The Statutes in questions are the *Housing Acts, 1957* (as amended by the *Housing Act, 1969*), *1961* and *1974*.

Under s. 6 of the *Housing Act, 1957*, in any contract made on or after July 6, 1957, for the letting of a house for human habitation at a rent not exceeding in London £80 and elsewhere £52 per annum, there is, notwithstanding any stipulation to the contrary, an implied condition that at the commencement of the tenancy the house will be fit for human habitation, with an undertaking that it will be so kept by the landlord during the tenancy. (For earlier contracts the rent limit is lower. The test of human habitation is explained in Chapter 2.)

This condition cannot be contracted out of, i.e. it cannot be excluded by any contractual stipulation. It is not, however, implied if the contract is for not less than three years with a stipulation that the premises should be put by the tenant into a state fit for human habitation and if the lease cannot be terminated before the expiration of three years.

The landlord has a right to enter the premises in order to inspect them after giving 24 hours' notice. Despite the right of entry the tenant cannot recover damages in respect of injuries caused by disrepair unless the landlord has received notice of the defect (*McCarrick v. Liverpool Corporation*, 1946). In this case the tenant's wife fractured her leg by falling on two stone steps leading from the kitchen into the back scullery. By reason of the condition of these steps the house was admitted to be unfit for human habitation. It was held that the tenant was not entitled to recover special damages, because the landlord had not received notice of the state of this disrepair. Since this case was decided, however, the liability for unsafe premises has been recast. If the landlord is under an obligation to repair or maintain the premises, he will be responsible for any personal injury or damage caused by the defective premises if he knows or ought to have known of the relevant defect. This duty is owned to all who may be affected by defects in the state of the premises, and this clearly includes the tenant and his family (*Defective Premises Act, 1972*, s. 4).

It should be stressed that the local authority has the duty to take administrative action (described in Chapter 2) against the person in control of the houses unfit for human habitation. The tenant would be better advised to initiate action against the landlord by reporting the facts to the local authority, than to rely on the covenant implied by s. 6. The administrative channel will normally be more effective than an action for breach of covenant.

SS. 32 and 33 of the *Housing Act, 1961*, provide that in any lease of a dwelling house granted after October 24, 1961, for a term less than seven years, there is to be an implied covenant by the landlord:

(*a*) To keep in repair the structure and exterior of the dwelling house (including drains, gutters and external pipes).

(*b*) To keep in repair and proper working order installations in the dwelling house:

for the supply of water, gas and electricity and for sanitation (including basins, sinks, bath and sanitary conveniences, but not, except as aforesaid, fixtures, fittings and appliances for making use of the supply of water, gas and electricity), and for space and water heating.

Any covenant by the tenant for the repair of the premises is to be of no effect as far as it relates to the matters mentioned above.

This covenant, however, does not impose on the landlord any obligation to rebuild or reinstate the premises in the case of destruction by fire, tempest, flood or other inevitable accident. In particular, the landlord is not responsible for damage caused by the tenant's failure to use the premises in the tenant-like manner (s. 32(2) of the *Housing Act, 1961*).

A possible doubt as to what is meant by the 'exterior of the house' has been resolved by the Court of Appeal in the case of *Hopwood v. Cannok Chase D.C.* (1975), where it was stated that the yard at the back of the house was not part of the exterior of the house. However, access to the front of the house is covered by the Act (*Brown v. Liverpool Corporation*, 1969).

Here again the landlord has a right to inspect the premises after giving

24 hours' notice. The landlord's liability to repair arises only when a defect becomes patent and is made known to him (*O'Brien and Another v. Robinson*, 1973).

The County Court may, if the parties consent and it is considered reasonable in all the circumstances to do so, make an order authorising the inclusion in a lease of provisions which exclude or modify the repairing obligations imposed by the Act.

The obligations imposed by ss. 32 and 33 of the *Housing Act, 1961*, do not depend on the amount of the rent paid.

It should be noted, however, that s. 32 does not apply to a landlord who is a specified educational institution (see page 63), a registered housing association, a local authority, or a government department (s. 80 of the *Housing Act, 1980*).

12.4   Express Covenant of Repair

A covenant to repair, expressed in general terms, usually obliges the tenant to keep the premises in a state of substantial repair, having regard to their age and nature, but the tenant is not responsible for deterioration of the premises due to 'fair wear and tear'. Such a covenant does not extend to the rebuilding of the premises as a whole if necessitated by old age or inherent defect, but it involves the obligation to rebuild premises destroyed by fire, earthquake or other similar causes. For this reason a tenant who accepts such a covenant is well advised to insure the premises even if there is no express covenant obliging him to do so. Destruction by enemy action has been excluded from the obligation to repair by the *Landlord and Tenant* (*War Damage*) *Act, 1939*.

The extent of the landlord's liability if he accepts the responsibility for repair is illustrated by *Jeune v. Queens Cross Properties Ltd* (1973). The landlord covenanted 'to maintain, repair and renew the structure of the property including the external walls thereof'. The Court decided that the landlord had not complied with the covenant since he failed to reinstate a balcony situated at the front of the property in the form in which it existed prior to its partial collapse.

An interesting example of the extent of the tenant's liability is shown by the case of *Lurcott v. Wakely* (1911). A house in London which was some 200 years old was let for a term of 28 years. The tenant covenanted 'well and substantially to repair and keep in thorough repair and good condition all the said premises' and at the end of term to yield them up so repaired. Just before the lease expired the front wall of the house was found in dangerous state and was condemned by the County Council, who required the wall to be taken down and rebuilt with a new concrete foundation, footing and damp course in accordance with the *London Building Act, 1894*. The landlord rebuilt it after the lease had expired and sued the tenant for the cost. Both the Divisional Court and the Court of Appeal expressed the view that the tenant was liable for the cost of taking down and rebuilding the wall. It seems clear, therefore, that when the tenant enters into such a repairing covenant he is bound to renew any part that cannot be otherwise repaired, whether it be a door handle, a door itself, a floor or a wall.

But the tenant is not responsible for an inherent defect in the house let. Thus in *Litter v. Lane* (1895) the house was built upon boggy soil and was 100 years old when let. Owing to the original faulty construction and the passing of time, the house got into a very bad condition and was condemned by the District Surveyor. The tenant was held not liable to rebuild under the covenant 'to repair, uphold, sustain, maintain, amend and keep the demised premises'. Lord Esher in the Court of Appeal said: 'If a tenant takes a house which is of such a kind that by its own inherent nature it will in course of time fall into a particular condition, the effects of that are not within the tenant's covenant to repair. However large the words of the covenant may be, a covenant to repair the house is not a covenant to give a different thing from that which the tenant took when he entered into a covenant. He has to repair that thing which he took; he is not obliged to make a new and different thing.'

However, if the tenant covenants 'to put the premises into repair', here by implication he undertakes to put the premises into a better state of repair than that in which he found them and to make them reasonably fit for occupation by the class of persons who would be likely to inhabit them. Age, character and locality dictate the standard of repair. But the fact that the neighbourhood may have deteriorated during the tenancy does not decrease the standard of repair.

Thus in *Calthorpe v. McOscar* (1924) a 99 years' lease was granted in 1825 of three new houses in Grays Inn, London, the tenant covenanting to repair and to yield up in repair. In 1825 Grays Inn was a rural neighbourhood; by 1920 it had become a slum. At the end of the lease a dispute arose as to the standard of repair expected from the tenant; the Court stated that the relevant time for applying the 'character' and 'locality' part of the text was the beginning of the lease.

Although usually the Court is not prepared to order specific performance to carry out repairs, whether they should be done by the tenant or the landlord, there is one exception to this rule. Under s. 125 of the *Housing Act, 1974*, in any proceedings in which a tenant of the dwelling sues his landlord for breach of a repairing covenant, the Court may, in its discretion, order specific performance of this covenant.

13

ASSIGNMENT AND SUBLEASES

13.1 Enforcement of Covenants after Assignment

It is important to understand the difference between assignment and subleases.

An **assignment** of a lease is a transfer of the whole interest (i.e. the whole term) in the land assigned. The party may assign the entire interest either in the whole or in part of the land being the subject of the lease.

A **sublease** arises when a tenant creates a shorter lease than that which he holds himself, for a subtenant.

The person assigning his interest is called the **assignor**, and the person to whom the assignment is made is the **assignee**.

In everyday language it may be said that when the landlord assigns his interest in land (i.e. his reversionary estate) he sells his land subject to the existing lease. If the tenant assigns his leasehold estate it may be said that he sells the leasehold of the property.

Every landlord and every tenant has the right to assign his interest, and every tenant to create a subtenancy, provided there is no covenant against assignment or subletting.

The assignment is a conveyance, i.e. transfer of an estate in land. A deed, therefore, is required to effect the transfer of the legal lease, even if the lease has been created informally. An agreement to assign a lease is within the scope of s. 40 of the *Law of Property Act, 1925*, and therefore is not enforceable unless there is a note or memorandum evidencing it or some act of part performance.

A lease is a contract, but it is unique because it creates two nexus, or ties, between the landlord and the tenant. These are termed **privities**. They arise between landlord and tenant after they contract a lease. First there is privity of contract, because they have mutual contractual obligations (as in other types of contract). Secondly, there is privity of estate, existing independently of the contract, which arises by the mere fact that the same piece of land 'belongs' to two persons, or, strictly speaking, that two different estates in the same piece of land belong to two persons: the landlord's estate being a fee simple in reversion, and the tenant's a leasehold in possession. In order to appreciate the rights and duties of the parties after the assignment, the concept of the two privities should be well understood.

As long as the original lease subsists, the two privities continue between the two original contracting parties, and there is no need to distinguish them. After the assignment by the tenant, however, the two privities are split. There is still privity of contract between the landlord and the assignor, but there is no longer privity of estate between them, because the latter privity now exists only between the landlord and the assignee. Thus on assignment the privity of estate moves from the original tenant to the assignee.

If the lease is assigned for a second time by the assignee of the first assignment (now the assignor of the second assignment), privity of contract continues to exist between the landlord and the original tenant, but the privity of estate now exists between the landlord and the new assignee. The first assignee disappears completely from the picture, as there is no longer any privity between him and the landlord. There is no privity of contract, because he did not contract with the landlord; the privity of estate has now disappeared, because the first assignee no longer has any estate in the land, the freehold of which belongs to the landlord and leasehold to the second assignee.

This may be illustrated by the following three diagrams (-------- denotes privity of contract, ... denotes privity of estate):

(*a*) *Privities before any assignment:*
   landlord

   tenant

(*b*) *Privities after first assignment:*
   landlord

   tenant   *first assignee*

(*c*) *Privities after second assignment:*
  landlord

  tenant *first assignee*   *second assignee*

In order to understand what happens to the tenant when the lease is assigned, it should be appreciated that all covenants may be divided into two categories. Some covenants relate to the land (or, as is often stated, 'touch and concern the land'); others, although contained in the contract of lease, are of a personal character and do not refer to the land which is the subject of the lease. This distinction was made in the leading *Spencer's case* (1583) and put on a clear statutory basis by s. 79 of the *Law of Property Act, 1925*, which states that the burden of a covenant entered into by the tenant or landlord relating to the land binds the legal assignee of the lease or reversion. Covenants which do not refer to the land are treated as strictly personal obligations and bind only the original parties and not the assignee.

The following covenants have been accepted by Courts as 'touching and concerning the land' and as such 'running with the land':

By the landlord: covenant for quiet enjoyment; for further assurance; for renewal of the lease; allowing in certain circumstances reduction of rent; imposing an obligation on the landlord to erect a new building in place of an old one; to provide a housekeeper to clean the flat, etc.

By the tenant: to pay rent; to pay rates and taxes; to repair; to insure; to use the house as a private dwelling only; against a particular trade; against assignment without licence; to pay a fixed sum towards redecoration in lieu of damage for wear and tear; to reside on the premises; to erect buildings on the land leased; in the case of land near the sea to maintain a sea-wall, even if the wall is not situated on the lease land.

On the other hand, the following covenants are considered to be personal only and as such do not run with the land:

By the landlord: right of re-entry should the tenant be convicted on an arrestable offence; granting the tenant the right to exercise an option to take a lease of other property.
By the tenant: to build a house on land other than that which is the subject of the lease; to pay rates and taxes for land not leased, etc.

13.2　Assignment of Reversion by Landlord and of Lease by Tenant

A landlord may always assign his reversion. The contract of assignment must be evidenced in writing, as provided by s. 40 of the *Law of Property Act, 1925*, and the assignment itself must be made by deed in order to pass the legal estate to the assignee. The benefit and the burden of a covenant entered into by the tenant which relates to the land passes to an assignee of the reversion unless a contrary intention is expressed in the lease.

A tenant has the right to assign his lease if there is nothing in the lease restraining him from doing so; the assignment must, of course, be by deed in order to pass the legal estate to the assignee. The assignment, it is stressed, is a transfer of the whole period for which the tenant possesses the property, as a transfer of the property for any period shorter than that which the tenant holds would be a sublease and not an assignment.

It is possible, however, to assign part of the land which the tenant holds under the lease. If this is done, the rent will be apportioned and the assignee will be responsible to the assignor for payment of his part of the rent, and for complying with the other covenants running with the land. The landlord's rights cannot be affected and he can demand the whole rent from either lease-holder, unless he agreed to the apportionment of the rent. Under s. 190 of the *Law of Property Act, 1925*, a person paying rent which it is the duty of another to pay, is entitled to be indemnified by that other person.

The assignment of the lease by the tenant does not prejudice the personal contract between the landlord and the assignor. The assignor, unless released by the landlord from his obligations, remains responsible for all covenants entered into when the original lease was created, as privity of contract still exists between the assignor and the landlord. The assignee, however, is bound by law to indemnify the assignor against any damage which may be suffered by him through the assignee being in default in performing the obligations which he accepted by the assignment (s. 77 of the *Law of Property Act, 1925*). This means that if the original tenant is sued by the landlord, he can seek an indemnity from the assignee at fault.

As privity of estate now exists between the landlord and the assignee, the latter is responsible to the landlord for those covenants which 'touch and concern' the land. In respect of these covenants the landlord can choose whether to sue the assignor or the assignee. Personal covenants, however, do not run with the land and it is only the assignor who is responsible for them.

13.3 Covenants against Assignment, Underletting or Parting with Possession

This covenant is usually expressed in the above form, which has a wider meaning than a covenant against assignment only.

Although this covenant is not implied, many leases expressly contain it in one form or another. Such a covenant is construed strictly against the landlord, for whose benefit it is stipulated, and therefore it does not cover an involuntary assignment—for example, in the case of death or bankruptcy. The landlord may have a remedy if there is a proviso for termination of the lease on the occurrence of such an event. A covenant against assignment is broken only by a legal assignment of the lease. To prevent avoidance of such a covenant, the obligation not to sublet is usually expressly added, thus including parting with a term shorter than the entire residue. The obligation 'not to part with possession' is added to include non-legal, informal assignments, which may not otherwise be covered by the prohibition. Although an equitable assignment is, therefore, caught, the tenant may still allow other persons to use the premises as long as he retains possession.

This covenant may be so worded as to forbid the assignment absolutely, or it may prohibit this unless the consent of the landlord is first obtained. The covenant, as formerly worded, is called an 'absolute' covenant against assignment, etc.; the latter is called a 'qualified covenant'. Whichever form the restraint takes, an assignment in breach of the covenant is not void. It is effectual in transferring the lease to the assignee, but the landlord may treat the forbidden assignment as a ground for forfeiting the lease, provided that the covenant is accompanied by a proviso for re-entry in such a case.

Until the *Landlord and Tenant Act, 1927*, such a qualified covenant gave the landlord an unrestricted right to refuse permission to assign, but s. 19(1)(a) of that Act provided that every covenant, condition or agreement against assigning, underletting or parting with possession of the leased premises without licence or consent is made subject to an implied proviso that the consent must not be unreasonably withheld.

The tenant must not assign, etc., without asking for consent, otherwise he would be in breach of the covenant. Consent must be asked for but, if it is refused and in the tenant's opinion the refusal is unreasonable, he can do one of two things: he can proceed with the assignment using the unreasonableness of the refusal as a defence against a possible action by the landlord for damages or forfeiture; alternatively, he may apply to the Court for a declaratory judgment that the consent has been unreasonably withheld. The second course of action is safer from the point of view of the tenant, as once he has such a declaratory judgment he can assign safely.

The older cases tended to accept that it was reasonable to refuse permission only on grounds connected with status or character of the assignee. Recently, however, the Courts have adopted a less restrictive view and consent may now be considered to be reasonably withheld:

(*a*) When the personality of the assignee is objectionable for some personal or financial reason. Under s. 5(1) of the *Race Relations Act, 1965*, withholding of consent on the grounds of colour, race, ethnic or racial origins is to be treated as unreasonable.

(*b*) When the assignee's intended use of the property would differ from the original, and when the intended use (even if not forbidden by any covenant of the original use) would be detrimental to the premises demised or other property of the lessor.

(*c*) When the primary object of the assignment is to provide the assignee with a protected tenancy upon the termination of the lease proper (*Lee v. Carter*, 1949). This case concerned a limited company which sought consent to assign the lease of the flat to one of the directors, who would then have held it under a protected tenancy.

It has been accepted, however, that the consent of the landlord is unreasonably withheld if he refuses consent in order to get some advantage for himself as, for example, to obtain a surrender of the lease or to prevent the assignee from giving up other premises belonging to the landlord.

The burden of proof is on the tenant to show that the consent was been unreasonably withheld.

One type of lease, however, is freely assignable. An assignment, underletting or parting with possession is allowed by s. 19(1)(b) of the *Landlord and Tenant Act, 1927*, if the lease is for more than 40 years and is made in consideration wholly or partially of the erection or the substantial improvement, addition or alteration of buildings (and the lessor is not a Government Department or local or public authority). For assigning, subletting or parting with possession taking effect more than seven years before the end of the term no consent or licence is required; only a notice of the transaction should be given in writing to the landlord within six months after the transaction is effected. Thus long-term building leases are freely assignable, and only 'end-leases' for a remaining period of less than seven years require consent. The consent in respect of end-leases is required because the lessee is under an obligation (often very burdensome) to hand over the premises in the same state as let, and the landlord may be prejudiced by the assignment of the end-lease to a financially unstable person.

14

TERMINATION OF LEASES

14.1 Frustration

It is not possible to enumerate or to classify all the circumstances in which contracts can be terminated by frustration. Frustration occurs when unforeseeable contingencies prevent the attainment of the purpose of the contract intended by the parties. It may be described as the 'stultification of the contract by subsequent events' (Cheshire).

The most common cause is accidental destruction of the subject matter of the contract before performance falls due. The contract of lease is, generally speaking, not susceptible to frustration because it is not only a contract, but also a conveyance of an estate in land, which is indestructible. This was decided in the case *Paradine v. Jane* (1647). Shortly after the lease had been granted, Roundheads occupied the land. Nevertheless, it was held that the rent was due even for the period when the tenant was forced out of the possession.

A more recent example of the same principle is *Cricklewood Property and Investment Trust Ltd v. Leighton Investment Trust Ltd* (1945). In May 1936 a building lease was granted to the tenant for 99 years. Before any building was erected, war broke out and restrictions imposed by the Government made it impossible for the tenant to erect the shops that they covenanted to build. In an action brought against them for the recovery of rent, it was pleaded that the lease was frustrated, but it was held unanimously by the House of Lords that, even if the doctrine of frustration were in some circumstances applicable to a lease, it did not apply in the circumstances in question. One of the Law Lords said *obiter* that there was a possibility of termination of a lease by frustration in a 'rare occurrence' (*obiter* indicates statements not part of a decision but given by way of explanation or illustration).

Some authors (for example Treitel) consider that the doctrine of *Paradine v. Jane* is outdated, that the contractual aspect of the lease should have preference before the conveyance aspect and that, therefore, frustration of leases should be accepted in suitable circumstances, particularly in short leases.

However, recently, in the case of *National Carriers Ltd v. Panalpina* (*Northern*) *Ltd* (*The Times*, December 16, 1980) the House of Lords expressed their unanimous view that frustration of leases was possible. (Lord Hailsham was reported as being of the opinion that though such cases might be rare, the doctrine of frustration was capable of application in leases of land, though it must be applied with proper regard to the fact that a grant of a legal estate was involved.)

14.2 Termination of Leases under Common Law

When considering the various methods by which the lease may be terminated at Common Law, it should be borne in mind that 'social' legislation protects many types of tenancies (residential, business and agricultural), granting tenants security of tenure and limitation of rent. This complex problem is discussed in later chapters. However, should such statutory protection not apply, Common Law principles come into operation and the lease is terminated according to Common Law rules. Hence the Common Law is still basically applicable despite the superimposition of social legislation.

A tenancy may be terminated in one of the following ways:

(a) By effluxion of time

Only leases for fixed terms are determined by the expiration of the time for which they have been created. However, this does not fully apply to tenancies protected by legislation, when after the termination of the contractual term a statutory tenancy arises.

(b) By exercise of an express power

A lease for a fixed term may contain a proviso giving powers to one or either party to terminate the lease prematurely.

(c) By disclaimer

Disclaimer may be effected either by a trustee in bankruptcy (or liquidator of a company) or by the tenant himself. Disclaimer by a trustee in bankruptcy is dealt with by the *Bankruptcy Act, 1914*. The trustee in bankruptcy may disclaim—that is, terminate—the lease if he comes to the conclusion that the lease of which the bankrupt is tenant is onerous to the estate. Such disclaimer is, of course, a breach of contract and damages may be claimed by proving for them in the bankruptcy proceedings. Disclaimer by the tenant is a breach of implied covenant (page 34), but in addition such behaviour terminates the lease.

(d) By merger

A lease is terminated by merger when the reversion and the lease become vested in the same person and there is no evidence that the person did not intend a merger. In this case the lesser estate (the leasehold) becomes merged in the greater estate (the freehold). A simple example of merger is when the tenant acquires the freehold from his landlord.

(e) By surrender

A lease is terminated by surrender when the tenant yields up the term to his immediate reversioner. A surrender may be express or by operation of law. An **express surrender** must be by deed or, if the lease is under three years, in writing. A **surrender by operation of law** occurs when the tenant acts in a way which is inconsistent with the continuation of the tenancy. The most usual instances of such inconsistent acts are: (i) delivery of possession to the landlord; (ii) a grant of a new tenancy to the tenant if this new tenancy overlaps with the old one; (iii) disappearance of the tenant without leaving an address or abandoning the subject of lease. Surrender must be accepted by the landlord.

(f) By forfeiture

This method is also called 'the exercise of the right of entry' or, more popularly (particularly in respect of periodic tenancies), **eviction**. As this type of termination is available to the landlord only in the case of breach of covenant, it will be discussed later amongst the remedies of the landlord for breach of covenant (Chapter 16).

(g) *By notice to quit*

It is only in respect of periodical tenancies that the lease may be terminated by a notice to quit. The general rule is that the notice must correspond with the period of the tenancy. Thus weekly tenancy requires a weekly notice, a monthly tenancy a month's notice, but yearly tenancies require only a six months' notice. This is the longest notice required by Common Law.

There are, however, three exceptions to this rule: (i) agricultural tenancies require 12 months' notice (*Agricultural Holdings Act, 1948*); (ii) s. 5. of the *Protection from Eviction Act, 1977*, provides that any notice in respect of a dwelling-house should be given four weeks before the end of intended termination, even if it is a weekly tenancy; (iii) business tenancies are also subject to special provisions in respect of the length of service of notice, which will be discussed in Chapter 23.

A notice to quit must expire at the end of the period of the tenancy. Thus a weekly tenancy from Saturday to Friday may be terminated by a notice expiring on Friday and a monthly tenancy corresponding to a calendar month may be terminated by a notice expiring at the last day of the month.

15

RIGHTS AND DUTIES OF THE PARTIES ON DETERMINATION OF LEASES

15.1 Landlord's Right to Possession

When a tenancy comes to an end, by whatever method, the position at Common Law is that the landlord has the right to possession of the land. Social legislation has restricted this right and, in some circumstances, extended the tenancy beyond the contractual term. However, when any tenancy finally comes to an end, it is the duty of the tenant to deliver up to his landlord vacant possession of the whole of the subject of the lease, together with all buildings, improvements and fixtures, unless he is entitled to remove them. If the tenant has sublet the premises or part of them, it is his duty to get rid of his subtenant before his own tenancy ends.

The obtaining of possession by the landlord must be peaceful as, under the *Protection from Eviction Act, 1977*, it is a criminal offence to force an entry. Therefore, the landlord cannot recover possession of dwelling-houses against the will of the tenant unless he obtains an order or judgment of the Court. In addition, under the *Protection of Eviction Act, 1977*, it is a criminal offence for anyone to harass or intimidate a person occupying premises as a residence with a view to forcing him to give up possession or to restrain him from pursuing any legal remedy open to him (page 84).

15.2 Tenant's Right to Remove Fixtures

A fixture may be defined as a thing of chattel nature annexed to the land. By annexation the thing ceases to be a chattel in the legal sense and becomes part of the land itself.

Annexation is not necessarily a matter of physical attachment. It may be direct, indirect or even constructive. Examples of these three types of annexation are gate posts which are directly annexed to the land; while the gate itself is indirectly annexed by being fixed to the posts; the key to the gate is annexed 'constructively'.

Sometimes it is not easy to decide whether a chattel is a fixture or not. The true test relates to the object and purpose of annexation. The mode of annexation is only evidence helping to decide whether a thing is a fixture or not. Thus in the case of *Holland v. Hodgson* (1872), L.J. Blackburn stated: 'Articles not otherwise attached to the land than by their own weight are not to be considered as part of the land, unless the circumstances are such as to show that they are intended to be part of land, the onus of showing that they were so intended being on those who contend that they ceased to be chattels; on the contrary, any article which is affixed to the land even slightly is to be considered as part of the land, unless the circumstances are such as to show that it was intended all along to continue a chattel, the onus lying on those who contend that it is a chattel.'

In most cases common sense will clearly show what remains a chattel, although attached to the land to some degree, and what becomes a fixture. For example, a carpet nailed to the floor, a picture hung on the wall, a bookcase, or a grandfather clock secured to the wall are clearly chattels. The purpose of annexation and nature of the thing itself provides an answer. Also electric bulbs, a ship's anchor or a tent are not fixtures. On the other hand, domestic stoves and grates built into the house, chimneys, wainscoting, panelling, picture rails, fixed baths, wash basins, sinks and radiators connected with pipes, locks and bars, gas and electric light brackets and pendants are fixtures. Statues, ornaments and stone seats merely resting on the ground, but forming a part of the architectural design of the land, have been held to be fixtures.

Fixtures are divided into landlord's fixtures, which the tenant has no right to remove (even if he brought them onto the premises, as they became the landlord's property), and tenant's fixtures, which he is entitled to remove provided, of course, that they had been brought by him. He must remove them before leaving the premises or (in some circumstances) within a reasonable period thereafter.

It is the general rule that fixtures must not be removed and that they have become landlord's fixtures ('whatever has been affixed to the land, goes with the land'). This rule, however, is subject to three exceptions where the fixtures become tenant's fixtures.

(a) Trade Fixtures

Common Law has relaxed the rule that a fixture necessarily becomes the property of the owner of the land in the case of trade fixtures. Thus, if the chattel has been affixed for the purpose of trade, the tenant is entitled to remove it, provided that it is a chattel perfect in itself, independently of the union with the soil, and can be removed without being entirely demolished or losing its essential character or value. This relaxation of the rule has been allowed to encourage trade and industry.

Examples of trade fixtures are machinery attached to the premises, pumping apparatus at a petrol station, etc. If removal would cause irreparable damage to the premises, then even trade fixtures cannot be removed and in any case any damage caused by the removal must be made good, as otherwise the tenant would be responsible for waste or breach of the implied covenant to surrender the premises at the end of tenancy in a proper state.

(b) Agricultural Fixtures

At Common Law (*Elwes v. Maw*, 1802) the relaxation in respect of trade fixtures did not extend to agricultural holdings. However, under the *Agricultural Holdings Act, 1948* (consolidating in this respect the *Landlord and Tenant Act, 1851*), the right of removal of agricultural fixtures was given to the tenant to roughly the same extent as in the case of trade fixtures. The tenant has a duty to give the landlord one month's notice and grant him a right to purchase the fixtures if the landlord so desires; the price, if no agreement is reached, is assessed by the Agricultural Land Tribunal.

(c) Domestic and Decorative Fixtures

Chattels which have been affixed by the tenant to the premises by way of ornament or for domestic convenience and utility are removable by the tenant, because it would not be equitable for the landlord to obtain ownership of articles which may be of great value. This is well illustrated by *Spyer v. Phillipson* (1931). The tenant had a lease of a flat for 21 years. Some years before the end of the lease the tenant installed some antique panelling, worth £5000 with chimney-pieces and fireplaces to match and friezes and a false ceiling to complete the decoration. The panelling was firmly attached by screws driven into the walls. The original fireplaces were removed and in one room the cornice was taken away. Parts of the brickwork were cut away to fix the new fireplaces. The tenant died and his executors claimed the right to remove panelling, etc. The landlord objected, but the Court of Appeal decided the case in favour of the executors. It was specifically stated that all damage done by the erection or removal of the fixtures had to be made good. The reason for this decision was that there was no intention in the part of the tenant that the panelling should become part of the premises. The proper inference was that the tenant intended to enjoy the panelling himself and not to benefit the premises.

Thus tapestry, mirrors, blinds and cornices are ornamental fixtures and stones, grates, pumps, furnaces, ovens, tubs, fences, cupboards and gas fittings are examples of domestic fixtures, both types of fixtures being removable by the tenant.

16

LANDLORD'S REMEDIES FOR BREACH OF COVENANTS

16.1 Non-payment of Rent

As there are different remedies for non-payment of rent and for breaches of other covenants, the two sets of remedies will be treated separately.

There are three remedies the landlord can resort to if the rent is not paid.

(a) Court Action for Recovery of Rent

A landlord may recover arrears of rent when there is a written, oral or implied agreement for payment of rent. When a person has been in occupation of land without an agreement fixing the rent, the landlord may bring an action for damages 'for use and occupation', under the *Distress for Rent Act, 1737*. This action is appropriate in cases of a tenant holding over after the contractual tenancy has ended, or where there is permissive occupation without any contract. An acceptance of or demanding a rent from a person in occupation of land by implication creates a tenancy; the landlord, therefore, must not accept rent from a tenant after terminating the lease by notice or after exercising the right of forfeiture. By provision of the *Limitation Act, 1939*, only six years' arrears of rent can be sued for.

(b) Distress

Distress is the taking of another person's chattel without legal process, as a pledge for performance of duty. However, under s. 147 of the *Rent Act, 1977*, no distress for arrears of rent let on a protected tenancy shall be levied except with the leave of the County Court (for further details see page 85). Of the various purposes for which distress could be made under Common Law, the most important is distress for the recovery of rent in arrears. By statute it is possible to distrain for arrears in rates (a warrant must be issued by Magistrates' Court) and taxes (the warrant must be issued by the General Commissioners—*Taxes Management Act, 1970*).

The general rule is that the landlord may distrain all chattels found on the demised land. Certain articles, however, are absolutely exempted from distress by Common Law or Statutes, while other articles are 'conditionally' privileged, which means that they may be taken only when there are no other chattels of sufficient value that do not enjoy any privilege.

The most important categories of chattels absolutely privileged are:

(a) Property of the Crown.

(b) Property of persons enjoying diplomatic immunity.

(c) Property already impounded in execution; the landlord, however, may notify the bailiff of the arrears of rent and the 12 months' arrears of rent have a prior claim (*Landlord and Tenant Act, 1709*). In the case of bankruptcy of the tenant, six months' arrears of rent constitute a privileged debt. The balance may be proved in bankruptcy.

(*d*) Property delivered to a person carrying on a public trade to be dealt with in exercise of the trade. Goods sent to a warehouse to be stored or goods sent to an auctioneer to be sold which are deposited in the premises in question are examples.

(*e*) Clothing, bedding and tools of the tenant's trade up to the value of £50. This amount may be increased by the Order of Lord Chancellor. 'Bedding' and 'tools of trade' are widely interpreted. A sewing machine hired by a husband for the use of his wife, who earned money as a seamstress to help cover household expenses, was accepted as privileged under this heading. It has been held that so long as clothing and bedding have not exhausted the amount privileged, a cab used by a taxi driver can be accepted as an implement of trade, and so was a piano used by a music teacher.

(*f*) Some other goods not belonging to the tenant. There are so many exceptions under the Common Law and the *Law of Distress* (*Amendment*) *Act, 1908*, that it is easier to state which articles not belonging to the tenant may be distrained. These include chattels belonging to the husband or wife of the tenant, chattels comprised in a hire-purchase agreement (but only if the agreement has not been terminated), goods in possession of the tenant under such circumstances that the tenant is the 'reputed owner' of the goods, goods of the partner of the tenant. Thus goods belonging to subtenants and lodgers are privileged.

The following goods are subject to conditional privilege:

beasts of the plough;
sheep;
instruments of husbandry;
the tools of the man's trade (if not protected absolutely under the rules explained above)—the axe of a carpenter, the books of a scholar and the stocking frame of a weaver have been held to be within this rule.

It may be seen that logic is not the prime characteristic of the distinctions as regards privilege.

As a general rule distress may be levied only on goods found on the demised premises, but if the tenant has fraudulently or clandestinely removed the chattels, the bailiff may, within 30 days after removal, seize them as a distress wherever they may be found, provided that they have not been sold *bona fide* to any person not aware of the fraud (*Distress Act, 1737*).

Only six years' arrears of rent may be subject to distress, but in agricultural land only one year's arrears may be realised by this method (s. 18 of the *Agricultural Holdings Act, 1948*).

A landlord may distrain either personally or through a bailiff. No person may levy distress as a bailiff unless certified by a County Court judge (*Law of Distress Amendment Act, 1888*).

The distrainor may seize chattels by actually taking them into possession, or by preparing a list of the distrained articles and leaving the list with the tenant. Leaving the goods on the premises (the usual procedure nowadays) is called **walking possession**. Distrained goods are considered to be in custody of the law.

Distrained goods may be sold in the free market for the best price available, but usually sale is by auction in order to avoid any complaint from the tenant that the price was not the best available. Neither the bailiff nor the landlord can buy the distrained chattels, even if they are sold by auction.

If the distress was illegal for any reason (if the rent was not due, if there was an irregularity in procedure, or if the distress was excessive), the tenant may either ask the Court for an injunction to stop the procedure or, if the distress was completed, he may sue for damages. There is also the possibility of taking an ancient action called **replevin**. This is an action to obtain a re-delivery of chattels wrongly distrained on providing sufficient security for the rent and costs of the action, and on the owner undertaking to bring an action to determine the right to distrain without delay.

One interesting procedure was introduced by the *Law of Distress Amendment Act, 1895*. It has been mentioned that clothes, bedding and tools of the tenant's trade up to a specified sum are absolutely privileged against distress. In order to provide a cheap and quick remedy against distress wrongful in this respect, a Magistrates' Court, on complaint that the goods and chattels exempted from distress have been taken, may by summary order direct that the goods and chattels be restored. If they have been sold already, the Court may direct that a sum determined by the Court, representing the value of the things sold, should be paid to the complainant.

(c) Forfeiture

A properly drafted lease contains a proviso ('forfeiture clause') allowing the landlord to terminate the lease and re-enter on the occurrence of specified breaches of contract by the tenant. Such breaches do not make the lease void, but only voidable, as it is up to the landlord to exercise his option to determine the lease if he wishes.

A forfeiture clause for non-payment of rent must be expressly reserved in the lease. It is usually inserted in shorter leases but not in long, building leases, as in such leases the capital payment is high and covers virtually the cost of building, and the rent itself ('ground rent') is comparatively low and may be easily realised by other means (described above under (*a*) and (*b*)).

It has long been settled that Equity may provide relief against forfeiture for non-payment of rent, whenever appropriate, considering a proviso for re-entry a mere security for obtaining the rent.

At Common Law a demand for rent was necessary before invoking the forfeiture clause, but, under the *Common Law Procedure Act, 1852*, a landlord is not required to serve a demand if rent is six months in arrears and there are insufficient goods to be distrained. The same Act provides for more extensive relief. Even if proceedings for forfeiture have already been initiated, the tenant may stay all further proceedings by paying the arrears of rent and costs to the landlord or to the Court. Moreover, there is a further discretionary remedy for the tenant. Even if judgment and execution have been obtained against the tenant in an action for ejectment for non-payment of rent, the tenant can nevertheless proceed to ask for relief in Equity within six months after the date the execution was issued. But if the Court considers that the tenant has been guilty of unreasonable delay in applying for relief, the judge may well refuse it, particularly if the landlord has relet the premises to a new tenant.

Further relief in respect of protected tenancies of dwelling-houses is explained below, as it refers to forfeiture actions for a breach of any covenant covered by a forfeiture clause.

16.2   Breaches of Covenant other than Payment of Rent

The landlord has two remedies for breaches of covenants other than payment of rent: (*a*) action for damages, which is available to the landlord whenever a covenant is broken; (*b*) forfeiture (action for re-entry) which is available to the landlord only if a proviso for forfeiture has been expressly reserved in the lease.

(*a*) *Action for Damages*

The most common covenant which gives ground for an action for damages is the covenant to repair the premises by the tenant. In such cases, in the absence of a proviso for re-entry, this is the only remedy. Specific performance will not be granted for the simple reason that supervision is extremely difficult, as 'standard of repair' is a matter of opinion.

The measure of damages depends on the following circumstances:

(*a*) If the action is brought during the currency of the lease, the damages amount to the diminution in the value of the landlord's reversion that results from the breach.

(*b*) If the action is brought after the termination of the lease, the old rule was that the measure of damages was the sum it would take to put the premises into repair. Now, however, it is provided by s. 18 of the *Landlord and Tenant Act, 1927*, that the damages must in no case exceed the amount by which the value of the reversion is diminished. Thus, no damages are recoverable if the premises are shortly to be pulled down, or if the repairs covered by the covenant are for any other reason valueless to the reversion.

Damages for breach of any other covenant amount to the loss resulting from the breach, as in the case of any other contract (the rule in *Hadley v. Baxendale*, 1854).

(*b*) *Forfeiture*

In an exceptional case re-entry may be sought (even without an express covenant) upon the conviction of the tenant under the *Sexual Offences Act, 1956*, for allowing the premises to be used as a brothel. The landlord is entitled to require the tenant to assign the lease to a person approved by the landlord (this approval must not be unreasonably withheld). If the tenant fails to assign within three months, the landlord may determine the lease.

Apart from this, the right of re-entry must be reserved in the agreement.

Before the right of re-entry can be enforced, the landlord must serve on the tenant a notice under s. 146 of the *Law of Property Act, 1925*. The notice must specify the breach, give reasonable time for remedy of the breach if at all possible and demand damages if appropriate. Such a notice, if in respect of breach of the covenant for repair, is called a **schedule of delapidations**. This notice must be drafted with caution. The demand in the notice must reasonably correspond to the obligations in the covenant which have been broken. If the notice demands anything in excess of the obligations in the covenant, the whole notice may be struck as bad.

This is illustrated by the case of *Guillemard v. Silverstone* (1908). At that time the *Conveyancing Act, 1881,* contained identical provisions to those of s. 146 of the *Law of Property Act, 1925.* The notice in this case set out the general covenant to repair, and then two further special painting covenants which the lease did not contain. The notice had annexed a schedule of jobs to be done, some of which were not required by the general covenant. In these circumstances the whole notice was held to be bad.

In another case, however (*Silvester v. Ostrowska, 1959*), a notice to remedy a breach of covenant to repair that also alleged the breach of a non-existing covenant against subletting was held to be good.

It is not necessary to give detailed specifications of the work to be done (although it is advisable). Thus in the case of *Fox v. Folly* (1916) a row of houses was subject to one lease and to one repair covenant. The notice stated that the covenant to repair had been broken and dealt with the repairs required under various headings such as 'roofs', without specifying which particular house or houses were referred to. It was held by the House of Lords that sufficient information had been given to satisfy what is now s. 146.

S. 147 of the *Law of Property Act, 1925,* provides a special form of relief in respect of the covenant to perform internal decorative repairs. The tenant may apply for relief and the Court—if satisfied that the notice requiring redecoration is excessive or unreasonable in all the circumstances, including the length of the tenant's term remaining unexpired—may relieve the tenant wholly or partially from liability for such repairs.

In respect of the tenant's contractual duty to repair the premises further relief is provided by the *Leasehold Property Repair Act, 1938.* In the case of any property other than an agricultural holding held on a lease for a term of seven years or more (with three years unexpired), when a notice is served under s. 146 in respect of repair, the tenant may serve a counter-notice within 28 days claiming the benefit of the Act. In this situation no proceedings for the enforcement of the repair covenant may be started without the leave of the Court, which, generally speaking, is given only when it is equitable that such a leave should be given (s. 1(5)).

Under s. 100 of the *Rent Act, 1977,* an application for possession of a dwelling subject to a protected or statutory tenancy may be adjourned, or postponed and the execution stayed or suspended by the Court, or an order may be issued conditionally, or after being issued rescinded on application of the tenant. This extremely wide discretion means that in practice in an action for ejection of the tenant for breach of any covenant (be it payment of rent, repair or other covenant) the County Court can make the following decisions:

(*a*) The judge may simply adjourn the case in order to give the tenant time to pay arrears of rent or to comply with other covenants.

(*b*) He may grant possession suspended on condition that the tenant pays the current rent and some additional sum towards arrears; this is an effective measure, as it compels the tenant to pay not only arrears by instalment, but also current rent if he wants to avoid eviction.

(*c*) He may grant possession, not immediately, but after a fixed period in order to give the tenant time to find other accommodation (it is usual, barring exceptional circumstances, to grant possession of a dwelling house only after at least 28 days have expired).

Forfeiture, whether for non-payment of rent or for breach of other covenant, is presumed to be waived (i.e. given up) by the landlord if he acknowledges the continuance of the tenancy for the period after the forfeiture. Accepting rent which has accrued since the forfeiture, distraining for such rent or suing for it amount to a waiver of the right to forfeit. Such an acceptance of or demand for the rent for the period after the forfeiture, even under protest or 'without prejudice', amounts to a waiver (*Segal Securities Ltd v. Thoseby*, 1963; *Central Estate (Belgravia) Ltd v. Woolgar*, N.2., 1973).

17

SOCIAL LEGISLATION PROTECTING TENANTS

17.1 Scope of Social Legislation

Since 1915, when the first *Increase of Rent and Mortgage Interest* (*War Restrictions*) *Act* was passed, social legislation protecting tenants has been with us in one form or another and it is certain it will remain for many years to come.

Social legislation protects three types of tenancies, albeit in different ways. As defined by the Acts, these, taken together, include virtually all tenancies which exist at present—namely, tenancies of dwelling-houses, business premises and agricultural holdings.

In all three types of tenancies protection entails the limitation of rent and security of tenure. The two have to go together, because limitation of rent would be of little value to the tenant if the landlord were able to terminate the tenancy at will; similarly, security of tenure would not be worth much to the tenant if not accompanied by a limitation of rent. In addition, in business and agricultural tenancies it is very important to encourage the tenant to improve his holding in order to make the business (or agriculture) as efficient as possible and for this reason in these two types of tenancies it is provided that the tenant (under specified conditions) may claim compensation for improvements made by him.

In addition, there is a need for a number of ancillary provisions in respect of dwelling tenancies, either to give the tenant additional protection or to ensure that he is not subject to devious stratagems by the landlord. These provisions include the obligatory issue of rent books, the giving of extended periods of notice to terminate tenancies, provisions against harassment and the conferring of a wide discretion to the Court to grant various reliefs.

The problem of social legislation will be dealt with as follows: first the protection of dwelling-houses in both the private and public sector will be considered; secondly, attention will be given to business tenancies; and lastly a short account will be given about the main provisions pertaining to agricultural holdings. This last type of tenancy will be dealt with in bare outline as it is too technical to be considered in more detail here.

A short historical outline is given about each type of protection, as only by tracing the history of the legislation is it possible to understand it fully and appreciate its meaning and significance.

A word of warning: the legislation covered here is so complex that it can be discussed in outline only by explaining the main principles. We are dealing (as one judge commented) with 'a jungle of legislation, sometimes ill designed, causing endless litigation' (*Central Estates* (*Belgravia*) *Ltd v. Woolgar*, 1971). The student who wants to master the subject thoroughly in all its details should consult more detailed treatises.

17.2 History of the Rent Acts and Allied Legislature

Until the First World War the supply and demand of houses were fairly well balanced and there was therefore no need for the Government to intervene by introducing any regulatory measures.

At the beginning of the First World War several factors contributed to an acute shortage of accommodation in towns. The nation's effort was directed towards the production of war materials and so the building of new houses virtually stopped. There was a great migration of the rural population to the towns to work in factories. Houses were not repaired and maintained. The Government was anxious to maintain the value of the pound and to fight inflation. For these reasons the first Rent Restriction Act was passed as a temporary measure for the duration of the First World War. However, hopes that the shortage of accommodation would disappear after the war were not realised, and therefore a number of Rent Restriction Acts were passed between the wars covering rents in houses of rather low rateable value and therefore concerning less affluent tenants.

As a result, many houses were let at rents which bore no relation to the open market value of the houses and eventually—by the *Housing Act, 1980*—these **controlled tenancies** (as they were called) were abolished.

Since the *Rent Act, 1965*, however, we have another kind of protection of tenants: **regulated tenancies**. This Act considerably extended the scope of tenancies protected and attempted to introduce a more flexible and sensible policy in respect of rent. Regulated tenancies covered all tenancies of dwelling-houses with the exceptions stated by the Act. The regulated tenancies were visualised as a long-term expedient, although it was provided that the Secretary of State may, by order, provide for partial or total exemption from protection of dwelling-houses in a given area. However, no such order has been issued and it is not expected that any will be issued in the foreseeable future, as the shortage of accommodation is still with us.

The *Rent Act, 1965*, was amended on several occasions, the most important being: the *Housing Act, 1969*, the *Housing Finance Act, 1972*, the *Counter Inflation Acts, 1972* and *1973*, the *Rent Act, 1974*, and the *Housing Rent and Subsidies Act, 1975*. The *Rent Act, 1965*, and the subsequent amendments were consolidated for the first time by the *Rent Act, 1968*, but as a result of subsequent piecemeal amendments the law became so complex that it was advisable to consolidate again the existing Acts covering protected tenancies of dwelling houses.

This has been done by two Acts:

(*a*) The *Rent Act, 1977*, which consolidated the 1968 Act and those parts of other Acts which dealt with protected tenancies. Virtually the whole of statutory law dealing with the protection of tenancies of dwelling-houses was covered by this Act (long tenancies not protected by Rent Acts are dealt with by the *Landlord and Tenant Act, 1954*, and by the *Leasehold Reform Act, 1967*, discussed in Chapter 26).

(*b*) The *Protection from Eviction Act, 1977*, which consolidated the *Rent Act, 1965*, in so far as it was not repealed, i.e. sections dealing with protection against harassment and other ancillary matters. This Act applies to all tenancies of dwelling-houses, irrespective of their rateable value or of the fact that they may be exempted from protection for other reasons.

In 1980, as a result of the Conservative Government coming into power, a radical change of policy regarding protection of tenants of dwelling-houses was introduced by the *Housing Act, 1980*.

The old controlled tenancies (with admittedly unrealistically low rent) have been abolished. Two new concepts have been created: ss. 51–55 made provision for **shorthold tenancies**; landlords are able to let dwellings at a fair rent for fixed terms of between one and five years, at the end of which they have the right to regain possession. SS. 56–58 and Schedule 5 introduced **assured tenancies**. 'Approved landlords' are able to let newly constructed dwellings outside the protection afforded by the Rent Act. 'Approved landlords' means a body specified for the purpose of the Act by an Order to be issued by the Secretary of State.

This short historical outline deals only with the protection of dwelling-houses covered by the *Rent Act, 1977*. Additional chapters (22–24) deal with long tenancies, business tenancies and tenancies of agricultural holdings.

17.3 Protected and Statutory Tenancies

A tenancy under which a dwelling-house (which may be a house or part of a house) is let as a separate dwelling is a **protected tenancy** for the purposes of the Act (s. 1 of the *Rent Act, 1977*). Thus the general rule is that all tenancies of dwelling-houses are protected unless exempted by the Act.

Whether a tenancy at will is within the Rent Act is debatable. In an early case decided in 1943 (*Francis Jackson Developments v. Stamp*) the Court of Appeal accepted a tenancy at will as being within the Rent Restrictions Acts, but this case was decided on peculiar facts and it is far from clear whether such a tenancy would be within the *Rent Act, 1977* (see Meggary, *Rent Act*, Vol. 1, page 510).

A dwelling-house (be it a separate building or flat) must be let as a separate dwelling in order to be protected. A tenancy does not enjoy full protection (but will be protected to a limited extent, as explained on page 66) if any vital living accommodation—for example, a living-room or bedroom—is shared with the landlord. However, the sharing of ancillary parts, such as the hall, a lavatory or a bathroom, does not deprive the dwelling of its separate character and such dwellings are fully protected. In some cases (e.g. the sharing of a kitchen) it is a matter of degree whether the dwelling is deemed to be shared or not.

If the tenant has the exclusive occupation of any accommodation and uses other accommodation in common with another person not being the landlord, the separate accommodation is deemed to be a dwelling let on a protected tenancy.

Statutory tenancies come into existence in the following two circumstances:

(*a*) A tenant whose contracted tenancy has come to the end and remains in possession owing to the protection given by the Act (perhaps against the will of the landlord) is called a statutory tenant (s. 2 of the 1977 Act).

(*b*) If the original tenant dies, then the first and second successors are protected in the same manner as the original tenant and become statutory tenants

(s. 2 and Schedule 1). The widow of the tenant is a statutory successor if she resided in the dwelling-house immediately before the death of the original tenant. Any other member of the tenant's family must have resided in the dwelling-house for six months preceding the tenant's death in order to obtain a status of successor. In the case of *Dyson Holdings Ltd v. Fox* (1976) Lord Denning said: 'In view of the change in the social climate the so-called "common law wife" [cohabitee] should be considered as having been a member of the tenant's family.'

Although a statutory tenant enjoys the same security of tenure as a protected one, his legal position is quite different. A statutory tenant has no estate or property in the land, but merely a personal right to remain in the dwelling-house. His interest is nothing more than a status of 'irremovability'; his landlord may terminate such a tenancy and obtain possession of the property, but only on a court order in specified circumstances described below. A statutory tenant must occupy the dwelling himself, unless prevented from living there temporarily, in which case he must evince a clear intention to return to it as soon as he can. The terms and covenants of the previous contractual tenancy (e.g. in respect of subletting, repair, etc.) bind the statutory tenant as if he were still a protected (i.e. contractual) tenant.

17.4   Exceptions from Protection

There are a number of tenancies that are expected from protection owing to their terms, to the character of dwelling, or to the status of the landlord (ss. 4–16 of the 1977 Act and ss. 152 *et seq.* of the *Housing Act, 1980*).

(a) Dwelling-Houses above a Certain Rateable Value

A tenancy is not a protected tenancy if the rateable value of the dwelling-house exceeds the limit prescribed by the Act. The limit refers to the rateable value at the 'appropriate day', i.e. either March 23, 1965, or the first day on which the dwelling appears on the valuation list, whichever is the earlier (s. 25(3)).

For all dwellings (disregarding their 'appropriate day') the limit is £1500 in London and £750 elsewhere—under the valuation which existed on April 1, 1973, or, if its first appearance on the valuation list falls after that date, on the date of listing on the valuation list.

If the appropriate day falls between March 22 and March 31, 1973, it is sufficient if the rateable value of the dwelling falls below £600 in London or £300 elsewhere under the valuation valid at that time (even if under the valuation existing after April 1, 1973, it exceeds £1500 or £750 as the case may be).

If the appropriate day falls before March 22, 1973, then another alternative is added: the rateable value may be under £400 in London or £200 elsewhere (under the valuation valid until March 31, 1973).

Thus, in the first instance, it should be checked whether the rateable value of the dwelling is under £1500 or £750 according to the valuation existing on April 1, 1973; only if the house is above this limit should the second or third alternative be considered.

(b) Tenancies at a Low Rent

A tenancy is not protected if under the agreement either no rent is payable or the rent payable is less than two thirds of the rateable value of the house on the appropriate day.

As the rent may be variable, taking into account service or maintenance charges, s. 5(4) provides that these charges should be disregarded in determining whether the rent is low.

This exclusion refers in the main to the long, building leases, where the initial payment covers the cost of the building and the rent (the 'ground rent') represents an acknowledgement of the landlord as a reversioner, rather than being a commercial rent. As long tenancies are protected in a different manner, no injustice arises from this exclusion.

If, exceptionally, such a tenancy is not a long one, then if the rent is low it is probably a family or charitable arrangement not deserving protection.

(c) Dwelling-Houses Let with Other Land

A tenancy is not a protected tenancy if the dwelling is let together with land which exceeds 2 acres.

(d) Tenancies with Board and Attendance

A tenancy is not a protected tenancy if the dwelling is *bona fide* let at a rent which includes payment in respect of board (i.e. food) or attendance. The value of board may be negligible, as long as it is *bona fide*, but the value of the attendance must form a substantial part of the rent.

(e) Lettings to Students

If the landlord is a specified educational institution, and the tenant is a student, then the tenancy is not protected. 'Specified institutions' means institutions enumerated in two Statutory Instruments: *Protected Tenancies (Exceptions) Regulations, 1974* (S.I. 1974/1366), and *Protected Tenancies (Further Exceptions) Regulations, 1976* (S.I. 1976/905). Thus, generally speaking, halls of residence of universities, polytechnics, colleges of education, homes run by students' welfare associations, etc., are exempted.

(f) Holiday Lettings

A tenancy is not protected if it is a holiday letting. The tenancy must be a genuine holiday letting, as the courts look behind any label given in the agreement at the intention of the parties (*Buchman v. May*, C.A., *The Times*, May 6, 1976).

(g) Agricultural Holdings

A tenancy is not protected if the dwelling is comprised in an agricultural holding and is occupied by a person responsible for the control of the farming of the holding. The agricultural workers, however, are protected to some extent under a separate Act (the *Rent (Agriculture) Act, 1976*, summarised in Chapter 24).

(h) Licensed Premises

A tenancy of a dwelling which consists of or comprises 'premises licensed for the sale of intoxicating liquors for consumption on the premises' (i.e. pubs) is not a protected tenancy.

(*i*) *Resident Landlords*

Tenancies granted by resident landlords are not protected, but they enjoy a lower degree of protection under the rules for 'restricted contracts' (see page 65).

(*j*) *Landlord's Interest Belonging to the Crown*

If the landlord is the Crown itself, the Duchy of Lancaster, the Duchy of Cornwall or a Government department, such a tenancy is outside protection.

(*k*) *Landlord's Interest Belonging to Local Authorities, etc.*

If the landlord is a local authority, the Commission for the New Towns, a development corporation, or the Development Board for Rural Wales, the tenancy is not protected. However, Part II of the *Housing Act, 1980* (Security of Tenure and Rights of Secure Tenants) grants some protection to the tenant in the public sector, which will be described in Chapter 20.

(*l*) *Landlord's Interest Belonging to Housing Associations, etc.*

A tenancy is not a protected tenancy if the landlord is a housing association fulfilling the conditions set out in s. 15(3), the most important being that the association should be registered in the Register of Housing Associations established under the *Housing Act, 1974*, maintained by the Housing Corporation.

A tenancy is also not protected if the landlord is the Housing Corporation or a housing trust registered as a charity within the meaning of the *Charities Act, 1960*.

(*m*) *'Assured Tenancies' (ss. 56–58 of the Housing Act, 1980)*

The *Housing Act, 1980*, established one type of tenancy which is exempt from protection. A tenancy under which a dwelling-house is let as a separate dwelling is an assured tenancy and not a protected tenancy (or, as the case may be a housing association tenancy) if the following conditions are met:

(i) The landlord must be an 'approved body'. This means one of the descriptions of bodies specified by an Order made by the Secretary of State.

(ii) The dwelling-house was to be constructed (i.e. construction work first began) after the passing of the Act. Thus only newly erected houses may be subject to this tenancy.

(iii) Before the tenant first occupied the dwelling-house under the tenancy, no part of it had been occupied by any person as his residence except under an assured tenancy.

Assured tenancies are protected to the same extent as business tenancies (i.e. under Part II of the *Landlord and Tenant Act, 1954*—see Chapter 23). Some modifications set out in Schedule 5 to the *Housing Act, 1980*, amend the 1954 Act to make it relevant to residential lettings.

This blanket provision allows the Secretary of State to exempt from protection any houses built in the future. 'Approved bodies' may be housing associations, pension funds, insurance companies, or even private firms. The first body obtaining this status has been the Abbey Housing Association Ltd (Approved Tenancies (Approved Bodies) (No. 1) Order, 1980, S.I. 1980/1694). The efficacy of this exemption is reduced by the fact that in future, on a change of Government, these tenancies may be taken under protection. It is assumed that a private developer will be reluctant to invest a large amount of capital in such a venture.

17.5 Tenancies and Contracts Exempted from Protection as being Restricted Contracts (ss. 19 and 20 of the *Rent Act, 1977* and ss. 69–72 of the *Housing Act, 1980*)

The term 'restricted contracts' applies to a contract whereby one person grants to another, in consideration of a rent, a right to occupy a dwelling as a residence (if the contract belongs to one of the classes enumerated below). This wide definition covers not only leases, but also occupational licences. Thus the Act gave Parliamentary approval to the view expressed by Lord Denning in the case *Luganda v. Service Hotels Ltd* (1969), where it was held that occupational licences are within the term 'letting' although not within the concept of 'tenancies', which expression means leases only.

The concept of restricted contracts originated in the restricted protection which existed since the Second World War in respect of furnished lettings. It was only after the end of the Second World War that it was considered necessary to protect furnished tenancies. The *Furnished Houses (Rent Control) Act, 1946*, provided for the limited protection of dwellings let at a rent which included payment for board, attendance or use of furniture, provided that the amount of rent attributable to attendance or use of furniture (but not board) formed a substantial part of the whole rent. This Act was originally intended to continue until the end of 1947 only, but it was extended and eventually included into the *Rent Act, 1968* (Part VI). Hence this limited protection was called 'Part VI protection' after the 1968 Act.

The distinction between the protection afforded to unfurnished dwellings and to furnished ones has always been criticised for the following reasons:

(*a*) First, there seemed to be no logical reasons why furnished lettings in buildings belonging to large companies should be protected to a much lesser extent than dwellings let as unfurnished.

(*b*) Secondly, the boundary between furnished and unfurnished tenancies was blurred, rendering the court's decisions unpredictable. Thus in the leading case of *Palser v. Grinling* (1946) the Court of Appeal expressed the view that 20 per cent of the whole rent would be a substantial portion, but on appeal the House of Lords refused to lay down a hard and fast rule. In the case of *Goel v. Sagoo* (1969) it was said: 'In deciding what portion of the total rent is fairly attributable to attendance or the use of furniture, the Court must be guided by common-sense considerations rather than by any formula: the cost to the landlord is a relevant factor, though the primary factor is the value for the tenant.' Thus for years the courts accepted that if the flat was furnished suitably, the letting was furnished, even if the portion of rent attributable to the use of furniture was quite low (due to the cheapness of second-hand furniture and the rise of the rents).

More recently, however, in the case of *Woodward v. Docherty* (1974), the Court of Appeal accepted that there may be many occasions when even a reasonably furnished flat should be treated as unfurnished. Applying the *Palser v. Grinling* principle, Lord Denning said: 'It is hard to accept that the provision of £100 worth of furniture for the use by a tenant of a flat the rent of which is £10 a week enables the landlord to establish that the amount of rent fairly attributable to the use of that furniture is a substantial part of the rent.'

This decision would have created havoc amongst lawyers practising in landlord and tenant law, but for the *Rent Act, 1974*, which rendered it virtually immaterial whether the letting was furnished or unfurnished, particularly in respect of tenancies which have been created since that Act came into operation.

The criterion whether the situation between the occupier of the dwelling and its owner falls under the concept of tenancies (protected) or restricted contracts (not protected) has been changed by the *Rent Act, 1974*. Restricted contract now covers the following tenancies, lettings and contracts:

(*a*) Under s. 21 of the *Rent Act, 1977*, where the tenant shares living accommodation with the landlord.

(*b*) In cases of furnished possessory licences, which give residential occupation to the licensee (*Luganda v. Service Hotels Ltd*, 1969).

(*c*) Tenancies with attendance, if the amount of rent attributable to the attendance forms a substantial part of the rent.

(*d*) Tenancies with board, if the amount of rent attributable to the board is not substantial (otherwise it would be completely outside any protection).

(*e*) Lettings by resident landlords (s. 12 and Schedule 2 of the *Rent Act, 1977*).

The last category is the main, crucial amendment introduced by the *Rent Act, 1974*, and now consolidated in the *Rent Act, 1977*. The previous division between furnished and unfurnished dwellings has been replaced by one governed by a new criterion—namely, whether the landlord lives in the same building as the tenant or not.

This change in the law seems to be rational, as the division between furnished and unfurnished dwellings was always rather arbitrary. Parliament considered that living in the same building might create problems between the landlord and tenant and for this reason it was better to treat such situations differently, irrespective of whether the dwelling is furnished or unfurnished. Understandably this new division applies only to lettings created after August 14, 1974, when the *Rent Act, 1974*, came into operation.

This comparatively simple rule, however, is complicated by some exceptions and qualifications and also by the necessity of issuing rather complex transitional rules.

The 'restricted contracts' rules apply mainly to cases where the landlord lives in the same building as the tenant. Although 'building' is not defined, it appears that even a house converted into self-contained flats is still a building. Protection is afforded to the tenant only if it is a 'purpose-built block of flats', even if the landlord lives in the same building (s. 12(1)(a) of the *Rent Act, 1977*). If, however, the tenant occupies a part of the same flat as the landlord in a purpose-built block of flats, then such a situation falls into the category of restricted contracts (s. 65 of the *Housing Act, 1980*).

The landlord must be a resident landlord not only at the beginning of the contract, but also at all times during the continuation of the contract. This condition (continuity of residence) is relaxed in three circumstances (s. 12 and Schedule 2 of the *Rent Act, 1977*, as amended by s. 65 of the *Housing Act, 1980*):

(*a*) In the case of transferring the property *inter vivos* (between living persons), 28 days' interruption does not break the continuity.

(*b*) In (*a*) above if the purchaser notifies the tenant within 14 days of his intention to occupy the premises, the 28 days' period is extended to six months.

However, it should be noted that during these periods of grace when, temporarily, there is no resident landlord, the tenant may be deprived of possession only on the grounds on which protected tenants may be evicted, i.e. only on the grounds stated in Schedule 15 to the *Rent Act, 1977* (see page 68).

(*c*) Lastly, if the landlord dies, the continuity is not broken if the successor occupies the premises within two years. The restrictions mentioned above do not apply.

The changes introduced by the *Rent Act, 1974*, do not affect unfurnished tenancies with a resident landlord existing on August 14, 1974, since it was considered unfair to deprive them of protection. On the other hand, furnished tenancies with no resident landlord not fully protected before August 1974, have become protected since that date.

There might have been a possibility of depriving the protected tenant of his protection if (by mutual agreement) his protected tenancy existing on August 14, 1974, was terminated and a new tenancy created which would be not protected as it was created after the 1974 Act came into operation and with the resident landlord. To make this rule ineffective it is stated that the tenant is protected if his tenancy is granted to a person who, immediately before it was granted, was a protected or statutory tenant of that dwelling house, or of any other dwelling house in that building.

This is the scope of restricted contracts. The extent of their very restricted protection will be dealt with in Chapters 18 and 19.

18

SECURITY OF TENURE OF PROTECTED TENANCIES AND RESTRICTED CONTRACTS

18.1 Protected Tenancies

Security of tenure within the meaning of the Rent Acts means that after the tenancy has been terminated under Common Law (by effluxion of time, notice to quit or some other reason), the tenancy survives as a statutory tenancy and the landlord may obtain possession of the dwelling only by a court order obtained in accordance with Part VII of the *Rent Act, 1977*.

It should be noted that under the *Protection from Eviction Act, 1977*, the landlord cannot recover possession of any dwelling-house (even if the tenancy is not protected) against the will of the tenant, unless he obtains an order of the court. Under s. 69 of the *Housing Act, 1980*, this applies also to any restricted contract which creates a licence.

Security of tenure is identical for all protected tenancies, be they 'regulated', 'statutory' or (created by the *Rent Act, 1974*) 'furnished regulated' (i.e. with no resident landlord).

Security of tenure is not absolute. There are circumstances in which the Court grants possession. In some cases it is within the discretion of the Court whether to grant possession; in some cases the Court, if asked, must grant possession.

With reference to the first group of reasons (Court's discretion), under s. 98 of the *Rent Act, 1977*, the Court shall not make an order for the possession of a dwelling-house which is let on a protected tenancy, or is subject to a statutory tenancy, unless the Court *considers it reasonable* to make an order and either:

(*a*) The Court is satisfied that suitable alternative accommodation is available for the tenant; or

(*b*) The circumstances are as specified in any of 10 cases in Part I of Schedule 15 to the Act.

The first requirement is that the Court must come to the conclusion that it is reasonable to grant an order for possession. The Court has to consider a wide range of circumstances in deciding 'reasonableness'; no exhaustive list can be made, but the personal circumstances of the tenant are clearly to be taken into account. In the case *Redspring v. Francis* (1973) an elderly woman renting a flat in a quiet street was offered, as an alternative accommodation, a flat in a noisy street with a cinema and shops in the vicinity. The Court did not consider it reasonable to grant her landlord an order for possession of the quiet flat.

Once the reasonableness has been established, the Court has to consider whether condition (*a*) or (*b*) above is satisfied.

The condition (*a*)—'alternative accommodation'—is inserted into the Act itself rather than the Schedule, because it seems this condition is the basic one. The purpose of the Act is obviously to protect only those tenants who are in need of a roof over their heads. In order to decide whether the new accommodation is suitable, the Court is given the following rules (Part IV of the Schedule 15):

(i) A certificate of the local authority of the district that the authority will provide alternative accommodation for the tenant will be conclusive evidence for the Court that the accommodation is suitable.

(ii) The accommodation must be suitable regarding its size.

(iii) The accommodation must be suitable in respect of security of tenure, i.e. must be either a protected tenancy or with equivalent security (e.g. a local authority letting).

(iv) The accommodation must be suitable with regard to the proximity to the tenant's place of work.

(v) The rent must be reasonable. This means that the rent must be within the tenant's means and corresponding to the standard of the accommodation offered.

The 10 cases under condition (*b*) above by which the court may give possession (if in all the circumstances it considers it reasonable), are:

(1) Where any rent lawfully due from the tenant has not been paid, or any obligation of the tenancy has been broken or not performed. Thus the tenant can be sure that security of tenure will be afforded to him only if he performs all the covenants binding him.

(2) When the tenant or any person residing or lodging with him or any subtenant of his has been guilty of conduct which is a nuisance or annoyance to adjoining occupiers, or has been convicted of using or allowing the dwelling house to be used for immoral or illegal purposes.

(3) Where the tenant has committed waste or neglected the premises or defaulted in their maintenance. If this behaviour is of the lodger or subtenant it is a defence for the tenant to show that he has taken all reasonable steps for the removal of the lodger or subtenant.

(4) In furnished tenancies, where the condition of any furniture has deteriorated owing to ill-treatment by the tenant or any person residing or lodging with him. Here again a similar defence is available to the tenant as in case (3).

(5) Where the tenant has given notice and, in consequence, the landlord has contracted to sell or let the dwelling and would be seriously prejudiced if he could not obtain possession.

(6) Where without the consent of the landlord the tenant has at any time after:

March 22, 1973, in the case of a tenancy which became a regulated tenancy by the rateable value of the dwelling protected being increased;
August 14, 1974, in the case of a regulated furnished tenancy;
December 8, 1965, in the case of any other tenancy,

assigned or sublet the whole of the dwelling-house. The reason for this seems to be that if the tenant relinquishes possession of the whole dwelling, apparently he does not need the dwelling and if so, does not deserve protection.

There may, however, be exceptional circumstances (temporary absence) when subletting may be justified and for this reason it is left to the discretion of the Court whether to grant possession to the tenant.

(7) In off-licence premises, if the tenant commits an offence as holder of the licence or conducts the business in an unsatisfactory manner. This case is now out of date, as it applied only to mixed (business and dwelling) controlled tenancies, which were abolished by the *Housing Act, 1980*. Mixed regulated tenancies are not protected by the Rent Acts, but are subject to protection under the *Landlord and Tenant Act, 1954*, as business premises (see Chapter 23).

(8) Where the premises are required by the landlord for the full-time employee already engaged and the tenant to be evicted was, but ceased to be, in employment with the landlord.

(9) Where the dwelling is reasonably required by the landlord for occupation as a residence for himself, any child of his over 18 years of age, his parents or his parents in law. This case for obtaining possession does not apply to landlords who became owners after the tenancy became protected. Thus the landlord should not have become landlord by purchasing the dwelling-house after:

> November 7, 1957, in the case of controlled tenancy (or, due to the abolition of controlled tenancies, in the case of tenancies which were controlled in 1977);
> March 8, 1973, in the case of a tenancy which became a regulated tenancy by virtues of s. 14 of the *Counter-Inflation Act, 1973* (which enlarged the scope of regulated tenancies);
> May 24, 1974, in the case of a regulated furnished tenancy;
> March 23, 1965, in the case of any other protected tenancy.

In addition, Part II of Schedule 15 to the *Rent Act, 1977*, added yet another condition ('greater hardship consideration'): the court must come to the conclusion that greater hardship would be caused for the landlord or his family if possession were refused, than for the tenant if possession were granted.

(10) Where the tenant has sublet the premises for an excessive rent, i.e. in excess of the amount appropriate for regulated or regulated furnished tenancies, if the subletting is one of those tenancies. In restricted contracts the landlord should not charge a rent in excess of the rent allowed under Part V of the *Rent Act, 1977*, dealing with restriction of rent for restricted contracts.

In the above 10 cases it is within the discretion of the Court whether possession should be given. In the next 10 cases contained in Part II of Schedule 15 to the *Rent Act, 1977* (as amended by the *Housing Act, 1980*, which added the very important and comprehensive 19th case) the Court must grant possession if satisfied that the conditions stated in these cases are fulfilled. One further condition exists which applies to all these cases: the landlord has to give the tenant notice that possession might eventually be recovered under the case in question. The notice must be given at the commencement of the tenancy in question, so that the tenant would realise that his tenancy is subject to the possibility of termination.

Cases 11 and 12 have been considerably amended by the *Housing Act, 1980*.

These are as follows:

(11) Where a person who occupied the dwelling-house as his residence let it on a regulated tenancy and:

(*a*) not later than at the beginning of the tenancy the landlord gave notice in writing to the tenant that possession might be recovered under this case;
(*b*) the Court is of the opinion that of the conditions set out in Part V of Schedule 15 to the *Rent Act, 1977*, one of those in paragraphs (a) and (c) to (f) is satisfied.

(12) Where a person who acquired the dwelling-house with a view to occupying it as his residence at such time as he might retire from regular employment, let it on a regulated tenancy before he has retired and:

(*a*) not later than at the beginning of the tenancy the landlord gave notice in writing to the tenant that possession might be recovered under this case;
(*b*) the Court is of the opinion that of the conditions set out in Part V of Schedule 15 to the *Rent Act, 1977*, one of those in paragraphs (b) to (e) is satisfied.

The conditions set out in Part V of the Schedule formulated by the *Housing Act, 1980*, enlarged the possibility of obtaining possession and are as follows:

(*a*) The dwelling-house is required as a residence for the owner or any member of his family who resided with the owner when he last occupied the dwelling-house as a residence.

(*b*) The owner has retired from regular employment and requires the dwelling-house as a residence.

(*c*) The owner has died and the dwelling-house is required as a residence for a member of his family who was residing with him at the time of his death.

(*d*) The owner has died and the dwelling-house is required by a successor in title as his residence or for the purpose of disposing of it with vacant possession.

(*e*) The dwelling-house is subject to a mortgage, made by deed and granted before the tenancy, and the mortgagee

is entitled to exercise a power of sale;
requires the dwelling-house for the purpose of disposing of it with vacant possession in exercise of that power:

(*f*) The dwelling-house is not reasonably suited to the needs of the owner with regard to his place of work, and he requires it for the purpose of disposing of it with vacant possession and of using the proceeds in acquiring as his residence a dwelling-house which is more suitable to those needs.

There is an interesting proviso pertaining to the last two cases. If the Court comes to the conclusion that it is equitable, it may grant possession even if no notice was given to the tenant.

These two cases have become much less important since the *Housing Act, 1980*, introduced case 19 ('shorthold tenancies'), described below.

(13) Where the dwelling-house is let under the tenancy for a term certain no longer than eight months and the dwelling was at some time within the period of 12 months preceding the beginning of the tenancy occupied under a right to occupy it for a holiday.

(14) This case covers a similar provision (of a tenancy for a term certain up to 12 months) in respect of premises usually let to students by educational institutions.

(15) This case applies to parsonage houses if they are required for occupation by the successor (this case has its application also when the parson does not occupy the premises himself, but has let it—*Bishop of Gloucester v. Cunnington*, 1943).

(16)–(18) and (20) These cases are of special character, covering tenancies of houses occupied by persons employed in agriculture or let by soldiers.

(19) **Shorthold tenancies** are of extreme importance. They virtually allow contracting out of the provisions of *security of tenure* existing under the *Rent Act, 1977* (but not from the limitation of rent; it still has to be 'fair').

Section 52 of the *Housing Act, 1980*, reads:

'A protected shorthold tenancy is a protected tenancy granted after the commencement of this Section which is granted for a term certain of not less than one year nor more than five years and satisfies the following conditions:

(*a*) it cannot be brought to an end by the landlord before the expiry of the term, except in pursuance of a provision for re-entry of forfeiture for non-payment of rent or breach of any other obligation of the tenancy; and

(*b*) before the grant the landlord has given the tenant a valid notice stating that the tenancy is to be a protected shorthold tenancy; and

(*c*) either a rent for the dwelling house is registered at the time the tenancy is granted or . . . a certificate of fair rent has been issued and . . . an application for the registration of a rent is made within 28 days after the beginning of the term.'

Only new tenants may be granted a shorthold tenancy, as a tenancy would not be a shorthold tenancy if it is granted to a person who, immediately before it was granted, was a protected or statutory tenant of that dwelling-house.

After an original shorthold tenancy ends it may be followed by another tenancy either for a further fixed term or by year-to-year tenancy. The tenant is a protected shorthold tenant until the end of the tenancy.

The tenant may bring tenancy to an end before the expiry of the term certain by notice in writing by the tenant to the landlord; and the appropriate length of the notice is one month if the term certain is two years or less, or three months if it is more than two years.

If a shorthold tenant sublets or assigns part or whole of the subject of the tenancy, the assignee or subtenant is not protected against the head landlord (this is a different situation than in other protected tenancies, where a lawful subtenant is usually protected against the head landlord even if the tenant is evicted—ss. 137 and 138 of the *Rent Act, 1977*).

Thus shorthold tenancies, as defined by s. 52 may be brought to the end by an appropriate notice given by the landlord to the tenant and, if proceedings for possession are commenced by the landlord, not later than three months after the expiry of the notice. The following conditions must be fulfilled for the notice to be appropriate:

(*a*) It is in writing and states that proceedings for possession under this case may be brought after its expiry.

(*b*) It expires not earlier than three months after it is served or, if, when it is served, the tenancy is periodic tenancy, before that periodic tenancy could be brought to an end by a notice to quit served by the landlord on the same day.

(*c*) It is served:

in the period of three months immediately preceding the date on which the protected shorthold tenancy comes to an end; or if that date has passed, in the period of three months immediately preceding any anniversary of that date.

(Thus, if a shorthold tenancy for, say, three years is not brought to an end by a notice of either party, it is automatically extended as a yearly tenancy, which may be brought to an end by three months' notice given by either party expiring at the end of each consecutive year.)

(*d*) In a case where a previous notice has been served by the landlord on the tenant and that notice was an appropriate notice, it is served not earlier than three months after the expiry of the previous notice. (This rather awkwardly phrased provision seems to mean that if the landlord, after properly serving a notice, does not start an action for possession within three months, he cannot serve another notice until three months after the expiry of the previous notice.)

Here again, as in cases (11) and (12), the court has a discretion to accept that the tenancy is a shorthold, even if the landlord did not give the appropriate notice to the tenant before the tenancy has started, or if condition (c) of the s. 52 is not complied with (registration of fair rent).

The Protected Shorthold Tenancies (Notice to Tenant) Regulations, 1980 (S.I. 1980/1707), prescribe the requirements with which a notice must comply in order to be valid.

18.2 Restricted Contracts (ss. 103–106 of the *Rent Act, 1977*)

The provisions of the *Rent Act, 1977*, for security of tenure in these contracts have been repealed by the *Housing Act, 1980* (s. 69), but only in respect of contracts entered into after the commencement of this Part of the 1980 Act. Thus in new restricted contracts there is no security of tenure whatsoever; even the discretion of the Court to grant relief to the tenant when sued for possession has been restricted by s. 106A of the *Rent Act, 1977* (as amended by the *Housing Act, 1980*, s. 69/2) to three months. This suspension may be made conditional with regard to payment by the tenant of arrears of rent or payments in respect of occupation after termination of the tenancy. The Court may impose any other condition as it thinks fit.

However, the abolition of ss. 103–106 of the *Rent Act, 1977* (security of tenure of restricted contracts) applies only to contracts concluded after the *Housing Act, 1980*, came into operation. Contracts existing at that time still enjoy the limited security of tenure formulated in ss. 103–106 of the *Rent Act, 1977*, and for this reason a short summary of these provisions is included.

Security of tenure in these contracts is given solely by deferring the effect of the notice to quit and for this reason it does not apply to fixed-term tenancies (where notice is not necessary to terminate the contract). Under the *Rent Act,*

1977, a second fixed-term contract granted to the same tenant in the same building was fully protected, thus disallowing the landlord from granting a succession of fixed-term contracts. However, the *Housing Act, 1980*, now allows this. Eviction in fixed-term contracts requires a court order and the tenant may ask for relief, which may be granted up to three months.

With regard to security of tenure in restricted contracts existing at the time when the *Housing Act, 1980*, came into operation, the provisions apply in two separate sets of circumstances:

(*a*) Where the notice to quit is given by the landlord after there has been a reference to the Rent Tribunal by the tenant asking for reduction in rent.

(*b*) Where the notice to quit has been given by the landlord and the tenant subsequently (but before the notice expires) applies to the Rent Tribunal asking for a postponement of the efficacy of the notice.

In the first case the landlord's notice to quit (given after the reference of the case to the Rent Tribunal by the tenant) does not take effect until the end of six months after the decision of the Tribunal. The delay is automatic and does not require any specific decision of the Tribunal. However, the Tribunal has the power to direct that the delay shall be for a shorter period in the circumstances of the tenant's default described below.

In the second case (when the landlord served a notice to quit before the tenant referred the case to the Tribunal), the Tribunal may defer the date on which the notice to quit will have effect for any period up to six months. The delay is not automatic; it must be applied for by the tenant and the delay may be granted by the Tribunal in exercise of its discretion.

In both cases, when the Tribunal orders possession within a period shorter than six months, at least seven days' grace must be given.

Thus, initially, the jurisdiction of the Tribunal extends only to granting security of tenure for a period of up to six months. Before the expiration of the six months (or shorter period established by the Tribunal), the tenant may apply again for a further extension of up to six months, and so on. Therefore, in theory, the tenant who performs his obligations may enjoy unlimited security of tenure as a result of his right to apply for an extension. In practice, however, the Rent Tribunal is reluctant to grant more than one, or perhaps two, extensions. Thus the security of tenure in restricted contracts (made before the *Housing Act, 1980*, came into operation) is severely limited.

Although the tenant is entitled to a six months' delay of notice to quit, the landlord may apply to the Tribunal asking for a reduction of that period on certain grounds, namely:

(*a*) That the tenant has not complied with the terms of the contract.

(*b*) That the tenant, or a member of his household, has been guilty of conduct which is a nuisance or annoyance to adjoining occupiers, or has been convicted of using the dwelling for immoral or illegal purposes.

(*c*) That the condition of any furniture provided for the use of the tenant has deteriorated owing to ill ill-treatment.

19

LIMITATION OF RENT IN REGULATED TENANCIES AND RESTRICTED CONTRACTS

19.1   Regulated Tenancies (Parts III and IV of the *Rent Act, 1977*, as amended by ss. 59–63 and Schedule 6 to the *Housing Act, 1980*)

Limitation of rent in regulated tenancies is visualised as a permanent feature of our law, although under s. 143 of the *Rent Act, 1977*, if there is no scarcity of dwellings in a given locality, the Secretary of State may issue an order taking dwellings out of the scope of protection, or lower the rateable value limits. Such an order has to be approved by both Houses of Parliament and so far none has been made and it is not expected that any will be issued in the foreseeable future.

Limitation of rent means that the rent for a dwelling-house subject to the limitation should be a **fair rent**. In fixing the fair rent all the circumstances (other than personal ones) should be taken into account, and in particular:

(*a*) The age, character, locality and state of repair of the dwelling-house.

(*b*) If any furniture is provided for use under the tenancy, the quality, quantity and condition of the furniture.

The 'scarcity element' should be disregarded. This means it should be assumed that the number of persons seeking to become tenants of similar dwelling-houses in the locality on the terms (other than those related to rent) of the regulated tenancy is not substantially greater than the number of such dwelling-houses available for letting.

In addition the following should be disregarded:

(*a*) Any disrepair or other defect attributable to a failure by the tenant under the regulated tenancy or any predecessor in title of his to comply with any terms of the tenancy.

(*b*) Any improvement carried out, otherwise than in pursuance of the terms of the tenancy, by the tenant of the regulated tenancy or any predecessor in title of his.

(*c*) Any amenity provided in the locality by a person other than the landlord or by any public body.

(*d*) Any deterioration in the amenities of the locality (other than a deterioration attributable to the act or omission by the landlord).

(*e*) If any furniture is provided by the landlord, any improvement or deterioration in the state of furniture attributable to the action of the tenant (improvement includes the replacement of any furniture or fittings).

The institution of **rent officers** is the machinery for assessing the fair rent. A rent officer (or rent officers) for any 'registration area'—which in London are the boroughs and outside Greater London the county councils—is nominated by the appropriate local authority, in accordance with schemes prepared by the Secretary of State.

Rent officers do not face an easy task; the Francis Committee on the working of the Rent Act in their report of March 1971 unanimously praised the work done by the rent officers.

In performing their task, rent officers accept as a useful guidance the rent determined as fair for the letting of comparable properties, or they calculate the capital cost of the property and a fair return on the capital spent; sometimes they look at an open market rent, deducting from it the 'scarcity value'.

In the case of *Anglo-Italian Properties Ltd v. London Assessment Committee* (1972) it was held by the court that where a fair rent is determined by considering a percentage of the capital cost and the actual cost of repair, it is not appropriate to deduct a percentage for scarcity value. The rent, as assessed by the rent officer, is registered in a register of dwellings subject to regulated tenancies, maintained by the rent officer.

Not all dwellings are registered, and therefore not all dwellings are subject to the assessment of a fair rent by the rent officer. If neither party applies for registration, the tenancy may exist and the rent be paid without any intervention by the rent officer.

Rent for regulated tenancies is treated differently, depending on whether the fair rent is registered or not.

Fair Rent not Registered

If fair rent is not registered by the rent officer, the rent as paid in December 1965 (when the regulated tenancies were created) is valid rent, unless changed under the procedure prescribed by the *Rent Act, 1977*. In this situation changing the rent is a reasonably simple matter and it may be effected in one of two ways:

(*a*) Either party may apply to the rent officer for the assessment of the fair rent. This method, which is the same whether the rent is already registered or not, will be discussed later.

(*b*) The parties may enter into a 'rent agreement with the tenant having security of tenure'. Such an agreement is an agreement increasing the rent payable by the tenant or granting to a tenant a new regulated tenancy at a rent exceeding the rent under the previous tenancy. Such an agreement must be in writing, signed by the landlord and the tenant and the document must contain the following statements:

(i) that the tenant's security of tenure under the Act will not be affected if he refused to enter into the agreement (this is done to ensure that the tenant really voluntarily agrees to the increase of the rent), and

(ii) that entry into the agreement will not deprive the tenant or the landlord of the right to apply at any time to the rent officer for the assessment and registration of the fair rent.

These statements must be set out at the head of the document and must be in characters not less conspicuous than those in any other parts of the document.

After the expiration of the contractual term the landlord and tenant are free to make a further rent agreement fulfilling the conditions mentioned above.

If the rent is not registered, the rent may be adjusted in the following circumstances (even during the continuation of the agreement):

(*a*) Any change in the responsibility for repair.
(*b*) Any change in the provision of use of furniture.
(*c*) Any change in the burden of rates (if paid by the landlord).
(*d*) Any change in the cost services (if provided by the landlord).

Fair Rent Registered

If the fair rent has been registered, or, if it is not registered but the parties have not made a 'rent agreement with tenants having security of tenure', described above, the only way in which the fair rent may be changed is by application to the rent officer for reassessment of the fair rent. The tenant, the landlord, or both parties jointly may apply to the rent officer for the determination and registration of the fair rent in the register maintained by the rent officer. The application must be made in the prescribed form (Rent Regulation (Forms, etc.) Regulations, 1978, S.I. 1978/495) and must:

(*a*) Specify the rent which is sought to be registered.
(*b*) Where the rent includes any sum payable by the tenant to the landlord for services and the application is made by the landlord, specify that sum and be accompanied by details of the expenditure incurred by the landlord in providing those services.
(*c*) Contain such particulars as may be prescribed (s. 67(2) of the *Rent Act, 1977*, as amended by s. 59(2) of the *Housing Act, 1980*, and by Schedule 6 of the latter Act).

If the rent officer requires additional information from either party he may call for it. If the application has been made jointly by both parties and the rent officer is satisfied that the rent applied for does not exceed the fair rent, he will register it forthwith. If the application is made by one party, the rent officer serves the notice of the application to the other party; this party may make representation within the time given by the rent officer, which must be at least seven days. If no representations have been received and the rent officer is satisfied that the rent is fair, he will register it.

If the other party makes representation, or if the rent officer is not satisfied that the application states the fair rent, he invites both parties (giving them at least seven days' notice) to appear at a specified time and place before him. After a hearing (and, if necessary, after visiting the premises), the rent officer determines the fair rent and notifies both parties. A statutory instrument (Regulated Tenancies (Procedure) Regulations, S.I. 1980/1696) prescribes the procedure to be followed by rent officers on an application for the registration of rent.

A party may within 28 days raise objections to the determination and in this case the rent officer refers the matter to the **Rent Assessment Committee**. The Committee decides the issue after asking, if necessary, for further information and after an oral hearing, which is arranged either on the Committee's initiative or if either party asks for it. A party may appear either personally or be represented (not necessarily by a lawyer). The Committee may view the premises in the presence of both parties or their representatives. The decision of the Rent Assessment Committee is final and may be challenged in the High Court only by applying for an Order of Judicial Review (as in the case of other judicial decisions taken by other administrative tribunals or inferior courts).

Chairmen of the Rent Assessment Committees are nominated by the Lord Chancellor; the members by the Secretary of State. The procedure of the Committee is prescribed by the Rent Assessment Committees (England and Wales) Regulations 1971, S.I. 1971/1065, as amended by the Rent Assessment Committees (England and Wales) (Amendment) Regulations, 1980 (S.I. 1980/ 1699).

The rent, as determined by the rent officer or by the Rent Assessment Committee, is registered. The registration of a rent for a dwelling-house takes effect, if the rent is determined by the rent officer, from the date when it was registered. If a rent for a dwelling-house is determined by the Rent Assessment Committee, the registration of that rent takes effect from the date when the Committee made their decision.

The rent as registered is not immutable. It may be changed in one of two ways: either by a fresh application to the rent officer every two years (or even earlier on a change of circumstances), or the parties may jointly make an application to the rent officer for the cancellation of the registration. (The three years' period prescribed by the *Rent Act, 1977*, has been reduced to two years by the *Housing Act, 1980*; under the latter Act the Secretary of State may shorten this period by a Statutory Instrument.) If the registration is to be cancelled, the parties must enter into a 'rent agreement with tenants having security of tenure', as described above.

In order to obtain the cancellation of an existing registration, the following two conditions must be satisfied:

(*a*) The application for cancellation must be made not earlier than the expiration of two years since the last registration of rent.

(*b*) The new agreement must last at least 12 months (without prejudice to the landlord's right to terminate the agreement in the case of non-payment of rent or breach of other terms of the tenancy).

The rent officer must be satisfied that the rent payable under the new agreement does not exceed the fair rent; he will then cancel the registration. The cancellation is without prejudice to a further registration at any time of the application of either party. Rent Allowance (Cancellation of Registration of Rent) Regulations (S.I. 1980/1698) prescribe the procedure to be followed by rent officers in the cancellation of the registration of rent.

The *Rent Act, 1977* (consolidating in this respect the *Housing Finance Act, 1972*, and the *Furnished Lettings (Rent Allowances) Act, 1973*) imposes on local authorities a duty to grant rent allowances to needy tenants in order to help them with the payment of rent. Rent Rebates and Rent Allowance Schemes (England and Wales) Regulations, 1980 (S.I. 1980/780), and Rent Allowances Schemes (England and Wales) (No. 2) Regulations, 1980 (S.I. 1980/1555), give details of the schemes. But local authorities, faced with the duty to pay rent allowances, are interested in ensuring that the rent is not excessively high. Therefore the local authority may apply to the rent officer for consideration and registration of the fair rent for any dwelling in its area. If the rent officer reaches the conclusion that the rent paid by the tenant exceeds the fair rent, he then determines and registers it. The tenant has to pay only the registered rent. The landlord may ask for the case to be referred to the Rent Assessment Committee, as in all other cases of the determination of the fair rent by the rent officer.

19.2 Regulated Tenancies: Certificates of Fair Rent

It may happen that a person intends to provide dwelling accommodation by the erection of a new house, or the conversion of an existing house, or intends to make some improvements in a dwelling-house already let, or let the premises for the first time, where no fair rent is determined. In these circumstances, before incurring expenses and before taking the final decision, he may like to know what will be the fair rent he will able to charge.

For this reason s. 69 of the *Rent Act, 1977*, allows such a person to apply to the rent officer for a certificate known a **certificate of fair rent** which specifies a rent which, in the opinion of the rent officer, would be a fair rent. Schedule 12 to that Act covers the procedure governing the application for this certificate and the action expected from the rent officer. The application may refer:

(*a*) To a house which is not ready yet for occupation (a house to be built or converted).

(*b*) To a house already subject to a regulated tenancy, but which is to be improved.

(*c*) To a house which is unoccupied and ready for letting, but in respect of which there is no fair rent determined, or determined more than two years ago.

In all three cases the application has to be accompanied with appropriate plans and specifications, and the rent officer, after asking, if necessary, for additional information, may determine the future fair rent. In case (*b*) an appropriate notice should be served on the tenant and the tenant is entitled to be present during any consultations. Either party, if not satisfied with the rent officer's determination, may ask for a reference of the case to the Rent Assessment Committee.

In case (*c*), where the house is ready for occupation, if the rent officer is satisfied that the rent asked for is a fair rent, he registers it; if he is not so satisfied, he considers the application in consultation with the applicant. Here again the applicant, if not satisfied with the determination of the rent officer, may refer the case to the Rent Assessment Committee.

When a certificate of fair rent has been issued in respect of a dwelling-house, an application for registration of a rent in accordance with the certificate may be made within two years.

Under Part II of Schedule 11 the rent officer, on receiving an application for the registration of a rent which has been determined by a certificate of fair rent, has to check whether the works specified in the application have been carried out according to the plans and specifications submitted and whether the condition of the dwelling-house is the same as that at the date of the certificate. If he is so satisfied, he registers the rent; if not, he notifies the applicant accordingly and at the applicant's request, or on his own initiative, refers the matter to the Rent Assessment Committee. The Committee, if satisfied that the works have been carried out as undertaken, will direct the rent officer to register the rent; if not, it will direct the rent officer to refuse the application for registration.

The provisions about the certificate of fair rent are useful, as they may induce owners to convert their houses into self-contained flats, or improve them, thus creating more and better houses for letting.

19.3   Restricted Contracts (ss. 76–95 of the *Rent Act, 1977*)

A party to a restricted contract—either the lessor or the lessee (as they are termed by the Act), or the local authority—might refer the contract to the **Rent Tribunal** for the district in question. Rent Tribunals had been set up in each local housing authority area.

Until recently there were two tribunals dealing with tenancies of dwelling houses: Rent Assessment Committees (whose jurisdiction covered regulated tenancies) and Rent Tribunals (which dealt with restricted contracts). As it was inconvenient that two separate tribunals had been constituted to deal with these two types of tenancies and contracts, the *Housing Act, 1980* (by s. 72), abolished the Rent Tribunals. The functions of the Rent Tribunals have been entrusted to the **Rent Assessment Committees**, and the Committees, when constituted to carry out functions so entrusted, are still known as Rent Tribunals. The Rent Assessment Committee (England and Wales) (Rent Tribunal) Regulations, S.I. 1980/1700, deal with the procedure to be followed by Rent Assessment Committees when carrying out functions formerly conferred on Rent Tribunals.

Both jurisdictions are, however, strictly separate and in the case of *Goel v. Sagoo* (1969) the High Court stated that it is not proper for a tenant to apply to the Rent Tribunal in respect of (then called) furnished tenancy and, after obtaining a reduction of rent, to apply to the court for the protection of the tenancy as if it were a regulated one.

The Rent Tribunal, after making the necessary inquiries and after giving both parties an opportunity to be heard, can either approve the rent, reduce it, or (since the *Rent Act, 1974*) increase it. The local authority, after being notified of the assessment of the rent, registers it separately from the regulated tenancies—in a register of restricted contracts. Only the registered rent may be charged for the accommodation in question. Every two years (or more often on a change of circumstances) either party may apply to the Rent Tribunal for a reassessment of rent.

The *Housing Act, 1980* (s. 71), inserted a new Section 81A to the *Rent Act, 1977*, allowing the cancellation of the registration of rent in restricted contracts. On an application made by the lessor, the Rent Tribunal will cancel the entry in the register of restricted contracts if the following conditions are satisfied:

(*a*) No less than two years have elapsed since the date of entry.

(*b*) The dwelling is not for the time being subject to a restricted contract.

(*c*) The application is made by the person who would be lessor if the dwelling were subject to a restricted contract.

Cancellation of the registration is without prejudice to a further registration of a rent at any time after the cancellation.

20

PROTECTION OF TENANTS IN THE PUBLIC SECTOR

20.1   Secure Tenancies

SS. 28–50 of the *Housing Act, 1980*, created a new concept: 'secure tenancies'. Secure tenancies are certain tenancies which were excluded from protection given by the *Rent Act, 1977*, but now enjoy some protection. The term 'tenants in the public sector' is somewhat misleading, as the concept covers a larger field.

The definition of a secure tenancy is somewhat complex— s. 28(1) of the *Housing Act, 1980*, reads:

'A tenancy under which a dwelling-house is let as a separate dwelling is a secure tenancy at any time when the conditions described below as the landlord condition and the tenant condition are satisfied, but subject to the exceptions in Schedule 3 to this Act and to subsection (5) below and sections 37 and 49 of this Act.'

The tenant condition is simple. It means that the tenant is an individual and occupies the dwelling house as his only or principal home. (In joint tenancies it is sufficient if one of them occupies the dwelling-house as his only or principal home.)

The landlord must be:

(*a*)   A local authority, or
(*b*)   The Commission for the New Towns; or
(*c*)   A development corporation; or
(*d*)   The Housing Corporation; or
(*e*)   A housing trust which is a charity within the meaning of the *Charities Act, 1960*; or
(*f*)   The Development Board for Rural Wales; or
(*g*)   A housing association (if it is excluded from protection of *Rent Act, 1977*, being registered with the Housing Corporation—for details see page 17); or
(*h*)   a housing cooperative.

Schedule 3 contains exceptions formulated broadly on similar lines as protected tenancies (long lease, premises occupied under contract of employment, temporary housing accommodation granted by local authority on land acquired for development, temporary accommodation for homeless persons, temporary accommodation for persons seeking employment, other short-term arrangements, temporary accommodation during works, agricultural holdings, licensed premises—i.e. pubs, student lettings, business premises, almshouses).

S. 37 states that secure tenancies assigned or totally sublet cease to be secure unless assignment is on the death of the tenant and the dwelling is disposed of in the course of the administration of his estate.

S. 49 is less important. It excludes from assured tenancies those which are granted by a housing association registered under the *Industrial and Provident Societies Act, 1965.*

Succession on death is similar to that in protected tenancies, but only one succession is allowed. If the tenancy is granted for a fixed term, after its expiration it becomes a periodic tenancy with the periods corresponding with the frequency of rent paid.

20.2   Security of Tenure of Secure Tenancies

A secure tenancy cannot be brought to an end by the landlord except by obtaining an order of the court. Court proceedings may be taken only after a four weeks' notice to quit was given (which is valid for 12 months). The notice to quit must specify the reasons for which it is given.

Schedule 4 to the *Housing Act, 1980*, gives 13 grounds on which an order for possession may be given by the Court. These are divided into three parts:

(*a*) Grounds 1–6, when the Court must be satisfied that it is reasonable to make an order:

rent arrears;
nuisance or annoyance to neighbours;
deterioration of the condition of the dwelling-house or common parts;
damage to furniture in furnished tenancies;
false statement by the tenant in order to obtain the tenancy;
accommodation was given temporarily for the duration of improvement works in permanent house and the works have been completed.

(*b*) Grounds 7–9, when the court must be satisfied that suitable alternative accommodation will be available for the tenant:

dwelling overcrowded (the tenant guilty of an offence—see page 8);
necessity of demolition of the dwelling-house occupied by the tenant;
the landlord is a charity and the status of the tenant conflicts with its object.

(*c*) Grounds when the court must be satisfied that both conditions mentioned under (*a*) and (*b*) are satisfied—i.e. reasonableness and alternative suitable accommodation:

the accommodation occupied by the tenant is suitable for a disabled person and the tenant is not disabled;
the landlord is a housing association or a housing trust and the tenant does not belong, or ceased to belong, to the category of tenants for whom the accommodation should be provided;
if accommodation is provided for other persons with special needs and the occupier ceased to belong to this category (e.g. 'battered wives'?);
the accommodation is too large for the needs of the tenant.

20.3   Terms of a Secure Tenancy ('Tenant's Charter')

The following terms are implied in secure tenancies:

(*a*) The tenant may allow members of his family to reside as lodgers.
(*b*) The tenant must not sublet or take in lodgers other than members of

his family without written consent from his landlord and such consent must not be unreasonably withheld.

(*c*) If a secure tenancy is assigned it ceases to be a secure tenancy unless:

the assignment is made under s. 24 of the *Matrimonial Causes Act, 1973* (transfer of property from one spouse to another); or the assignment is made to a person who would or might have taken the tenancy succession.

(*d*) The landlord has a power to compensate the tenant for the cost of improvements at the end of tenancy, if improvements have been made with the consent of the landlord. The rent should not be increased on account of any improvements made by the tenant.

20.4 Limitation of Rent in Secure Tenancies

A housing association may increase the rent by a notice given under s. 93 of the *Rent Act, 1977*, as long as the new rent does not exceed the fair rent.

Apart from this, the terms (including the rent) of a secure tenancy may be varied only by one of the following ways:

(*a*) By agreement between the landlord and tenant.

(*b*) To the extent only that it relates to rent or to payment in respect of rates or services by the landlord or the tenant in accordance with any provision in the lease. A notice about the variation must be given four weeks in advance. (It is assumed that every lease in respect of secure tenancies does contain clear provisions how the rent may be increased.)

20.5 Other Provisions Peculiar to Secure Tenancies

SS. 42–46 of the *Housing Act, 1980*, deal with the housing management of secured tenancies. Housing management relates to the management, maintenance, improvement or demolition of the houses, or to the provision of services or amenities in connection with dwelling houses representing a new programme likely to affect secure tenants. In all these matters it is the duty of the landlord to make arrangements to inform the tenants of the authority's proposals and to consider any representations of the tenants. Methods of housing allocation should be made public.

Under s. 48 provisions covering secure tenancies apply equally to occupational licenses.

Members of the tenant's family are defined in s. 50(3). It should be noted that persons living together as husband and wife are included into the definition of 'members of family' even if not married. The same applies to illegitimate children.

21

ADDITIONAL PROTECTION FOR RESIDENTIAL OCCUPIERS

Note: All references are to the *Protection from Eviction Act, 1977*, unless otherwise stated.

21.1 Introduction

The reasons why additional protections are contained in a separate Act and not in the *Rent Act, 1977*, are twofold: first they cover not only protected tenants, but all tenants of dwelling-houses, even if for reasons explained in Chapter 17 their tenancies are exempted from protection; and secondly because the *Protection from Eviction Act, 1977*, covers all 'residential occupiers'.

A 'residential occupier', i.e. a person protected by s. 1 of the Act, means a person occupying the premises as a residence, whether under a contract or by virtue of any enactment or rule of law giving him the right to remain in occupation or restricting the right of any other person to recover possession of the premises. The definition is sufficiently wide to protect occupational licences and other persons who occupy the premises under 'restricted contracts'.

21.2 Unlawful Eviction and Harassment of Occupiers

S. 1 defines two statutory offences punishable by fine or imprisonment (without prejudice to any liability or remedy under civil proceedings):

(*a*) If any person unlawfully deprives the residential occupier of any premises, unless the accused proves that he had reasonable cause to believe that the residential occupier had ceased to reside in the premises.

(*b*) If any person, with intent to cause the residential occupier of any premises to give up the occupation of the premises or to refrain from exercising any right or pursuing any remedy in respect of the premises, does an act calculated to interfere with the peace or comfort of the residential occupier, or persistently withdraws or withholds services reasonably required for the occupation of the premises as a residence.

SS. 2 and 3 state that it is not lawful to enforce the right of entry or evict the tenant otherwise than by proceedings in the Court. The Court during such proceedings may give similar relief to the tenant, as on application to levy distress (see page 85).

21.3 Rent Books

Under the *Landlord and Tenant Act, 1962*, it is provided that a rent book must be given to any residential tenant if the rent is payable weekly. The rent book must contain information given in s. 2 of the above Act and in the *Rent Book (form of notice) Regulations, 1976* (S.I. 1976/378). The Schedule attached to these Regulations contains separate forms of rent books for regulated tenancies and restricted contracts.

The information prescribed gives such useful data as the name and address of the landlord, his agent (if any) and describes appropriate provisions covering the most important aspects of the protection pertaining to both types of tenancy.

21.4   Notices to Quit

Under s. 5 a notice to quit in respect of any premises let as a dwelling is required for its validity to contain information prescribed by the Statutory Instrument *The Notices to Quit* (*Prescribed Information*) (*Protected Tenancies and Part VI Contracts*)— (now Restricted Contracts)—*Regulations, 1980*) (S.I. 1980/1624).

The information prescribed is as follows:

(*a*) Even after the notice to quit has run out, the landlord must get an order for possession from the Court before the tenant can lawfully be evicted;

(*b*) If the tenancy is a protected tenancy under Part I of the *Rent Act, 1977*, the Court can normally grant the landlord such an order only on the grounds set out in the Act.

(*c*) If the tenant does not know whether the tenancy is protected or is otherwise unsure of his rights, he can obtain advice from a solicitor. Help with all or part of the cost of legal advice and assistance may be available under the Legal Aid Scheme. He can also seek information from a Citizens' Advice Bureau, a Housing Aid Centre, a Rent Officer, or a Rent Tribunal Office.

21.5   Other Restrictions

Under s. 147 of the *Rent Act, 1977*, no distress for the rent of any dwelling-house let on protected tenancy or subject to a statutory tenancy shall be levied except with the leave of the County Court; and the Court shall with respect to any application for such relief have similar powers of adjournment, stay, suspension, postponement or otherwise as are conferred in relation to proceedings for the possession of such a dwelling-house (page 37).

It is a criminal offence under Part IX of the *Rent Act, 1977*, to require or receive a payment of any premium as a condition of the grant, renewal or continuance of a tenancy protected by the Act; the same applies to restricted contracts. Where the purchase of any furniture, fittings or other articles is required as a condition of the grant, renewal, continuance or assignment of a tenancy or contract subject to the Act, and the price exceeds the reasonable price of those articles, the excess is to be treated as a premium. In addition to imposing a penalty, the Court may order a refund of the premium paid.

How far the Court is vigilant to give effect to the provisions prohibiting the premiums, is shown by the case of *Ailion v. Spiekerman* (1976). Spiekerman was a tenant of a flat under a lease expiring in December 1976. The tenancy was a protected tenancy. In April 1974 he agreed to assign the lease to Ailion on payment of £3750 for chattels, which both parties knew were worth only a fraction of that price. Ailion successfully claimed specific performance of the agreement on payment only of a reasonable price for the chattels.

21.6   Disclosure of Landlord's Identity

SS. 121 and 122 of the *Housing Act, 1974*, introduced some additional provisions in order to improve the position of the tenant.

Any person collecting rent from the tenant has a duty (breach of which is a criminal offence) to disclose the name and address of the landlord if requested to do so in writing by the tenant.

If the interest of the landlord under a tenancy of premises which include a dwelling is assigned, the new landlord has a duty (breach of which is also a criminal offence) to give, within two months, notice in writing to the tenant notifying him of the assignment and giving the name and address of the new landlord.

These provisions are very useful for the tenant, as previously there were cases where the tenant had difficulty in finding out whom he had to approach if he had some legal grievance against the landlord. This often happened in the case of corporate landlord merging, and/or changing their names.

21.7 Jurisdiction

Under s. 141 a County Court shall have jurisdiction to determine any question:

(*a*) As to whether a tenancy is a protected tenancy or whether any person is a statutory tenant of a dwelling-house.

(*b*) As to the application of provisions relating to the limitation of rent and protection of party to a restricted contract.

(*c*) As to whether a tenancy is a protected, statutory, or regulated furnished tenancy, or any matter which is or may become material for determining any such question as above.

Under s. 86 of the *Housing Act, 1980*, a County Court has jurisdiction to determine any question in connection with secured tenancies (i.e. tenancies in public sector).

Where a Court makes an order for the possession of any land, the giving up of the possession should not be postponed for more than 14 days, or, in exceptional circumstances, for more than six weeks. This restriction, however, does not apply in an action for forfeiture of a lease (i.e. during its duration) in cases when the Court may grant possession under Part I of the Schedule 15 to the *Rent Act, 1977* (see page 68), and in restricted contracts, where the Court may postpone eviction to a date not later than three months after the making of the order.

22

LONG TENANCIES

22.1 Protection under the *Landlord and Tenant Act, 1954*

The Rent Acts have never applied to tenancies under which the tenant pays a rent less than two thirds of the rateable value of the house and they still do not apply to such tenancies. This exclusion (based on the appropriate day's rateable value—see Chapter 17) applies to all tenancies with one exception: if after the conversion of controlled into regulated tenancies under the *Housing Finance Act, 1972*, the rent (possibly in view of revaluation on April 1, 1973) falls below two thirds of the rateable value, the tenancy will, nevertheless, be protected (Schedule 17, para. 5).

Thus, if the rent is less than two thirds of the rateable value the tenant has no protection when his contractual tenancy ends, unless the tenancy is for a term exceeding 21 years, when Part I of the *Landlord and Tenant Act, 1954*, applies. As practically all low-rent tenancies are building leases, under which the tenant pays a large initial amount and afterwards a ground rent only (which is invariably under two thirds of the rateable value), it may be said that virtually all long tenancies fall outside the *Rent Act, 1977*, but within the *Landlord and Tenant Act, 1954*.

A tenancy, in order to be protected by Part I of the 1954 Act, must be a long tenancy (over 21 years) at low rent (under two thirds of the rateable value) and the rateable value must be within the limit imposed by the *Rent Act, 1977* (see page 62). In addition, the tenancy must be such that it would be within the Rent Act if it had not been at a low rent (for example, it must be a separate dwelling, the house must not be the subject of a 'restricted contract' only, and the landlord must not belong to certain public bodies set out in ss. 13–16 of the *Rent Act, 1977*). Putting it in a nutshell, we may say that the Act covers long tenancies at a low rent to which the *Rent Act, 1977*, would apply if the rent were not low.

There are elaborate procedural requirements as to the creation of a statutory tenancy after the contractual tenancy has been terminated. There is an important condition that the property has to be let as a dwelling-house and that the tenant has to occupy it as his residence.

The security of tenure given by the *Landlord and Tenant Act, 1954*, is very similar to the security afforded by the *Rent Act, 1977* (see Chapter 18). There is one additional ground for obtaining possession by the landlord, but only if the landlord is a local authority or other public body enumerated by s. 28(1) of the *Leasehold Reform Act, 1967*—namely, if the landlord intends to demolish or reconstruct the premises for purposes of redevelopment. On the other hand, three grounds of asking for possession are not included in the 1954 Act (Schedule 3 of that Act):

(*a*) The tenant has given notice to terminate his tenancy and, in consequence, the landlord has contracted to sell or let the premises.

(*b*) The tenant, without the consent of the landlord, has assigned or sublet the whole dwelling-house.

(*c*) The dwelling-house is reasonably required by the landlord for occupation by himself or members of his family.

With regard to the rent the tenant will have to pay after the termination of the contractual long tenancy, the procedure for the determination of the fair rent under the *Rent Act, 1977*, applies. The rent may be agreed between the parties or, if no agreement has been reached, the rent is determined and registered by the rent officer with the right of referring the case to the Rent Assessment Committee if the landlord or tenant is not satisfied with the rent officer's determination (s. 39 of the *Leasehold Reform Act, 1967*).

The provisions of the *Landlord and Tenant Act, 1954*, referring to long tenancies were of importance for some 13 years, until the *Leasehold Reform Act, 1967*, was enacted, which allows certain leaseholders either to acquire their freehold or to obtain an extension of their existing lease for an additional 50 years.

22.2   *Leasehold Reform Act, 1967: the Problem*

Note: In the rest of this chapter all statutory references are to the *Leasehold Reform Act, 1967*, unless otherwise stated.

The *Leasehold Reform Act, 1967*, was preceded by the White Paper 'Leasehold Reform in England and Wales' (Cmnd 2196), which discussed the problem of leasehold reform. The White Paper stated that experience had shown that the system of long leases worked very unfairly against the occupying leaseholder. It was considered indefensible that at the end of the term the law should allow the ownership of the house to revert to the freeholder, who got not only the land, but also the house, the improvements and everything else the leaseholder or his predecessor had added to it. In the Government's view, the occupying leaseholder was morally entitled to the ownership of the building and the freeholder to the ownership of the land only.

Although the main principle of this legislation seems simple enough, the Act in its detailed provisions creates many complex problems and here it is intended only to summarise the main provisions of the Act. A judge in the Court of Appeal in the case of *Central Estates (Belgravia) Ltd v. Woolgar* (1971) stated: 'It is an ill-designed piece of legislation, which has caused endless litigation. It was designed to help deserving tenants, where the leaseholder had in effect been paid the value of the house over and over again.' (The case concerned a tenant who was convicted of keeping a brothel and, in order to avoid forfeiture of the lease, submitted a claim for enfranchisement, i.e. buying the freehold. The Court accepted that the claim had not been made in good faith as required by the Act—i.e. with a genuine wish to obtain the freehold—but only in order to avoid the consequences of the tenant's misdeed. The Court therefore granted leave to the landlord to bring forfeiture proceedings under Schedule 3, para 4(a), of the Act, thus refusing the tenant's claim for enfranchisement.)

22.3 *Leasehold Reform Act, 1967*: **Qualifying Conditions**

SS. 1–4 set out the conditions which must be satisfied to give a tenant the right either to acquire the freehold ('enfranchisement') or to extend his lease ('extension'):

(*a*) The tenant must be a leaseholder of a leasehold house.

(*b*) The tenancy must be a long tenancy.

(*c*) The tenancy must be at a low rent.

(*d*) The rateable value must be below the limits imposed.

(*e*) The tenant has to occupy the premises as his only or main residence either for the last three years or for a period amounting to three years in the last 10 years.

(*f*) The house must not be let or occupied with other land or premises to which it is ancillary or comprised in agricultural holding within the meaning of the *Agricultural Holdings Act, 1948*.

Some of these qualifications require further comment.

House

The meaning of 'house' for the purpose of the Act is explained in s. 2. 'House' includes any building designed or adapted for living and reasonably so called, notwithstanding that the building may not be structurally detached, or solely designed for living in, or divided into flats and maisonettes. Thus:

(*a*) Where a building is divided horizontally, the flats or other units into which it is so divided are not separate 'houses', though the building as a whole may be.

(*b*) Where a building is divided vertically, the building as a whole is not a house, though any of the units into which it is divided may be.

Thus this definition includes semi-detached and terrace houses, but not flats or maisonettes. There is another limitation in respect of houses 'not structurally detached' (e.g. terrace and semi-detached): if a building is not structurally detached it would not fall within the Act if a material part of the building lies above or below a part of the structure not comprised in the house.

Any garage, outhouse, garden, yard and appurtenances let with the house are included in the property subject to enfranchisement.

The question of what building is 'reasonably called a house' creates some problems. There have been some cases in which the Court has had to consider the meaning of house under the Act. In the case *Lake v. Bennett* (1969) a leasehold property was built as a house some 100 years ago. The ground floor was let off (or, strictly speaking, sublet off) as a licensed betting shop and the tenant lived in the upper floor and basement. The building was accepted as a house for the purpose of the Act. In *Harris v. Swick Securities Ltd* (1969) it was held that if a person occupied a part of the house himself and sublet part of the house to four families, he still occupied the house as his residence and was entitled to take advantage of the Act.

S. 2 gives the landlord the right to exclude from the enfranchisement mines and minerals after ensuring proper support to the structure of the house. The landlord also has some rights to include in the premises or exclude from them some land which it is reasonable to include or exclude from the enfranchisement. If there is a dispute on this matter, the Court decides the issue.

Long Tenancy (s. 3)

A long tenancy is a tenancy granted for a term exceeding 21 years. Three special cases are included in the definition of long tenancy:

(*a*) A tenancy contracted for a term exceeding 21 years remains within the scope of the Act even if it is terminable before the end of its term by a notice given by the landlord to the tenant.

(*b*) A tenancy for a term not exceeding 21 years with a covenant for renewal without payment of a premium and if there has been one or more renewals so that the total of the term exceeds 21 years.

(*c*) Where a tenant of any property under a long tenancy at a low rent, on the coming to the end of that tenancy, becomes tenant of the property under another tenancy, then the latter tenancy shall be deemed to be a long tenancy irrespective of its duration. This provision also benefits anyone to whom the latter tenancy became assigned (*Austin v. Dick Richards Ltd*, 1975).

Any period during which the long tenancy continues under Part I of the *Landlord and Tenant Act, 1954*, is considered to be a long tenancy within the meaning of the Act.

However, the agreement cannot antedate the time the lease started. Thus in *Roberts v. Church Commissioners* (1971), on May 15, 1950, the tenant signed a contract for the grant to him of a lease of a house for a term of $10\frac{1}{4}$ years from September 1, 1950. By another lease, dated October 29, 1952, the premises were let for a term of $21\frac{1}{4}$ years from September 1, 1950 (retrospectively!). It was held that this lease was not a long tenancy, as at no time during the tenancy did the tenant actually have a term for 21 years.

Low Rent (s. 4)

Low rent means a rent which amounts to less than two thirds of the rateable value on the 'appropriate day'. The appropriate day is the latest of the three following dates:

(*a*) March 23, 1965 (the date of the White Paper preceding the Act);
(*b*) The date on which the premises first appear on the valuation list.
(*c*) The first day of the lease.

An exception is made for tenancies (other than building leases) which were granted between the end of August 1939 and the beginning of April 1963. These leases must have been under two thirds of the rateable value at the beginning of the tenancy even though this date falls before March 23, 1965. Thus pre-war tenancies may be accepted as at low rent, although at their creation the rent might have exceeded the limit, but this does not apply to tenancies created between the beginning of the Second World War and April 1963.

Rateable Value

In deciding whether the house fulfils this condition, an interesting problem arises when two houses are converted into one residence. Three cases explain the Court's attitude.

In *Peck v. Anicar Properties Ltd* (1971) the tenant held a long lease at a low rent of a building comprising a shop on the ground floor and residential accommodation above, where he lived. A staircase connected the shop with the dwelling accommodation. Entrances to the shop and to the dwelling accommodation were from different streets. The tenant was also a lessee under a separate agreement of the next door building, which was likewise a shop with dwelling accommodation above. A hole had been made in the wall between the two shops, which were used by the tenant as one business. There was no communication between the dwelling accommodation in the two buildings and the dwelling in the nextdoor building was sublet by the tenant to somebody else. Thus the tenant lived in one building and the other building was used by him in part as a shop and in part sublet. The tenant applied to acquire the freehold of the building where he lived. It was held by the Court of Appeal that a mere hole knocked through to the next building did not affect the fact that the first building where the tenant lived was a separate building and might be enfranchised (the two buildings taken together were over the rateable value limit).

Wolf v. Crutchley and Another (1971) concerned two adjoining terrace houses let by the defendant to the plaintiff. Each house taken separately was within the rateable value limits, but taken together they exceeded the limit. The plaintiff had taken steps to use the two houses together and made an opening at the first floor of the houses from one to the other. Since that time the plaintiff had used the two houses together and taken in girl students from a nearby ballet academy. Living herself in one of the houses, the plaintiff claimed to be entitled to enfranchise it. The defendant claimed that the two houses had become one and were outside the rateable value limit. The Court of Appeal decided that the house where the plaintiff lived was a separate house and the connecting door had not deprived the house of this character.

In the case *Gaidowski v. Gonville and Caius College, Cambridge* (1975) two adjoining houses were subject to one tenancy. Each house was under the rateable value limit, but taken together they exceeded the limit. An opening was made in the wall between the two houses at the ground-floor level and both rooms were used as one big drawing-room. It was held by the Court that, having regard to the structure of both houses, one house was a 'house' within the meaning of the Act and was occupied by the tenant as his residence.

Under the Act the rateable value of the house on the appropriate day must not have been more than £400 in London or £200 elsewhere. The 'appropriate day' means either March 23, 1965, or, if the house appeared in the valuation list for the first time after that date, the date when it was entered on the list. The *Housing Act, 1974* (s. 118), amended the rateable value condition. The wording of the amendment leaves some doubt about its meaning, but it is submitted that:

(*a*) In a case where the tenancy was created on or before February 18, 1966, the rateable value limit (under the valuation valid since April 1, 1973) is £1500 in London or £750 elsewhere (this, of course, will cover the vast majority of cases).

(*b*) In a case where the tenancy was created after February 18, 1966, the rateable value is:

either £1000 in London or £500 elsewhere, under the new valuation (valid since April 1, 1973), if the appropriate date falls after April 1, 1973; or £400 in London or £200 elsewhere, under the old valuation if the appropriate date falls before April 1, 1973.

Only or Main Residence

In *Fowell v. Radford* (1970) Lord Denning said: 'While it was unusual, there is nothing to prevent each spouse having his own residence for the purpose of the *Leasehold Reform Act, 1967*. This is a question of fact.'

With respect to the residence requirement, s. 7 provides that where the tenant of a house dies while occupying it as his residence, a member of his family resident in the house becomes tenant under the same tenancy and (provided that he himself satisfies the requirement as to residence) may apply for enfranchisement or extension of the lease. A member of the deceased family is widely defined and the definition includes a spouse, children and parents (and parents and children include parents-in-law and sons and daughters-in-law).

Under s. 5 a tenant who has given notice to the landlord claiming enfranchisement or extension can assign the tenancy with the benefit of the existing notice. The assignee may immediately proceed with the claim. If the assignor assigns without the benefit of the notice, the notice ceases to have any effect and the assignee (the new tenant) has to fulfil the condition of residence in his own right.

22.4   *Leasehold Reform Act, 1967*: Enfranchisement (ss. 8–13)

Where a tenant of a house fulfils the qualifying conditions, he has the right to acquire the freehold of the house free from encumbrances.

The price of the freehold may be agreed between the parties; if no agreement can be reached, it is the Leasehold Valuation Tribunal which assesses the price. The price is assessed on the assumption that the landlord's interest is restricted to the land and that the house ('bricks and mortar') belongs to the occupying tenant. However, it has been accepted that the value of land for the landlord depends on the length of the outstanding lease. Therefore, in order to achieve an equitable result the Act provides that the price is the amount which the house would realise on the open market on the assumption that the vendor is selling the freehold, subject to the existing tenancy, and that the tenancy was to be extended 50 additional years under the modern (i.e. presently appropriate) ground rent.

The first case decided by the Lands Tribunal (*Custin v. Heart of Oak Benevolent Society*, 1969) assessed the price of the freehold much higher than had been generally expected and it became clear that the interpretation of the Act as it stood defeated the intention of the Statute. For this reason the *Housing Act, 1969*, added an amendment (s. 82) to the effect that the sitting tenant and members of his family should not be considered as potential purchasers.

More assumptions have been added by the *Housing Act, 1974*, in cases where the rateable value of the house exceeds £1000 in London or £500 elsewhere. The most important is that there is no assumption that the lease has been extended for an additional 50 years, but only that, after the expiration of the contractual tenancy, a statutory one will exist under the *Landlord and*

Tenant Act, 1954 (s. 118). This, of course, increases the price of enfranchisement.

Another assumption worth mentioning is that the *price* should be diminished by the extent to which the value of the house has been increased by any improvement carried out by the tenant at his own expense. The *rateable value* of the house should be reduced by the amount attributable to these improvements, but only if these improvements are works amounting to structural alteration, extension or addition (Schedule 8 to the *Housing Act, 1974*).

Various methods of valuation have been adopted by valuers in submitting evidence to the Tribunal. Discussion of them is outside the scope of this book. It is interesting to note, however, that in cases where the unexpired lease amounted to 75 years, the Tribunal assessed the price as an amount equivalent to ten times the ground rent (*Jenkins v. Bevan Thomas*, 1972). This low price of enfranchisement increases sharply as the outstanding period of the lease decreases.

The tenant has the right to withdraw from the transaction when he has ascertained the amount of the price. In such a case he has to pay the landlord's costs incurred by him and cannot claim again his right to enfranchise for three years.

The tenant acquires the freehold free from encumbrances with the exception of those shown in the conveyance, but, of course, burdened by the existing easements and restrictive covenants. S. 10 contains detailed provisions giving the landlord the right to create new easements or restrictive covenants which are required by him as a result of dividing his property (if this is the case); on the other hand, the tenant acquires the freehold with the benefit of easements and restrictive covenants which are required by him after severance of the property acquired by him.

22.5   *Leasehold Reform Act, 1967*: Extension (ss. 14–16)

If the tenant fulfilling the qualifying conditions gives the landlord notice of his desire to have the lease extended, the landlord is bound to grant the tenant a new lease for a term expiring 50 years after the existing tenancy. Thus, if a tenant having, say, 20 years of existing lease to run, seeks to exercise his right to extension, the existing lease is terminated and a new lease is granted for 70 years. The landlord's costs connected with the granting of the new lease have to be borne by the tenant, who also has to pay off arrears of rent (if any).

Generally speaking, the new tenancy is on the same terms as the old one, with any necessary adjustments due to change of circumstances (e.g. the exclusion from the new tenancy of a part of the property).

The rent for the remaining period of the old lease remains unchanged, but for the extended period it is a 'modern rent', assessed in the last 12 months of the old period (as only then can the modern rent be ascertained due to the fluctuation of the value of money). The rent is a ground rent representing the value of the site (without the building which, according to the philosophy of the Act, belongs to the tenant). This rent may be revised after 25 years at the request of the landlord expressed not earlier than 12 months before the expiration of the first 25 years of extension.

Until the termination of the original tenancy occurs, the tenant can change his mind and ask for enfranchisement instead of extension of the lease. However, once the extension starts, the tenant cannot ask for enfranchisement. He has no further right to an extension after the termination of the 50 years provided by the Act and he is not protected by the *Landlord and Tenant Act, 1954*, or the *Rent Act, 1977*.

22.6 *Leasehold Reform Act, 1967*: Procedure and Jurisdiction

A tenant wishing to take advantage of the right to enfranchise or to extend the lease has to give notice to the landlord on a form prescribed by the Leasehold Reform (Notices) Regulations, S.I. 1967/1768, as amended by S.I. 1969/1481. There is a separate form of notice for acquiring a freehold or for demanding an extension of the lease. The landlord, within two months, should give a counternotice in the prescribed form stating whether he admits the tenant's right and, if not, on what grounds he objects. Otherwise it would be assumed that the landlord does not object to the tenant's request.

SS. 20 and 21, as amended by s. 142 and Schedule 22 to the *Housing Act, 1980*, establish jurisdiction in respect of disputes under the Act.

The County Court has jurisdiction in determining legal problems: whether a person is entitled to enfranchisement or extension, what provisions ought to be inserted in the conveyance or in the lease and generally speaking other legal questions which may arise.

The Rent Assessment Committee (which, when acting on problems of the *Leasehold Reform Act, 1967*, is known as a 'Leasehold Valuation Tribunal'), whose jurisdiction overlaps on some points with that of the County Courts, is responsible for the determination of the price of enfranchisement, the rent during the extended lease and for the assessment of compensation payable to the tenant under ss. 17 and 18 of the Act (see below). From the decisions of the Leasehold Valuation Tribunal appeal may be made to the Lands Tribunal.

Overlapping jurisdiction exists in respect of provisions which ought to be included in the conveyance, apportionment of rent if the premises are split, etc. There are provisions for the County Court to transfer a case to the Leasehold Tribunal in the case of overlapping jurisdiction, should this be considered convenient.

22.7 *Leasehold Reform Act, 1967*: Landlord's Rights Overriding the Tenant's Claim for Enfranchisement or Extension (ss. 17, 18, 19 and 28)

The tenant's rights under the Act are excluded under s. 28 of the Act if the landlord is a local authority or some other public body (e.g. Commission for New Towns, universities, Regional Hospital Boards, nationalised industries, port authorities, etc.). The condition for this exclusion is that the appropriate Minister certifies that the property will be required for relevant development within the next 10 years.

Some rights of the landlord take priority over the tenant's claim to take advantage of the provisions of the Act.

S. 17 applies only to cases where an extension has been granted, and not enfranchisement. Under this Section the landlord is empowered to apply to the County Court at any time during the extended period, or 12 months before it begins, for an order granting possession of the premises to him for the purpose of redevelopment, and the Court, on being satisfied that the landlord has established this ground, must make a declaration that he is entitled to possession. The tenant is entitled to compensation for the loss of the premises, which (as stated in Schedule 2, para. 5) amounts to the price of the lease-hold of the house if sold in the open market by a willing seller on the assumption that the lease has been extended for 50 years.

S. 18 applies to the cases of both enfranchisement and extension. When the tenant has given notice that he intends to exercise his right of enfranchisement or extension, the landlord may, at any time before effect is given to the notice (which probably means before the freehold is conveyed or the new lease granted to the tenant), apply to the Court for possession of his property. The land-lord has to fulfil certain conditions, the most important being:

(*a*) That he requires to occupy the premises as the only or main residence of himself or a member of his family.

(*b*) That the landlord's interest has been created or purchased before February 18, 1966 (this date was chosen because it was the date on which the White Paper on leasehold reform was published). This means that the land-lord acquired the interest in the expectation that the long lease would termin-ate at the end of contractual term (subject to the tenant's rights under the *Landlord and Tenant Act*, 1954).

(*c*) A 'greater hardship' proviso (similar to that under the *Rent Act, 1977* —see page 70) is to be applied by the Court.

Under Schedule 2, para. 2, the tenancy shall determine (and compensation becomes payable) on a date fixed by the Court, which cannot be earlier than four months and not later than 12 months after the termination of the con-tractual tenancy.

Here again the tenant is entitled to compensation assessed on similar lines as under s. 17 explained above.

S. 19 ('Retention of Management Powers for General Benefit of Neighbour-hood') allows the landlord to retain powers of management of any area which may be subject to enfranchisement in order to preserve the benefits which are at present enjoyed in well managed estates (e.g. Dulwich Estate in London). The powers of the landlord, covenanted in the long leases to ensure the upkeep for the general good of the neighbourhood, would be lost on enfranchisement were these special provisions not preserved. This Section applies if there is an area which at the commencement of the Act was occupied directly or indirectly under tenancies held from one landlord. The landlord's application had to be made within two years after the commencement of the Act to the Secretary of State for the Environment. In the case of a house which might have been enfranchised only after the *Housing Act, 1974*, extended the right of the en-franchisement (by increasing the rateable value limits), the two-year period is counted since August 20, 1974.

The Secretary of State, after considering the reasonableness of the applica-tion, may issue a certificate allowing the landlord to retain powers of manage-ment after enfranchisement. These powers should be clearly defined in the 'Scheme of Management', attached to the application. As the Scheme limits the rights of the owner of the freehold, such a certificate requires the approval of the High Court and afterwards is registered under the *Land Charges Act, 1925*, as a local land charge and can be enforced as if it were a restrictive covenant. However, the provisions of the Scheme of Management may go further than the restrictive covenants, as they may be positive in their contents, imposing on the future freeholder various positive duties, including payments of contributions towards the upkeep of the area covered by the Scheme. The previous landlord of the land now covered by the Scheme may assign his rights and powers to somebody else (e.g. local authority or association of the previous tenants, now the owners of the houses involved).

With reference to the two-year period in which the Management Scheme should be submitted it has been decided in the case of *Cadbury v. Woodwards and Others* (1972) that if the original submission was made within the statutory time, but the amended submission was made later (after the Court rejected the original Scheme), the Scheme could be approved as amended.

23

BUSINESS TENANCIES

23.1 Introduction

Being the least controversial of all branches of social legislation, the law of business tenancies has, perhaps for this reason, produced the best results. It has remained largely outside politics as it has been generally acknowledged that some kind of statutory protection for tenants of business tenancies is necessary or hardship to tenants and damage to business could occur in the circumstances pointed out in Adkin's book on landlord and tenant:

(*a*) Tenants of business tenancies might in some cases expend large sums of money upon making improvements, but on the determination of their contractual tenancies the benefit of such improvements would pass to their landlords, who may be able to obtain an increased rent. Such a situation would not encourage the tenant to make improvements which would benefit the business.

(*b*) Tenants might have agreed not to alter the premises without the consent of their landlords and the consent might be unreasonably refused.

(*c*) Tenants may, in the course of years, build up a good trade in connection with the premises and at the end of the lease the landlord might ask for a greatly increased rent owing to the goodwill attached to the premises.

Thus it may be seen that whereas in tenancies of dwelling-houses the two problems that arise are security of tenure and limitation of rent, in business tenancies, although limitation of rent to a reasonable amount is of some importance, the two main problems are security of tenure and compensation for improvements.

These two aspects are the concern not only of the tenant, but also of the community at large, which is interested in having as modern and efficient business establishments as possible. Tenants must be induced to modernise their premises, which they will do if they are, at least to some extent, sure that the tenancy will not be inequitably terminated. Also, the tenant will be induced to modernise only if—provided that the improvements are reasonable—he will be entitled to compensation for the money spent at the termination of the tenancy.

Until 1927 there was a completely free market in business tenancies, and it was only in that year that the *Landlord and Tenant Act, 1927*, was passed, which provided in Part I for the payment of compensation for improvement and for loss of goodwill to a tenant of a business lease on termination of his tenancy. The provisions of the 1927 Act never worked properly in relation to compensation for loss of goodwill and were eventually replaced by more comprehensive protection in the *Landlord and Tenant Act, 1954*, which in Part II deals with business premises.

Fifteen years after the passing of the 1954 Act it appeared necessary to amend it considerably, mostly to plug some loopholes ingenious lawyers found in the Act and used for avoidance of its provisions. These amendments were introduced by the *Law of Property Act, 1969*.

Thus the following Acts now deal with business tenancies: the *Landlord and Tenant Act, 1927*, in respect of compensation for improvement and the *Landlord and Tenant Act, 1954* (as amended by the *Law of Property Act, 1969*), in respect of security of tenure and limitation of rent.

23.2 Definitions and Exclusions from the Act

S. 23 of the *Landlord and Tenant Act, 1954*, stating that Part II of the Act applies to any tenancy where the property is occupied for the purposes of a business, does not define 'business', but provides that it includes a trade, profession or employment, and includes any activity carried by a body of persons, whether corporate or incorporate. The wording is extensive and eliminates the need of distinguishing between the various kinds of activities that may qualify for protection.

There is a number of cases explaining what is meant by 'business'. Thus the following activities have been accepted as being within the protection afforded by the Act: a school, a private hospital, a tennis club carried on by a society, a 'home' where working girls are boarded without payment, the taking of lodgers or paying guests, subletting of premises as apartments. The last activity, however, is included only in the 1954 Act and not in the 1927 Act; thus such tenancies enjoy protection in respect of security of tenure and limitation of rent, but are not entitled to compensation for improvement.

The following categories of tenancies are excluded from the provision of the 1954 Act (they are, broadly speaking, very similar to the exclusions from the 1927 Act, although there are some insignificant differences):

(*a*) Mining leases (because, it is submitted, it is reasonable to suppose that it is not intended that a tenant who obtained a lease allowing him to extract minerals should have the right to renew it for an indefinite period).

(*b*) Agricultural holdings (as they are protected under separate legislation— see Chapter 24).

(*c*) Tenancies created by reason of office or employment.

(*d*) 'On-licence' premises (i.e. pubs), except premises where the sale of alcohol does not form a major part of business (restaurants, hotels or refreshment rooms at railway stations).

(*e*) 'Short tenancies'. Originally, under the 1954 Act, tenancies for a period not exceeding three months were excluded, but the *Law of Property Act, 1969* (s. 12), amended this provision. Now a tenancy is exempted if it is for a term certain of not more than six months, provided that the tenant has not been in occupation for a period which exceeds 12 months (this period includes any period during which the predecessor in the carrying on of the business was in occupation). Protection of short tenancies after 12 months' occupation has been introduced to prevent the stratagem by which the landlord granted to a tenant a succession of short tenancies, thus evading the provisions of the 1954 Act.

(*f*) Tenancies 'at will'. These are rather quasi-tenancies, of unspecified duration, lasting only as long as both parties do not wish to terminate them at any time. In the case of *Hagee* (*London*) *Ltd v. A. B. Erikson and Larson* (1975) Lord Denning said: 'Seeing that the legislation [1969 Act] has opened up a way of contracting out of the 1954 Act, I feel no hesitation in accepting that an express contract for a tenancy at will is not within the 1954 Act. Such a tenant has no right to a new lease when his tenancy at will terminates. I would only add that a tenancy at will of this kind is very rare.'

23.3 Compensation for Improvement

The tenant is not entitled to compensation for improvements in the following circumstances:

(*a*) If he made them before March 25, 1928 (the date when the 1927 Act came into operation); the reason for this exclusion is that the landlord might have agreed to some improvements not expecting to be compelled to compensate for them. If such a duty were consequently imposed on him, he would suffer unexpected loss. The tenant is not injured in any way as he made these improvements without expecting any compensation.

(*b*) If he made them before October 1, 1954, in pursuance of a statutory obligation. This exclusion, introduced by the 1927 Act, was removed by the 1954 Act, but only in respect of future improvements.

(*c*) If he completed them before October 1, 1954, and less than three years before the expiration of the tenancy. Before the 1954 Act came into operation (and before a degree of security of tenure was given to tenants) it was considered improvident to allow the making of improvements in the last three years of the contractual tenancy. If the making of such improvements were allowed, not only would the tenant lack sufficient time to profit from them, but also the landlord would be saddled with improvements of a nature he might not approve and with the obligation to compensate for them. The situation has been radically changed after 1954, as now the tenant can in most cases expect a new tenancy after the contractual tenancy has ended.

(*d*) If he made them in carrying out a contractual obligation. It may be safely assumed that if the tenant accepted an obligation to make certain improvements detailed in the lease agreement, he obtained some concession (e.g. reduced rent) for accepting this burden.

Apart from these situations the tenant is entitled to compensation provided that he uses the proper procedure both in making the improvements and in claiming the compensation.

Neither the 1927 nor the 1954 Act defines what improvement entails; s. 1 of the 1927 Act includes in improvement the erection of any building and those fixtures which the tenant has affixed but is not entitled to remove on the termination of the tenancy. Some court cases illustrate further what is understood by improvement. Thus the demolition of an existing building and the erection of a new one to be used for a new and different business may constitute an improvement (*National Electric Theatres v. Hudgell*, 1939).

In order to be able to claim compensation for intended improvement the tenant must serve on the landlord a notice of his intention to make the improvements with a specification and plans.

If the immediate landlord is himself a tenant, he should serve a copy of this notice on his superior landlord, until the notice reaches the freeholder. Copies of all documents during the ensuing proceeding should be similarly served and in this case the immediate landlord, when his tenancy terminates, will be able to obtain compensation for improvements which he paid to his tenant.

The immediate or superior landlord has, on receipt of the notice, three courses of action open to him:

(*a*) He may offer to carry out the intended improvements himself. Such an offer must be accepted by the tenant and in this case the landlord is entitled to increase the rent as appropriate. If there is no agreement between the parties, the amount of the increase is determined by the Court.

(*b*) The landlord may reach an agreement with the tenant as to the work to be done by the tenant.

(*c*) The landlord may, within three months of receiving the notice, serve on the tenant a counternotice objecting to the tenant's intention. The tenant may then apply to the Court for a certificate that the improvements proposed by him are 'proper improvements'.

In order to be recognised as proper, improvements have to possess the following features (s. 1(1) of the 1927 Act):

(*a*) They must be of such a nature as would, on termination of the tenancy, increase the *letting* value of the holding. Thus the effect of the improvements must last beyond the time of the lease.

(*b*) They must be reasonable and suitable in view of the nature of the holding. This is a matter for the Court to decide.

(*c*) They must not be such as would diminish the value of any other property belonging to the same landlord or to any superior landlord from whom the immediate landlord directly or indirectly holds.

If the certificate that the improvements are proper has been issued (either by the landlord on the request of the tenant or by the Court on the tenant's application), the tenant may make the improvements notwithstanding anything in the lease to the contrary.

When the work has been completed the tenant may require the landlord to give him a certificate that the improvements have been properly executed. If the landlord refuses to issue this within one month from the demand, the tenant may apply to the Court for such a certificate. If the landlord issues the certificate when asked by the tenant, the latter has to pay the costs (e.g. surveyor's fee). If the Court issues it, the costs are within the discretion of the Court.

If by reason of the executed improvements rates or insurance premiums are increased, these additional amounts should be borne by the tenant, even if according to the contract of lease it is the landlord who has been made responsible for these payments.

When the tenant has completed the improvements and obtained the certificate, he acquires the right to claim compensation from the landlord on quitting the premises at the determination of the tenancy. He will be paid the compensation when he actually vacates the premises and not when his original tenancy ends but is extended by the Court.

When the end of the tenancy is approaching, the tenant must follow carefully the correct procedure in making his claim. The time of making the claim is now governed by s. 47 of the 1954 Act, which amends s. 1(1) of the 1927 Act:

(*a*) When the tenancy is about to end through the effluxion of time (see Section 14.2) and the tenant does not intend to take advantage of his right to extend the tenancy (see below), the claim should be made not earlier than six and not later than three months before the ending. The reason for this early claim is that the landlord must be made aware of the intention of the tenant so as to make the necessary arrangements to meet the claim.

(*b*) When the tenancy is terminated by forfeiture, the claim should be made within three months from the Court order of forfeiture or within three months from the vacating of the premises if it is effected without Court order.

(*c*) If the tenancy is terminated by a notice to quit, the period is three months from the date of such notice.

In the last case we face a difficulty. If a notice to quit is given by the tenant, his claim for compensation should be made. If, however, the landlord serves the notice to quit and the tenant intends to object to it (as he is entitled to do in the situation described in Section 23.4), the problem arises whether the tenant should serve a claim for compensation (as he must do in order to obtain compensation) and whether, should he do so, he is estopped from fighting the notice to quit. That the tenant was so estopped has been argued by the landlord in some cases, but the argument was rejected. (*Adler v. Blackman*, 1952: 'Claiming compensation by the tenant does not mean that he accepts the landlord's notice as a valid one.') (See also *Davis W.* (*Spitalfields*) *Ltd v. Huntley*, 1947.)

The landlord and tenant should try to reach an agreement on the amount of compensation. If no agreement is reached, the Court decides the issue.

The sum due as compensation is *the lesser* of the two following amounts (s. 1(1) of the 1927 Act):

(*a*) The net addition to the value of the holding as a whole, which may be determined to be the direct result of the improvements at the termination of the tenancy.

(*b*) The reasonable cost of carrying out the improvements at the termination of the tenancy, after deducting the costs (if any) of putting the works constituting the improvements in a reasonable state of repair.

The net addition to the value signifies that if improvements diminish the value of the holding in some respects, such diminution should be set against the accretion in value (*National Electric Theatre v. Hudgell*, 1939).

In both amounts indicated above, the words 'at the termination of the tenancy' protect the tenant against devaluation of the money spent some years previously by him on improvement.

In determining the amount of compensation regard should be paid to the landlord's intended use of the premises. If he intends to demolish them, the compensation may be reduced or even completely refused, depending on the time between the termination of the tenancy and demolition.

23.4 Security of Tenure

Note: In this paragraph all statutory references are to the *Landlord and Tenant Act, 1954*, unless otherwise stated.

The object of the 1954 Act is to give a general and automatic but limited security of tenure (quite different from the protection afforded by the Rent Acts in respect of dwelling houses) to business tenancies that are within the scope of the Act. When the contractual tenancy ends, a statutory tenancy arises between the landlord and tenant, since the Act expressly states (s. 24(1)) that 'a tenancy to which this Part of the Act applies shall not come to an end unless terminated in accordance with the provisions of this Part of the Act'.

Before discussing the methods by which business tenancies may be terminated, the concept of 'competent landlord'—i.e. the landlord for the purposes of the 1954 Act—should be explained. S. 44(1) states that the landlord for the purposes of the Act means not necessarily the immediate landlord, but the landlord (nearest to the tenant if there is a chain of tenancies and sub-tenancies) who holds either a reversion of at least 14 months' duration, or the fee simple. Thus, if the reversion of the immediate landlord is only, say, of nine months' duration, the tenant has to deal with the next superior landlord who fulfils this condition.

There are three possible methods of terminating tenancies of business premises:

(*a*) Tenant's notice to terminate (s. 27).
(*b*) Landlord's notice to terminate (s. 25).
(*c*) Tenant's request for a new tenancy (s. 26).

In addition, the tenant may terminate the lease by surrender (but see page 48) or the landlord by forfeiture due to breach of any covenant fortified by a proviso of re-entry (see page 55).

Tenant's Notice to Terminate

The tenancy ends if the tenant gives notice to terminate it. A three months' notice is required either before the end of a tenancy which was contracted for a fixed term, or of a statutory tenancy, i.e. a tenancy extended under the Act. In business tenancies even fixed-term tenancies require notice, because otherwise the landlord may expect that it will be extended automatically. If the tenancy is a periodical, contractual tenancy, the tenant may during the term give a valid notice according to the agreement or, in default of agreement, according to Common Law (see page 49). If the tenant terminates the lease by his notice or surrenders the lease and the surrender is accepted by the landlord, he cannot take advantage of the provisions of the Act giving him the right to ask for a new tenancy.

S. 4 of the 1969 Act added a proviso that a notice to quit or an act of surrender by the tenant executed before the tenant has been in occupation of the premises for a period of one month is ineffective. This provision was enacted in order to prevent the landlord obtaining surrender by the tenant (or obtaining a notice to terminate the tenancy from the tenant) before the tenancy started, thus virtually evading the provisions of the 1954 Act.

Landlord's Notice to Terminate

If the landlord gives a notice to terminate (which should be given not more than 12 and not less than six months before the intended termination but not earlier than the end of a tenancy for a fixed term), he should indicate in the notice whether he requires the premises to be vacated or is prepared to grant a new tenancy, but is dissatisfied with the terms of the present tenancy and wants to change them. The notice should be given in the prescribed form (Landlord and Tenant (Notices) Regulations, S.I. 1957/1157). It is the tenant's duty to notify the landlord within two months whether he is willing to give up possession, or wants to continue the tenancy. Like the tenant, the landlord must not give the notice before the tenant has been in occupation of the premises for one month. If it were otherwise, the landlord may be tempted to give the tenant notice before the contract for tenancy was effected and the tenant may be compelled to accept the notice in order to obtain the tenancy. In such a manner the provisions of the Act could again be evaded.

Apart from the notice to terminate, the landlord may also forfeit the lease if the tenant commits a breach of a covenant fortified by a proviso of re-entry. Here the general principles of the *Law of Property Act, 1925*, apply and the tenant may ask for relief under s. 146 of that Act (see Chapter 16).

Tenant's Request for a New Tenancy

A request for a new tenancy may be made by the tenant where the current tenancy is for term certain exceeding one year, or if such a term has expired and the tenancy has become a statutory tenancy.

It may seem superfluous to grant this right to the tenant if his tenancy does not terminate by effluxion of time and is automatically extended unless terminated by one of the methods discussed above. Nevertheless, it is sensible for the tenant to ask for a new tenancy if he intends to invest money in his business and hence requires full security of tenure for some time to come.

A tenant must request a tenancy which would begin not more than 12 and not less than six months from the date of the request. This is the same period required for the landlord to give notice to terminate the tenancy. The request must be made in the prescribed form, setting out the property to be let (which may be the whole or a part of the present subject of the tenancy), the rent proposed and other terms, including its duration. In *Bolsom (Sidney) Investment Trust Ltd v. Karmios (E) & Co. (London) Ltd* (1956) it was accepted that if the tenant did not suggest the duration of the new tenancy but requested a new tenancy 'upon the terms of the current tenancy', he proposes by implication a new tenancy of the same duration as the old one. The landlord has to notify the tenant of his objections to the granting of a new tenancy within two months, as otherwise it will be assumed (no relief being possible against this assumption) that the landlord agrees to the extension on the terms proposed by the tenant.

In the last two eventualities (where the landlord has given a notice to terminate the tenancy and the tenant has duly served a counternotice within two months as required by the Act, or where the tenant has asked for a new tenancy and no agreement has been concluded as to the new tenancy), the tenant may at any time (being not less than two and not more than four months after the landlord giving notice to terminate the tenancy or after the tenant's request for a new tenancy as the case may be) apply to the court for a new tenancy.

The Court must make an order granting a new tenancy for a period of up to 14 years, unless the landlord successfully objects to such a grant on the grounds specified in s. 30(1) of the Act. The Court must be satisfied:

(*a*) That the tenant ought not to be granted a new tenancy because he has failed to comply with his obligations to repair and maintain the premises; or

(*b*) That the tenant ought not to be granted a new tenancy in view of his persistent delay in paying rent which has become due. (Here the condition is more severe than in dwellings, as even *delay* in payment of rent is sufficient. Apparently only the punctual payee is protected.); or

(*c*) That the tenant ought not to be granted a new tenancy in view of any other substantial breach of his obligations or for any other reason connected with the tenant's use or management of the premises. (Here again there is a strict duty imposed on the tenant; even a lowering of the standard of business which may affect the value of the holding may be sufficient even if it does not amount to breach of any covenant.); or

(*d*) That the landlord has offered and is willing to provide suitable alternative accommodation; or

(*e*) That the tenancy was created by the subletting of part only of the property and the superior landlord may expect to obtain a higher rent by letting the holding as a whole and he requires possession of the holding in order to let it in such a manner or otherwise to dispose of it; or

(*f*) That the landlord intends to demolish or reconstruct the holding and cannot reasonably do so without terminating the tenancy. Before 1969 some landlords took advantage of this reason. They used it as a pretext to terminate the tenancy of the whole subject-matter of the lease, although they intended to carry out minor developments on part of the holding. For this reason s. 7 of the 1969 Act allows the Court to order the termination of the tenancy in respect of the part of the holding, if only a part is required by the landlord. If the landlord proves that he has a genuine intention to carry out development in a given manner and requires the whole holding, the tenant cannot insist that the intention may be reasonably carried out in such a manner as to leave a part of the holding to the tenant. 'Intended work' of the landlord means only genuinely intended and not 'reasonably' intended (*Decca Navigator Co. Ltd v. Greater London Council* 1974); or

(*g*) That the landlord himself intends to carry on a business or live on the premises. The landlord is not entitled to oppose an application for a new tenancy on this ground if his interest was purchased within the five years immediately preceding the termination of the current tenancy.

If the creation of the new tenancy has been agreed between the parties, but they cannot agree its terms, the Court determines them. If the tenant finds that the terms determined by the Court are too onerous for him, he may, within 14 days, ask for the revocation of the Court Order granting the new tenancy on those terms, in which case the Court gives the tenant reasonable time for terminating the tenancy and vacating the premises.

23.5 Terms of a New Tenancy

The terms of the new tenancy may be agreed between the landlord and the tenant and in default of agreement may be determined by the Court. Thus the Court determines, among other covenants, the duration of the new tenancy and the rent to be paid.

If the Court grant a new tenancy for a term of years certain, the tenancy must not exceed 14 years.

The rent, if determined by the Court, must be such as would reasonably be expected from the letting of the premises in the open market by a willing lessor, but the following considerations should be disregarded:

(a) The fact of occupation by the tenant or his predecessor *in title* (the tenant in possession may be prepared to pay an unduly high rent to avoid disturbance of his trade).

(b) Any goodwill attached to the holding by reason of the carrying on of the business by the tenant or his predecessor *in the business*.

(c) The value of any improvement carried out by the tenant or his predecessor in title. The following two conditions must be satisfied for the improvement not to be taken into account:

the improvements must not have been carried out in pursuance of an obligation accepted in the original tenancy agreement;
they should have been completed not more than 21 years before the application for the new tenancy was made.

Before the 1969 Act amended s. 34 of the 1954 Act, the improvements were disregarded only if they had been carried out during the 'current tenancy'. This often involved injustice to the tenant. If the new tenancy were granted for a comparatively short period (as was often the case)—say, for three years any improvements made by the tenant did not pay for themselves. This resulted in a reluctance on the part of the tenant to make improvements, and was therefore a detriment to himself, to the landlord, to the business and, in effect, to the community at large. For this reason s. 34 was amended and now the tenant is more prepared to carry out improvements knowing that (provided the new tenancy is granted by the Court) he will not face an increased rent due to improvements for the next 21 years. It should be noted, however, that this immunity from paying higher rent for 21 years since the improvements have been executed, applies only to the cases when *the Court* grants a new tenancy. If the parties contract a lease for, say, 21 years, with a provisio that the rent will be revised after each seven years, when an arbitrator assesses 'reasonable rent for the demised premises' the improvements made pursuant to the landlord's licence at the tenant's expense are taken into account, because the arbitrator assesses the rent for the premises as he finds them, which means with the improvements. This perhaps rather surprising decision was made by the House of Lords in the case *Ponsford and others v. H.M.S. Aerosols Ltd* (1978).

There is one unexpected result of this decision that should be taken into account. What would happen if, after the expiration of the contractual tenancy, the Court would assess the future rent and the improvements were not yet 21 years old? Apparently the rent would be lowered by the amount attributable to the improvements unless offset by an increase of the original rent due to inflation or other reasons not connected with the improvement effected by the tenant.

In the light of this decision it is imperative for the tenant, if he wants to enjoy immunity from an increase in rent for 21 years, even if the rent is reassessed during the contractual tenancy, to include an appropriate covenant in the lease or, before carrying out the improvements, to obtain the appropriate authority from the landlord.

Under the 1954 Act there was a proviso that the old rent should be paid until the new rent was agreed between the parties or determined by the Court. Inevitably this proviso was an inducement to a tenant facing a considerably higher rent in future to protract the procedure for granting a new tenancy. To make this stratagem futile, the 1969 Act inserted a new Section 24A into the 1954 Act, in which it is stated that the Court may order the payment of an 'interim rent', determined by the Court from the date on which proceedings have commenced, until the new tenancy is granted and the new rent assessed.

Under the 1954 Act the new rent should be determined for the whole period of the new tenancy and for this reason the Court was often reluctant to grant a new tenancy for the whole permitted period of 14 years as, due to inflation, this might have been inequitable for the landlord. The Law Commission recommended that a determination of a variable rent should be allowed and this has been effected by the new Subsection (3) of the s. 34 of the Act (an amendment made by the 1969 Act): 'Where the rent is determined by the Court, the Court may, if it thinks fit, further determine that the term of the tenancy shall include such provisions for varying the rent, as may be specified in the determination.' The Court may therefore decide that the rent should be increased at stated intervals by a given amount, or provide that the rent should be subject to reference to an arbitrator or Court. Thus it appears that the Court has a very wide discretion and there is no reason why it should not now grant longer tenancies. This is, of course, in the interest of business and the community.

Where the parties have agreed that the rent should be subject to revision during the contractual tenancy at the request of landlord, which should be made at given time (e.g. not earlier than six, not later than three months before the expiration of each seven-year period of the 21 years' tenancy) and the landlord neglected to serve the notice in time, the House of Lords decided that time is not of the essence in the contract and a notice given out of time may be effective (*United Scientific Holdings Ltd v. Burnley Borough Council*, 1977).

23.6 Compensation in Lieu of a New Tenancy

If the new tenancy is refused on one of the last three grounds given above, it is obvious that the tenancy comes to an end without any fault of the tenant, but only for the benefit or convenience of the landlord. For this reason in any of these three eventualities the tenant is entitled to compensation. The compensation amounts to $2\frac{1}{4}$ times the rateable value of the holding but if the tenant (including his predecessor *in business*) has been in occupation for a period exceeding 14 years, the compensation amounts to $4\frac{1}{2}$ times the rateable value (Landlord and Tenant Act, 1954 (Appropriate Multiplier) Regulations 1981,

S.I. 1981/69). Under s. 37 of the 1954 Act compensation was payable only when the Court decided that no order for a new tenancy should be made. This meant that an application to Court for a new tenancy had to be made even in hopeless cases to ensure the right for compensation. The 1969 Act gave the tenant a right to compensation in appropriate cases without the necessity of futilely applying to Court for a new tenancy. Thus now the tenant can elect to take compensation and quit the holding at the proper time without the need to apply for a new tenancy.

23.7　Contracting Out

S. 38 of the 1954 Act deals with the possibility of contracting out of the provisions of the Act. Two types of exclusions are allowed:

(*a*) Contracting out of the compensation for disturbance (i.e. 'compensation in lieu of new tenancy').
(*b*) Contracting out of the right to apply for a new tenancy.

Contracting out of compensation for improvements is not allowed in respect of any claim made after December 12, 1954 (Para. 7 of Schedule Nine to the 1954 Act).

Contracting out of compensation for disturbance is allowed provided that the tenant does not in fact occupy the holding for the period of five years or more. This provision does not affect an agreement as to the amount of compensation made after the right to compensation has accrued.

Contracting out of the right to apply for a new tenancy was absolutely forbidden by the 1954 Act. This was the reason why many stratagems were invented to evade the cumbersome provisions of the Act and why it was necessary to close the loopholes in the 1954 Act by the amendments effected by the 1969 Act. There may be cases, however, where the landlord does not require the premises for, say, five years, but afterwards he will need them. If there is a tenant who requires the premises for only five years and is prepared to contract out of the protection, it is reasonable that such an agreement should be allowed between businessmen, who should know what they are doing. Therefore a new Subsection (4) was added by the 1969 Act to s. 38, allowing limited contracting out. On the joint application of the future landlord and tenant before the contract has been concluded, or on the joint application during the tenancy, the Court may authorise an agreement for the surrender of the tenancy on such a date or in such circumstances as may be specified in the agreement.

23.8　Jurisdiction

The County Court has jurisdiction over problems pertaining to business tenancies if the rateable value of the premises does not exceed £5000 (*Criminal Justice Act*, 1973, s. 6(1), and Second Schedule; also Landlord and Tenant Regulations, S.I. 1973/702); otherwise it is the High Court which has jurisdiction (s. 63 of the 1954 Act). Any case may, by written agreement between the parties, be transferred from the County Court to the High Court or from the High Court to a specified County Court.

24

AGRICULTURAL TENANCIES

Note: In this chapter all statutory references are to the *Agricultural Holdings Act, 1948*, unless otherwise stated.

24.1 Introduction

This branch of landlord and tenant law contains so many technical provisions comprehensible only to persons possessing considerable knowledge of agriculture that only a short summary of the law, with the emphasis on procedural aspects, is attempted here.

The general law of landlord and tenant also applies to agricultural tenancies, but there are a few rules of Common Law exclusively pertaining to these tenancies. These may be summarised as follows:

(*a*) There is no implied warranty on the part of the landlord as to the fitness of the land for cultivation. Tenants of agricultural holdings are supposed to be professional farmers and it is up to them to inspect the condition of the farm (*Erskin v. Adeane*, 1873).

(*b*) The tenant has an obligation to manage and cultivate the land in a good and husbandlike manner according to the custom of the country. The 'custom of the country' does not imply a universal and immemorial usage (as legal customs do) but only a prevalent usage which has subsisted for a reasonable length of time in the neighbourhood. It is usually sufficient to prove such custom by showing that it is so well known and acquiesced to, as to be reasonably presumed to have been tacitly imported into the contract between the parties. This obligation has, however, become less important in recent times, as there are now many various methods of cultivation recognised as proper. This has been acknowledged by the *Agricultural Holdings Act, 1906*, which gives the tenant the right to farm how he pleases, notwithstanding any agreement to the contrary, provided that the holding does not deteriorate under his methods.

(*c*) The tenant had no right to remove any fixtures at the end of his tenancy. The only exception at Common Law was the right to emblements, which means that if the tenancy determined unexpectedly between seed time and harvest through no fault of the tenant, he was entitled to collect the crop he had sown. As this might be a bone of contention between the outgoing tenant and his successor, emblements have been virtually replaced by the 'tenant's rights' explained below.

24.2 Statutory Provisions

There are a number of Acts dealing with agricultural tenancies, starting with the *Landlord and Tenant Act, 1851*. At present the basic Act dealing with agricultural tenancies is the *Agricultural Holdings Act, 1948*, which consolidates previous provisions. This Act, as amended by the *Agricultural (Miscellaneous Provisions) Acts 1954, 1968, 1972*, and *1976*, the *Agricultural Acts, 1958, 1970*, and the *Agricultural Holdings (Notices to Quit) Act, 1975*, will be explained in outline.

Before the Second World War the legislature's intention was primarily motivated by the need to protect tenants against exploitation by landlords. In the 1940s, however, the legislature's main concern was to promote and secure as efficient an agricultural industry as possible.

It will be seen that the tenant is well protected against exploitation in the form of demands for an unduly high rent, against losing any investment put into the holding and against unnecessary disturbance or termination of the tenancy against his will, but only on condition that he performs his duties conscientiously and cultivates the land in a proper manner.

The questions of the proper cultivation of the land and of assessing a 'fair rent' to be paid by the tenant depend to large extent on technical and local knowledge, and are better decided by professional farmers who have extensive knowledge of agriculture and local conditions than by the Court. For this reason, as it will be seen, arbitration or the Agricultural Land Tribunals, and not the Courts, are in the first instance involved in all disputes arising in connection with these tenancies.

24.3 Creation of Tenancies and Limitation of Rent

The *Agricultural Holdings Act, 1948*, defines agriculture very widely as including horticulture, fruit-growing, dairy-farming and livestock breeding, and the use of land as grazing land, meadow land, osier land, market gardens and nursery grounds and the use of land for woodlands where that use is ancillary to the farming of the land (s. 84(1)). The agricultural holding includes the entire farm, farmhouse, cottages, etc.

There is no statutory requirement that all agreements for agricultural tenancies must be in writing, but the 1948 Act provides that if there is no agreement on 'specified matters', either party may request the other to enter into a written agreement containing all specified matters and if he fails to do so, may refer the terms of the tenancy to arbitration (s. 5 and Schedule 1). The more important 'specified matters' are:

(*a*) The names of the parties.
(*b*) Sufficient particulars of the holding.
(*c*) The period or the periods of the tenancy.
(*d*) The rent reserved and the dates on which it is payable.
(*e*) Liability for land taxes (not in existence now) and rates.
(*f*) Maintenance and repair of fixed equipment.
(*g*) The question of insurance of buildings against fire (usually the landlord's obligation).
(*h*) Fertilizing the soil with the full manure value of harvested crops;
(*i*) Proviso of re-entry on breach of covenants by the tenant.

With reference to (*d*), if rent is not determined by agreement between the parties, it is determined by arbitration. However, if the rent had been determined by agreement or arbitration more than three years ago, the tenant (or landlord) may again refer to arbitration for the determination of the new rent.

The new rent, as assessed, replaces the existing rent from the day on which the tenancy could have been terminated by notice to quit given at the date of reference. Both landlord and tenant may give a notice to quit of not less than one year, but no more than two years before the date fixed for the expiration of the tenancy (s. 3). Thus, practically speaking, the rent of agricultural holdings is subject to review at three-yearly intervals on the initiative of either party.

24.4 Security of Tenure

A letting of an agricultural holding for less than one year (with some minor exceptions) takes effect as a tenancy from year to year. Tenancies from year to year are protected by the Act. Moreover, a tenancy for a term of two years or more does not expire at the end of the term but is extended automatically until the statutory notice is given.

The combined result of these provisions is that all tenancies of agricultural holdings are protected with the single exception of tenancies for a fixed length between a year and two years. There would seem to be no policy justification for this and the lack of protection for such tenancies suggests a loophole in the Act. In *Cladstone v. Bower* (1960) the Court accepted that a tenancy for a term of 18 months did not enjoy the protection of the Act ('If the gap in protection given by the Act is accidental, it is for Parliament to remedy the matter.').

As was mentioned, a notice to quit must be given at least 12 months before the date on which the year of the tenancy ends (s. 23), but in the case of the bankruptcy of the tenant the tenancy may be ended immediately.

If a notice to quit is given by the landlord, the tenant may, within a month, serve a counternotice in which case the notice to quit shall not have effect unless the Agricultural Land Tribunal consents to the operation of the notice (s. 24(1) as amended by the s. 8(1) and Schedule 1, Para. 8, of the 1958 Act).

In some cases, however, the Agricultural Land Tribunal's consent is not necessary. There are seven such circumstances, the most important being:

(*a*) If the Agricultural Land Tribunal has consented to the operation of the notice to quit before the notice has been given (before it gives consent the tenant would have had a chance to appear before the Tribunal).

(*b*) If the land is required for development approved by the planning authority.

(*c*) If the Agricultural Land Tribunal certified not earlier than six months before the notice that the tenant was not fulfilling his responsibilities to farm the holding in accordance with the rules of good husbandry.

(*d*) If, in spite of a request, the tenant remained in arrears of rent for more than two months after a request has been served, or failed to remedy a breach of another covenant after being given notice of the breach.

(*e*) If the tenant becomes bankrupt or dies. The *Agricultural (Miscellaneous Provisions) Act, 1976*, amended the provision of the 1948 Act, which provided that a tenancy is ended by the death of the tenant. SS. 18 to 24 of that Act enacted provisions for succession on the death of the tenant. These rules are rather complex, but in outline they may be summarised as follows: only an 'eligible person' is entitled to succession, and an eligible person means a person fulfilling the following three conditions:

(i) he must be a member of the family of the deceased tenant (membership of the family is defined in s. 18(1));
(ii) in the preceding seven years his principal livelihood should have derived from his agricultural work on the holding (it is sufficient if during this seven-year period he was so occupied for five years);
(iii) he is not already a tenant of another agricultural holding.

The Agricultural Land Tribunal, before granting the consent, must be satisfied on a number of points given in s. 25; the most important are:

(*a*) That it is in the interests of good husbandry.
(*b*) That it is in the interests of sound management that the holding should be amalgamated with the estate of which it is a part.
(*c*) That greater hardship should be caused by withholding than by giving consent to the operation of the notice.

Thus security of tenure depends on the Agricultural Land Tribunal's views on the standard of farming by the tenant and hardship caused to either party as a result of their interests being in conflict.

24.5 Rights and Duties of Parties on Determination of Tenancies

The landlord has the following rights on determination of the tenancy:

(*a*) *The right to possession of the holding*; this right is common to all types of tenancy and does not require further comment.
(*b*) *The right to compensation for deterioration* of particular parts of the holding (s. 57) and for general deterioration of the holding (s. 58).

The claim under s. 57 refers to compensation for dilapidation of, deterioration of, or damage to any part of the holding caused by the non-fulfilment by the tenant of his responsibility to farm in accordance with the rules of good husbandry—for example, the wrong removal of dung, neglecting the repair of buildings, fences and gates, removing landlord fixtures, etc.

Under s. 58 (general deterioration of the holding) the landlord has to give a notice to the tenant at least one month before the end of the tenancy. Here the tenant is responsible for the depreciation in the value of the holding due to deterioration during the tenancy through the failure of the tenant to cultivate the land according to the rules of good husbandry or the terms of the contract. In this case it is not necessary to point out exactly what wrongs have been committed; it is sufficient if the arbitrator finds that the value of the holding has been depreciated due to poor farming, which may evade detailed specification.

The tenant has the following rights on the termination of the tenancy:

(*a*) *The right to remove his fixtures* (see page 51).
(*b*) *The right to emblements*. Emblements are crops which are harvested within the year of sowing (such crops include grain, hemp, vegetables or hops). The right to emblements has been considerably curtailed by Statute and virtually replaced by 'tenant's right', enacted by Schedule 4 to the Act.

(*c*) *The right to compensation for improvements*. The tenant is entitled to compensation for improvements, hence there is an incentive for him to improve the holding he maintains. The general principle for assessing compensation is that the compensation must correspond to a sum fairly representing the value of the improvements to the incoming, and not outgoing tenant. All improvements for which the tenant may claim compensation are fully listed in Schedules 3 and 4. They are divided into three categories:

(i) Improvements to which the consent of landlord is required (Part 1 of Schedule 3). These are of rather a permanent nature, which change the character of the holding. There are seven of them, the most important being the planting of hops, orchard or fruit bushes, and works of irrigation.

(ii) Improvements for which the consent of the landlord or the approval of the Agricultural Land Tribunal is required. There are 17 such improvements, which are mostly of a semi-permanent nature, and which may or may not be really useful to the holding. Examples are the construction of silos, making improvements to roads and bridges, land drainage, provision of means for sewage disposal, etc.

(iii) Improvements for which no consent is required. These are improvements which should be done in the course of day-to-day cultivation and which do not affect the character of the holding. They include the chalking of land, application of purchased manure (including artificial fertilizers), protection of fruit trees against animals, etc.

(*d*) *The 'tenant's rights'*. Part 1 of Schedule 4 provides for other matters for which compensation is payable. These are, however, not improvements, but old 'emblements', now called 'tenant's rights', established not by custom but by Statute. Thus the tenant has a right to claim compensation for growing crops, seeds sown and cultivations, pasture laid down by the tenant, etc.

(*e*) *Compensation for Increased Value of the Holding* (s. 56). When the tenant of an agricultural holding shows that by the continuous adoption of a system of farming the value of the holding has been increased, he is entitled to compensation amounting to the increase in value. This Section, being of residual nature, is little used, as it is difficult to prove that the system used by the tenant has really increased the value of the holding.

### 24.6	Compensation for Disturbance

Where a tenancy of an agricultural holding terminates by reason of a notice served by the landlord (other than owing to the tenant's death, bankruptcy or default) and the tenant vacates the holding, he is entitled to compensation for disturbance. This amount to a year's rent, but if the tenant notifies the landlord accordingly and proves a higher loss, he is entitled to a larger sum up to two years' rent. Compensation for disturbance is due in addition to any compensation for improvement and cannot be contracted out of. If no agreement is reached between the parties it is the County Court which decides the amount and orders its payment.

The *Agricultural* (*Miscellaneous Provisions*) *Act, 1968*, considerably improved the position of the outgoing tenant. SS. 9 *et seq*. of that Act provide that where a landlord has to pay compensation to the tenant under the *Agricultural Holdings Act, 1948*, he has to pay a further sum equal to four times the annual rent of the holding, the purpose being to assist in the organisation of the tenant's affairs. There are, however, exceptions, the more important being where the Agricultural Land Tribunal consents to the notice to quit by reason of the tenant's default, or where, owing to the 'greater hardship' rule, the Agricultural Land Tribunal decides the case in favour of the landlord. Under s. 12 in cases of compulsory purchase, the acquiring authority has the same duty as if it were the landlord.

S. 12 has no application if the tenant (having two years or more of the tenancy to run) is entitled to full compensation under the *Land Compensation Act, 1961* (see page 206).

As an alternative to a s. 12 payment, the *Land Compensation Act, 1973* (s. 35), provides a 'farm loss payment' to the tenant of leases granted or extended for a term of years certain, of which no less than three years remain unexpired. As the majority of agricultural tenancies are from year to year it is not often that this payment would be due to tenants. It amounts to one year's profit computed by reference to the profits of the last three years of the tenancy.

24.7 Jurisdiction

Many disputes arising between landlord and tenant regarding agricultural tenancies are referred to arbitration by the Acts. The rules governing this are contained in Schedule 6 to the 1948 Act, the 1963 Act and the *Agriculture (Miscellaneous Provisions) Act, 1972*. The arbitrator is a person appointed by agreement between the parties or, in default of agreement, by the Minister from among the members of the panel constituted for this purpose. Neither party has powers to revoke the appointment of the arbitrator without the consent of the other party. Schedule 6 to the 1948 Act deals with some points of procedure; otherwise the *Arbitration Act, 1950*, as amended by the *Arbitration Act, 1979*, applies to arbitration under the 1948 Act as amended.

A number of matters can be referred to the Agricultural Land Tribunal, the most important being: consent to the operation of notices to quit, certificates of bad husbandry, approval of long term improvements, etc. The Agricultural Land Tribunals have been established by the *Agriculture Act, 1947*, extensively amended by the 1958 Act (s. 8 and Schedule 1). There are eight Tribunals in England and Wales; the chairmen have a legal qualification and two other members are appointed, representing the interests of the owners and tenants of agricultural holdings respectively.

24.8 Protection for Tied Cottages of Agricultural Workers

In recent years special attention has been paid to agricultural workers living in 'tied cottages'. As the accommodation for such workers is closely connected with their work, they are licensees rather than tenants. Losing their work involved losing the accommodation, and they felt almost fixtures of the land since quitting their job meant making them homeless. On the other hand, giving them full security of tenure would create an insurmountable difficulty for the farmers, who were unable to employ new workers without accommodation for them.

SS. 32 and 33 of the *Rent Act, 1965* (as amended by the *Agriculture Act, 1970*), provided for the necessity of obtaining a Court Order to evict an agricultural worker and the Court had to defer the order for possession for six months, unless the farmer could prove that work on the farm would be seriously prejudiced.

These provisions were not quite satisfactory and for this reason the *Rent (Agriculture) Act, 1976*, was enacted. This is a complex Act containing 40 Sections and nine Schedules. It is virtually a rent code on similar lines to the *Rent Act, 1977*, but referring to agricultural workers.

As the agricultural worker is a licensee rather than a tenant, the Act calls him a 'protected occupier'. If, however, the worker's contract of employment comes to the end, he becomes a 'statutory tenant'. One statutory succession of such a statutory tenancy is allowed.

The statutory tenant enjoys a similar security of tenure to tenants under the *Rent Act, 1977*, with minor amendments. The most important difference is, however, contained in ss. 27–29 dealing with rehousing of workers. Before the farmer's application for rehousing of the statutory tenant can succeed, there are three conditions to be proved to the satisfaction of the Court:

(*a*) The cottage must be needed for a replacement worker.

(*b*) The farmer must have no suitable empty house available.

(*c*) The rehousing must be in the interest of efficient agriculture.

Generally, the worker will enjoy protection after two years' employment, but disabled workers qualify without this condition. Casual and seasonal workers are not protected even if they are housed by the farmer for a short period at a particular period of the year.

Rehousing means that the local housing authority must use their best endeavours to provide suitable alternative accommodation and once such accommodation is provided, the farmworker must move to it. It remains to be seen how well these provisions will work.

PART 3
TOWN AND COUNTRY PLANNING

25

HISTORICAL OUTLINE

Note: In this and subsequent chapters all references to Sections relate to the *Town and Country Planning Act, 1971*, unless otherwise stated.

25.1 Introduction

For centuries, until the Industrial Revolution, the task of Government was, generally speaking, rather simple, being limited to securing order within the realm and defence against invaders. It was only after the Industrial Revolution that the complexity of modern life compelled the Government to accept responsibility for many other problems, including the welfare of citizens, the condition of their homes, their education, health and even standard of living.

Within administrative law we can discern three categories of legislation dealing with the living conditions of the population. These are the Public Health Acts, which were enacted first as being the most urgent due to the unsanitary conditions of the towns, followed by the Housing Acts and lastly by the Town and Country Planning Acts.

The *Public Health Act, 1848*, was the first of a series of general Acts dealing with public health. The first comprehensive Act in this sphere was the *Public Health Act, 1875*. This enabled the local authorities to issue bye-laws with respect to new buildings, but it was the *Housing of the Working Classes Act, 1890*, which for the first time made provision for the removal of insanitary dwellings and for the supply of new houses for the working classes. Thus this Act marks the beginning of housing legislation.

However, the Public Health and Housing Acts deal only with individual houses which are unsatisfactory or otherwise unfit for human habitation and with groups of unfit or substandard houses. They do not consider the problem of the general environment of houses.

25.2 History of Planning Legislation up to 1946

The problems of houses built within the close vicinity of factories or factories built in residential areas were not tackled until 1909, when the *Housing, Town Planning, etc., Act* was passed. It was a timid step towards town planning. It gave local authorities powers to make 'town planning schemes' for suburban land, with the general object of 'securing proper sanitary conditions, amenity and convenience in connection with the laying out and use of the land and of any neighbouring lands'. Although the schemes did not yet accept the idea that development invariably required permission from the local authority, they could indicate the types of development which required application to and permission of the local authority.

Further acts developed the idea of planning. The Act of 1932 enabled local authorities to prepare planning schemes for any land in England and Wales, not merely suburban land as had previously been the case.

The Second World War brought air attacks and considerable destruction of towns. This created an opportunity to give considerable attention to the problem of town and country planning in connection with post-war reconstruction.

25.3 The First Comprehensive Planning Law: *Town and Country Planning Act, 1947*

The above considerations led to the setting up of a Committee on Compensation and Betterment under the Chairmanship of Lord Justice Uthwatt. The final Report of the Uthwatt Committee was published in 1942. The Report defined betterment as 'any increase in the value of land (including the buildings thereon) arising from central or local government action whether positive, e.g. by execution of public works or improvements, or negative, e.g. by imposition of restrictions on other land'. The Report, which was rather radical in its contents, suggested that all future betterment should belong to the society and, in this connection, as an incidental result it suggested that all development should be subject to the control of Government.

Implementing to a large extent the recommendations of the Uthwatt Report, the *Town and Country Planning Act, 1947*, was passed, introducing for the first time a comprehensive scheme of town and country planning.

Planning became not only the right, but also a duty of the local planning authorities (at that time the counties and county boroughs). The lay-out of the Act was logical and comparatively simple and it may be represented by the following principles:

First, the local planning authorities were entrusted with the duty of preparing development plans for their areas.

Secondly, in order to ensure that the development plan would be adhered to, a further important principle was introduced—namely, that any development (as defined in the Act) required the permission of the local planning authority. There were, however, some clearly defined exceptions, which are outlined later.

Thirdly, any unauthorised development might be subject to enforcement procedure under the Act.

Fourthly, there was a right of compensation in certain circumstances if the owner's rights were infringed due to the exercise of planning control; in some cases the owner was entitled to compel the local planning authority to buy the land from him if, due to the planning restriction, it was rendered incapable of reasonably beneficial use in the existing state.

Fifthly, the Act expropriated for the State the development value of the land accruing after the Act came into operation.

The 1947 Act also contained a number of provisions on other matters connected with planning (e.g. the conferring upon local authorities the power of compulsory acquisition of land required for development by the authority).

Whereas the first four principles are still with us with some amendments, the fifth principle did not survive the change of Government in 1951 (when the Conservative Party came into power) and this problem has become a bone of contention between the two main Parties.

25.4 Planning Legislation during the Post-1947 Era

The 1947 Act was amended on several occasions in subsequent years (1951, 1953 and 1959), until finally, in 1962, the main Act and subsequent amending Acts were repealed and consolidated in the *Town and Country Planning Act, 1962*.

In 1967, twenty years after the 1947 Act was enacted, experience had shown that the Act required considerable overhauling. A White Paper entitled 'Town and Country Planning' (Cmnd 3333), published in June 1967, pointed out those deficiences in the existing legislation and suggested changes: 'Three major defects have now appeared in the present system. First it has become overloaded and subject to delays and cumbersome procedures. Second, there has been inadequate participation by the individual citizen in the planning process and insufficient regard to his interest. Third, the planning system has been functioning better as a negative control, than as a positive stimulus to the creation of a good environment.... We must recognise that planning is now operating in a very different context from that immediately after the war. When the 1947 Act was being prepared, planning was based on the belief that our population was likely to remain stable and there was little appreciation at that time of the likely growth of motor traffic and still less of the impact that it would have on the structure of our towns and on the countryside....'

The White Paper's views were accepted by Parliament and the *Town and Country Planning Act, 1968*, was passed, amending the 1962 Act in many respects, the most important being the following:

Part II of the 1962 Act relating to the making, approval and coming into operation of development plans was repealed and replaced by Part I of the 1968 Act.
The enforcement of planning control was strengthened.
Some decentralisation and simplification of procedure in granting planning permission and in appeals against decisions was effected.

The Act also contained a variety of other changes of considerable importance in planning law.

Part I of the 1968 Act relating to the procedure for the making of development plans was intended to be introduced in various parts of the country as soon as the Secretary of State for the Environment was satisfied that the local planning authority was properly prepared to work the new procedure, as it gave the authority much more scope. For this reason both types of development plans—'old style' and 'new style'—are in operation, although a Statutory Instrument (S.I. 1974/1069) introduced the 'new style' in the remainder of England and the new style development plans are being prepared in the whole of England and Wales.

After the 1968 Act came into operation, town and country planning law again became too complicated. For this reason a new consolidating Act—the *Town and Country Planning Act, 1971*—was enacted and came into operation (with some minor exceptions given in s. 294) on April 1, 1972. This is the principal Act which is still in operation.

Containing 295 Sections and 26 Schedules, the Act is very comprehensive, consolidating the 1962 and 1968 Acts and a number of others as far as they deal with planning, the most important being the *London Government Act, 1963*, the *Control of Office and Industrial Development Act, 1965*, the *Industrial Development Act, 1966*, the *Civic Amenities Act, 1967*, and some others.

However, just seven days after passing the consolidating Act in 1971, Parliament started amending it and in July 1972 the *Town and Country Planning* (*Amendment*) *Act, 1972*, received Royal assent. This act makes several important amendments to the 1971 Act, the main purpose of these amendments being:

(*a*) To provide for joint structure plans, which may be made by two or more county councils if they wish to do so. This is sensible, as many items covered by structure plans refer to larger areas than those covered by a county council.

(*b*) To amend the procedure relating to the approval of structure plans by the Secretary of State for the Environment (see page 128).

(*c*) To dispense with structure plans in the London boroughs; now it is the Greater London Council which is responsible for making the structure plan for Greater London.

(*d*) To control demolition in conservation areas (see page 158). Now buildings in conservation areas are treated to a large extent as if they were listed (see page 157).

Since that Act a number of further Acts amended the town and country planning law in many important aspects.

The *Local Government Act, 1972*, which reorganised the system of local government and which came into operation on April 1, 1974, affected the *Town and Country Planning Act, 1971*, in some particulars.

The *Town and Country Amenities Act, 1974*, made more effective provisions for conservation areas and for 'listed buildings' (buildings of special architectural or historic interest).

The *Community Land Act, 1975*, affected planning law by complex provisions. The aims of the Act (as explained in the White Paper 'Land', Cmnd 5730) were twofold: namely, to enable the community to control the development of land in accordance with its needs and priorities and to restore to the community the increase in the value of land arising from its effort (the 'development value'). However, this Act was repealed by s. 101 of the *Local Government, Planning and Land Act, 1980*, even before it become operative in its entirety.

The *Town and Country Planning* (*Amendment*) *Act, 1977*, made the enforcement of control more effective by enlarging the scope of 'stop notices'.

The *Inner Urban Areas Act, 1978*, empowers the Secretary of State to specify any inner urban area as a 'designated district' and the district or county council covering the district may be made a 'designated district authority'. A Statutory Instrument (Inner Urban Areas (Designated Districts) (England and Wales) Order, 1978) specifies designated district authorities for the purposes of the Act. This is an enabling Act, giving the designated district authorities wide powers to make loans and grants for acquisition or works on land. The main aim of the Act is to extend the powers of selected local authorities to assist industry so that it is encouraged to maintain existing operations in inner urban areas and, where possible, to extend them.

Lastly, the *Local Government, Planning and Land Act, 1980*, in Part IX (ss.

86–92) and in Schedules 14 and 15, introduced a number of important amendments to town and country planning law. They are aimed at simplifying procedure and at reducing the control of central government.

This is the situation as far as the legislation enacted up to the end of 1980 is concerned. However, it should be realised that planning law is still and will be always subject to development and amendments necessitated by ever changing circumstances and variations of governmental policy.

26

PLANNING AUTHORITIES

26.1 Introduction

The main idea in the organisation of planning authorities is that day-to-day administration is entrusted to local authorities. Central Government's role is the harmonisation of the work of local authorities, its supervision and the determination of policy.

26.2 Central Authority

In central Government the Minister responsible for town and country planning is the *Secretary of State for the Environment* (s. 224(1)(d) and (2)).

The powers and duties of the Secretary of State are very great and may be considered under the following headings (A. E. Telling, *Planning Law and Procedure*, Chapter 3):

(*a*) Issuing of statutory instruments. The *Town and Country Planning Act, 1971*, may be considered a 'skeleton Act', since many technical and other important details are left to the statutory instruments issued by the Secretary of State. Thus many orders supplement the provisions of the Act and these will be mentioned in their proper place, but here it is appropriate to say that the General Development Order covers many aspects of planning law. For example, many classes of development are permitted by the General Development Order without the necessity of applying for planning permission (Town and Country Planning (General Development) Order, 1977, S.I. 289). The G.D.O. (as it is commonly called) also prescribes in detail the procedure for applying for planning permission.

(*b*) In some cases decisions of the local authority require approval by the Secretary of State. For example, the 'new style' structure plans have to be approved by the Secretary of State. There are many other matters requiring approval by him, which will be discussed at the appropriate place.

(*c*) In many instances a person aggrieved by a decision of a local planning authority has a right of appeal to the Secretary of State. For example, there is a right of appeal against the refusal of planning permission, against the granting of it subject to conditions, against an enforcement notice, etc. Although such appeals should be directed to the Secretary of State, Schedule 9 allows a number of appeals to be decided by a person nominated by the Secretary of State, i.e. by an inspector. This aspect will be discussed later.

(*d*) In some cases the Secretary of State may give directions, either in general, or in particular matters. For example, a direction may be given laying down the procedure to be followed where the planning authority wishes to grant planning permission which is not in accordance with the development plan. The Secretary of State may also issue a direction 'calling in' an application for planning permission in a particular case.

(*e*) If the Secretary of State considers that a local planning authority has failed to fulfil some duty under the Act, he may himself take action or entrust it to another local authority.

(*f*) Claims for compensation when planning decisions restrict new development (which may be made under Part VII of the Act) are dealt with by the Secretary of State (see Chapter 34).

(*g*) Some decisions of the Secretary are of a judicial nature, interpreting the existing law. Thus under s. 53 the Secretary of State may, on appeal from the local planning authority, or at first instance, determine whether planning permission is necessary.

In addition to these functions given by statute, the Secretary of State shapes the policy of the local planning authorities by advice and information, which is usually contained in circulars.

26.3   Local Planning Authorities

The local planning authorities are the county council for counties and the district council for districts (s. 1(1) and (2) as amended by the *Local Government Act, 1972*). This organisation of the local planning authorities came into existence on April 1, 1974).

The Secretary of State may by Order constitute a joint planning board for an area of any two or more local planning authorities. Thus there may be a joint planning board as a county planning authority covering areas (or part of the areas) of two or more county councils or as a district planning authority covering areas (or part of the areas) of two or more district councils. Such a joint planning board may be created only after holding a local inquiry unless all the councils concerned have consented to the making of the order. Schedule 1 contains detailed provisions in respect of the joint planning board. The members of the joint planning board will be appointed by the constituent councils and it shall be a body corporate having its own legal personality. Joint planning boards have been constituted for the Lake District and for the Peak District.

A local planning authority may establish a planning committee and the committee may exercise any of the planning functions within the delegated authority of the council except the power to borrow money or to levy precepts for rates. A planning committee may appoint subcommittees (S.lol of the *Local Government Act, 1972*).

Any two or more local planning authorities may concur in establishing a joint advisory committee for the purpose of advising these authorities on the preparation of the structure and of the local plans, provided that at least two thirds of the members are members of one or other of these authorities (s. 101(1)(a) of the *Local Government Act, 1972*).

Any of the local authorities' functions may be discharged by an officer of the authority, provided that arrangements to this effect are made by the local authority concerned and/or by the planning committee or subcommittee (s. 101(1)(a) of the *Local Government Act, 1972*).

All functions conferred on local planning authorities shall be exercised both by county and district planning authorities (s. 182(1) of the *Local Government*

Act, 1972). Schedule 16 to that Act divides the jurisdiction between the county and district planning authorities (see Chapter 36).

The Greater London area is organised differently for the purpose of carrying out the provisions of town and country planning law (see Chapter 36).

27

DEVELOPMENT PLANS

27.1 Introduction

In 1947 the local planning authorities were, for the first time, instructed to prepare development plans and the 1947 Act set out the detailed procedure under which the plans were to be made. This Part of the Act was later consolidated in the 1962 Act, and now appears in Schedules 5 and 6 to the 1971 Act.

The new procedure created by the 1968 Act replaced the 'old style' development plans. The 'new style' was initially introduced by stages for those local authorities who were sufficiently strong to undertake the much more responsible planning task. Moreover, as from August 1, 1974, the whole of England and Wales came under the provisions of Part II of the 1971 Act dealing with the 'new style' plans. However, until all structure and local plans are prepared, the 'old style' development plans still govern the policy of the planning authorities. For this reason a short note is necessary to explain the contents and function of the 'old style' development plans.

27.2 Old Style Development Plans

Para. 1 of Schedule 5 requires any local planning authority to submit a development plan for approval to the Secretary of State for the Environment. The plan should indicate:

(a) The manner in which the land covered by the plan is to be used.

(b) The stages by which the development plan is to be carried out.

The plan consists of a basic map and a written statement (both obligatory) together with such other maps as may be appropriate. Examples of these special maps are a town map, an inset map, a comprehensive development map, a street map or a programme map.

A development plan may:

(a) Define the sites of the proposed roads, buildings, airfields, parks, pleasure grounds, nature reserves and other open spaces.

(b) Allocate areas for agricultural, residential or industrial purposes (some areas not allocated out are usually shown as 'white areas'). Until 1968 the development plan could also designate areas subject to compulsory purchase, but this has been repealed by the 1968 Act, which conferred upon local authorities a straightforward power to acquire land compulsorily without the necessity of designating it in the development plan.

A development plan is prepared by the local planning authority (in this case the county council) and must be approved by the Secretary of State.

A notice of submission of a plan for approval by the Secretary of State must be given in the *London Gazette* and in local newspapers; the notice must indicate the place where copies of the plan may be inspected. A Regulation issued by the Secretary of State (Town and Country Planning (Development Plans) Regulations, S.I. 1965/1453) prescribes the detailed procedure regarding objections which may be made by any interested person and details of the procedure to be adopted in the preparation and approval of development plans. Persons objecting may send their objections to the Secretary of State within the time prescribed by the Regulations. The Secretary must either hold a local inquiry or give objectors a hearing before an inspector. The Secretary of State may afterwards approve the development plan with or without modifications. Under Para. 6(3) of Schedule 6 the Secretary of State is authorised to hold discussions with the local planning authority or any other authority without inviting objectors to be present. In this case the rule of natural justice, *audi alteram partem* as expressed in the case *Errington v. Minister of Housing and Local Government* (1936), is excluded.

Under Para. 3 of Schedule 6 any person aggrieved by a development plan approved by the Secretary of State may make an application to the High Court within six weeks, and the Court (apart from having the power of issuing an interim order suspending the operation of the plan) may quash the plan if satisfied that it is *ultra vires* (in excess of jurisdiction), or that the interests of the applicant have been substantially prejudiced by a failure to comply with any requirements of the Act or of any Regulations issued under the Act. Apart from this right of making an application to the High Court, a development plan cannot be questioned in any proceedings whatsoever.

The development plan must be reviewed every five years, or more often if the local planning authority wishes or the Secretary of State so instructs. The procedure of amending an existing plan is the same as for preparing the original plan.

The Secretary of State has a default power. If a local planning authority neglects any of its duties in connection with the preparation of the development plan, the Secretary of State may himself take the necessary action or authorise some other planning authority to act.

27.3 New Style Development Plans: Their Concept

The new style development plan is dealt with in Part II of the 1971 Act, ss. 6–21, as amended by the *Town and Country Planning (Amendment) Act, 1972*, ss. 1–4, the *Local Government Act, 1972*, ss. 182–4 and Schedule 16, and by ss. 88–9 and Schedule 14 of the *Local Government Planning and Land Act, 1980*.

As the new style plan entrusts to the local planning authorities much wider powers than the old style, it was introduced gradually although since August 1, 1974, all authorities have been entrusted with the task of preparing the new style development plans.

Up to the end of 1980, 66 structure plans (out of a total expected coverage for England of 72) were submitted to the Secretary of State for his approval. Of those 54 have been approved and 12 await approval. A further six structure plans had still to be submitted to him (Avon, Dorset—excluding South East, Hampshire—South West, Isles of Scilly, Lancashire—Central and North, Somerset). Some of the approved structure plans are already subject to proposals for alteration.

The reasons for introducing the new style development plans were stated in the White Paper as the advisability of simplifying procedure, decentralisation and the giving of a greater role to citizens in influencing the contents of plans.

Development plans are prepared in two stages: **structure plans** and **local plans**. The Secretary of State is required to confirm the structure plans only; local plans are prepared and approved by the local planning authority and sent to the Secretary of State solely for information purposes.

27.4   New Style Development Plans: Structure Plans

Under s. 6 the preparation of a structure plan is the responsibility of county councils and they institute the surveys on which the structure plan will be based, as it is recognised that reliable research is necessary before a structure plan is made. The survey does not necessarily have to be conducted by the authority itself: it may be entrusted to outside consultants.

The survey, once completed, must be kept under constant review, and the county council may at any time institute a fresh survey.

Matters to be examined in the survey must include the following points:

(*a*) The principal physical and economic characteristics of the area of the authority (including the principal purposes for which the land is used) and, so far as they may be expected to affect that area, any neighbouring areas.

(*b*) The size, composition and distribution of the population of the area (whether resident or otherwise).

(*c*) The communications, transport and traffic of the area and, if advisable, of any neighbouring areas.

(*d*) Any considerations which may be expected to affect the matters mentioned above.

(*e*) Any matters prescribed by the Secretary of State.

(*f*) Any changes projected and the effect of these changes.

Thus, in essence, the survey covers land, population and its movements.

There is also a duty on the county council to consult, if necessary, any other authority (e.g. a district council) about any matters that may affect it.

The county council must prepare and send to the Secretary of State a report on its survey and submit to him for his approval a structure plan for its area. This plan, which must be a written statement (it should be noted that it may not be a map), must:

(*a*) Formulate the local planning authority's policy and general proposals for the development and other use of land in that area (including measures for the improvement of the physical environment and the management of traffic).

(*b*) Contain such matters as may be prescribed by the Secretary of State.

The structure plan must be justified by the results of the survey and must have regard to:

(*a*) The current policies of the region as a whole.

(*b*) The resources available.

(*c*) Other matters as directed by the Secretary of State.

The written statement should be illustrated by such diagrams as may be prescribed, which would be treated as forming part of the plan. The structure plan should be accompanied by an explanatory memorandum summarising the reasons for the general proposals formulated in the plan; the memorandum should state the relationship of the plan to the neighbouring areas. It may contain such illustrative material as the local planning authority thinks appropriate.

Thus the structure plan and the memorandum are a general statement of policy and do not show how any particular piece of land is affected. It is therefore hoped that there would not be many objections by individual owners, but rather that problems of general policy only would be discussed during the procedure of the approval of the structure plan.

Whilst preparing a structure plan the planning authority must give adequate publicity to the matters which they propose to include in the plan and the proposed contents of the explanatory memorandum. The local authority must provide an opportunity to all persons to make representations if they wish. When the structure plan has been prepared and submitted to the Secretary of State for approval publicity should again be given to this and all persons should be made aware that they can make objections to the Secretary of State (s. 8). This is another important difference between the old and the new style procedure: the public at large is entitled to take part in preparing the plan by making *representations* and, in addition, can make *objections* against the draft of the prepared plan to the Secretary of State. In the old style only objections were allowed.

When submitting the plan to the Secretary of State, the local planning authority must show what steps have been taken to comply with the requirements regarding publicity, etc., and that consideration has been given to the views of the persons who made representations. If the Secretary of State is not satisfied that the local planning authority has acted properly in preparing the plan, he should return the plan for defects to be remedied (s. 9).

The Secretary of State may either approve the plan, with or without modifications, or reject it. If the plan is rejected, objections do not require to be considered. Otherwise, the Secretary of State must consider any objections. Under the 1971 Act, he had either to afford objectors an opportunity to be heard by an inspector, or to arrange a local inquiry to be held. In either case the local planning authority was entitled to be represented. But this procedure created a problem. The Greater London development plan inquiry, for example, had to look into some 21,000 objections and, of course the expense and delay were enormous. The Government came to the conclusion that the issues involved in the Greater London plan (or other structure plans) were mostly 'strategic' ones of little interest to the individual property owner, who would in any event be able to defend his rights by objections to the local plans at a later stage. Therefore a new procedure was introduced by s. 3 of the *Town and Country Planning* (*Amendment*) *Act, 1972*, which applies to structure plans and to those local plans which, exceptionally, have to be approved by the Secretary of State.

Under the amended procedure, anyone can submit a written objection and the Secretary of State must consider all such submissions. He will then select the 'broad strategic and key issues', according to his discretion, and those issues will be referred to a person or persons for examination in public. Neither the objectors nor the local authority responsible for the preparation of the structure plan will have the right to appear at the examination unless invited by the Secretary of State to do so, although the panel holding the examination will have power to invite additional bodies or persons to take part. The examination under these provisions will be under the supervision of the Council on Tribunals, but in other aspects will not be considered to be a public inquiry.

Thus these provisions limit, to some extent, the role of the citizens in planning advocated so eloquently by the White Paper in 1967.

Before eventually approving the structure plan, the Secretary of State, in a similar way to the old style, may consult with any local planning authority or other persons.

At any time after the approval of a structure plan, the local planning authority may submit to the Secretary of State an alteration to the structure plan. They have to take this action if so directed by the Secretary of State (s. 10).

It may happen that two or more local planning authorities responsible for the preparation of a structure plan come to the conclusion that it would be advisable to prepare a joint survey and report, and to prepare a structure plan covering two or more areas of the local planning authorities. For this reason s. 10A (introduced by the *Town and Country Planning (Amendment) Act, 1972*) states that two or more local planning authorities may apply to the Secretary of State for his consent to their areas or any part thereof being treated as a combined area for the purposes of the preparation of a structure or local development plan and, if the Secretary of State agrees, the local authorities concerned may institute a joint survey, submit a joint report on the survey and jointly prepare and submit to the Secretary of State a structure or local plan for the combined area.

S. 10B introduced by the *Town and Country Planning (Amendment) Act, 1972*, allows the local planning authority to withdraw the structure plan submitted to the Secretary of State for approval before it is approved.

27.5 Local Plans

The general rule is that local plans are the responsibility of district councils. There are, however, two exceptions to this rule:

(*a*) In respect of an area in a National Park, as in this case local plans are prepared by the county councils.

(*b*) The structure plan for an area or the 'development plan scheme' (see below) may provide that some local plans will be prepared exclusively by the county council (s. 2A of the Act as enacted by s. 182 of the *Local Government Act, 1972*, and s. 10C(5) of the Act as enacted by s. 183(2) of the *Local Government Act, 1972*).

When the structure plan has been approved, the local planning authority must as soon as practicable consider the desirability of preparing, and if appropriate prepare one or more, local plans (s. 11(1) and (2) of the 1971 Act as amended by Para. 1 of Schedule 16 to the *Local Government Act, 1972*).

A local plan consists of a map and a written statement and formulates proposals for the development and other use of land, including measures for the improvement of the physical environment and the management of traffic. The plan contains such diagrams, illustrations and descriptive matters as appropriate. The local planning authority may decide to establish an **action area** and in such a case a local plan is prepared for that area. An 'action area' is an area selected for early development. The Town and Country Planning (Structure and Local Development Plans) Regulations, S.I. 1974/1486, state that an area should be treated as an action area if development is intended to be carried out within 10 years. The local plan must conform generally to the structure plan. Different local plans may be prepared for different purposes for the same part of the area covered by the structure plan. Thus local plans are either plans with varying degrees of detail about a particular part of the area, or plans whose purpose concerns some particular aspect of planning for a rather wider area. There may be action area plans or district plans covering larger parts of the area of the local planning authority, or even much smaller local plans dealing with a particular problem of some area within the district.

The primary purpose of a local plan is to guide the authority and developer in respect of possible development of the land covered by the plan. The system is designed to be of utmost flexibility and the amount of detail which goes into any particular local plan will depend on the nature of the proposals it contains.

A local planning authority proposing the preparation of a local plan must give adequate publicity to this fact and allow the persons interested an opportunity to make representations which have to be considered by the local planning authority when the draft plan is being prepared (s. 12). When the draft of the local plan is ready, the local planning authority must make copies of the draft plan available for inspection and send a copy to the Secretary of State. Time must be given to the objectors to raise objections to the draft of the plan. The Secretary of State may direct the local planning authority to comply with the procedural requirements if he thinks that they have not been adhered to.

The local planning authority must consider objections that have been raised and must either hold a local inquiry or arrange a private hearing before a person appointed by the Secretary of State (s. 13).

After considering the objections and the report of the inspector who held the local inquiry or hearing, the local planning authority may by resolution adopt the plan. The Secretary of State does not, as a general rule, approve the local plan (it is sent to him for information only), but has a right to direct that a particular plan shall not take effect unless approved by him (s. 14).

A local plan may be amended at any time after complying with the procedure prescribed for the preparation of the original plan (s. 15).

If a local planning authority is in default in preparing any survey or structure plan, the Secretary of State may either take the action himself or entrust the action to another local planning authority (s. 17).

The Secretary of State has issued a statutory instrument on the form and content of structure and local plans and on the detailed procedure to be adopted in preparation of the plan (Town and Country Planning (Structure and Local Plans) Regulations, S.I. 1974/1486, as amended by the Town and Country Planning (Structure and Local Plans) (Amendment) Regulations, 1979, S.I. 1979/1738).

Where there is a conflict between any of the provisions of a local plan and the provisions of a structure plan, the provisions of a local plan prevail for all purposes. This interesting provisions introduced by Para. 10 of Schedule 14 to the *Local Government, Planning and Land Act, 1980*, is obviously dictated by the fact that people may rely on local plans in arranging their affairs.

27.6   Development Plan Schemes

This is a new concept, created by the *Local Government Act, 1972*, (s. 183, inserting s. 10C into the 1971 Act). The county planning authority in consultation with the district planning authorities of the county shall make, and afterwards keep under review (and amend if they think fit), a 'development plan scheme' for the preparation of local plans for those areas in the county which are to be covered by the local plans (with the exception of any part of the county which is included in a National Park).

The development plan scheme:

(*a*) Designates the authority responsible for the preparation of each local plan for the area in question, specifying the title and nature of each local plan for the area and giving an indication of its scope.

(*b*) Sets out a programme for the preparation of the several plans for that area.

(*c*) Indicates the relationship between the several local plans for that area.

A copy of the scheme should be sent to the Secretary of State for information.

If a district planning authority makes representations to the Secretary of State that it is dissatisfied with the development plan scheme, the Secretary may amend the scheme and any amendments so made shall have effect as if made by the county planning authority.

28

DEFINITION OF DEVELOPMENT

28.1 Operations

SS. 22–4 define development and set out the general principle that planning permission is required for the carrying out of any development of land.

Development means the carrying out of building, engineering, mining or other operations in, on, over or under land, or the making of any material change in the use of any building or other land (s. 22(1)).

Building operations include rebuilding operations, structural alterations of or any additions to buildings and other operations normally undertaken by a person carrying on business as a builder. 'Building' includes any structure or erection and any part of a building, as so defined, but does not include plant or machinery comprised in a building. **Engineering operations** are not defined as such, but s. 290 states that they include the formation or laying out of a means of access to highways. The words **mining operation** are not defined in the Act, but 'minerals' include all minerals and substances in or under land of a kind ordinarily removed by underground or surface working, except that it does not include peat cut out for purposes other than sale.

Other operations are not defined, but should be taken as acts which change the physical character of the land, or what is in, under, or in the air above it. In *Cheshire v. Woodward*, 1962, the Minister, on an enforcement notice appeal, held that the placing on the land of a coal-bagging hopper on wheels resting on concrete blocks and a mobile conveyor also on wheels, both in a coalyard, was not development (although the inspector reported that in spite of the fact that both structures were on wheels, it would be difficult to move them and that such movements were unlikely whilst they were in use). The Divisional Court held that the Minister had not erred in law. This case illustrates that the operation must create a permanent situation and that it must annex the building (or structure) to the land. For this reason the placing of caravans on land is not an operation, but a way of using the land (this means it is a development, but under the second part of the definition: 'material change in the use of any building or other land').

It is not easy to illustrate by examples what is meant by 'other operations', but no doubt removal of topsoil, so far as it is not included in 'engineering' or 'mining' operations, would be considered 'other operations'. The removal of an embankment surrounding an ammunition depot has been held to be development (*Coleshill and District Investment Co. Ltd v. Minister of Housing and L.G.*, 1969).

Whether the demolition of a building is an operation constituting development seems to be a debatable question. For some years it was assumed that the demolition of a building itself is not a development (unless it is a part of building operations, e.g. *Howell v. Sunbury on Thames U.D.C.*, 1963), but in a more recent case (Coleshill case, see above) Lord Upjohn said: 'There is nothing in Section 12 [now s. 22 of the 1971 Act] which makes it plain that demolition *per se* or *simpliciter* is necessarily excluded from the very wide words of Section 12.'

Some years ago the Secretary of State asked Dobry, Q.C., to prepare a report suggesting improvements in the procedure governing planning control. He suggested in his report that demolition should be made a controlled development. The Secretary of State, however, in the Circular considering the report, stated that he did not intend to seek further powers to control demolition, the main reason being the increased time needed for deciding planning applications and the necessity to secure additional local authority resources.

It should be noted, however, that listed buildings and (generally speaking) buildings in conservation areas are subject to control if their demolition is sought.

28.2 Material Change in the Use of Land

The second type of development is 'the material change in the use of a building or other land'. This definition creates considerable difficulties of interpretation, because it is a matter of degree whether the change in question is 'material' or not. It seems that the general test is whether or not the change in the use will completely alter the character of the land or building.

Sometimes the question will depend on the degree of intensification of use. Thus in the case of *Guildford R.D.C. v. Penny* (1959) an increase in the number of caravans from eight to 27 was accepted by the High Court as concerning a matter of fact and not law and as such was not subject to revision by the High Court on appeal from the Magistrates' Court on the case stated. The Magistrates did not consider it a material change. But in another case Lord Denning said that an increase from 24 to 78 caravans might well amount to a material change of use (*Esdell Caravan Parks Ltd v. Hemel Hempstead R.D.C.*, 1966). Moreover, in yet another case (*Birmingham Corporation v. Minister of Housing and L.G. and Habib Ullah*, 1963) the owner of two houses which had been in single family occupation installed several families in each. The Minister considered that there had been no material change of use as the houses remained residential. On appeal by the local authority the Court held that the Minister had erred in law saying that there could not be a material change in use if the house had remained residential. This is a matter of fact and degree in each case.

Another important consideration which may decide whether the change of use is material or not, is what 'planning unit' is accepted as the proper unit to be examined. Thus in the case of *De Mulder and others v. Secretary of State for the Environment* (1974) it was stated that a planning authority 'could not, by arbitrarily dividing up a site into a number of smaller areas and directing separate enforcement notices to each of them, impose more severe restriction on a land owner than might have been imposed on him by a notice applicable to the whole area'. In this case the proper planning unit was the whole farm and the enforcement notices were unduly restrictive in that in each of the separate areas the appellants were restricted to a use of the intensity found there in April 1970. If a single enforcement notice had been used, the increase in intensity would have been permissible, as the increase of use in one part of the farm was compensated by the reduction of use in another part.

The general definition of development as stated in s. 22, which is simple enough, is subject to some qualifications, and this makes the meaning of development, and particularly those developments which require permission, rather a complex one. The definition is qualified in the following respects:

(*a*) Some changes of use are a development even if not material (s. 22(3) and (4)).

(*b*) Some operations and changes of use are not considered to be a development within the meaning of the Act (s. 22(2)).

(*c*) Some changes of use, although they are developments, do not require planning permission (s. 23).

(*d*) Some developments are permitted by the General Development Order and do not require individual planning permission (s. 24).

28.3   Changes of Use which are a Development even if not Material

'For the avoidance of doubt' the following three changes in the use of land are declared to involve a material change and as such require planning permission:

(*a*) The use as two or more separate dwelling-houses of any building previously used as a single dwelling-house. In simple terms, the conversion of single dwelling-houses into flats requires planning permission in spite of the general rule that works which do not affect the external appearance of a building are not developments (see Section 28.4 below).

(*b*) The deposit of refuse or waste material on land notwithstanding that the land is already used for that purpose, if either the superficial area of the deposit is thereby extended, or the height of the deposit is thereby extended and exceeds the level of the adjoining land.

(*c*) The use of land for the display of advertisements on any external part of a building shall be treated as involving a material change of use (some advertisements, however, are permitted by a statutory instrument—Town and Country Planning (Control of Advertisements) Regulation, 1969 (S.I. 1532), as amended by the Town and Country Planning (Control of Advertisements) (Amendment) Regulations of 1972 (S.I. 489), 1974 (S.I. 185) and 1975 (S.I. 898)). This control is dictated by the possibility that the amenities of the area may be affected by undesirable advertisements.

28.4   Operations and Changes of Use not Considered to be Development

(*a*) The carrying on of works for the maintenance, improvement or alteration of any building which affect only the interior of the building, or which do not materially affect the external appearance of the building and are not works for making good war damage. But it has been held that the restoration to the same design of a building of which only the original foundation, damp course and two walls remained, was a reconstruction constituting a development and not only maintenance or repair (*Street v. Essex C.C.*, 1965). Also the replacement of a hedge by a fence is not maintenance, but development (*Scholes v. Minister of Housing and L.G. and Heysham B.C.*, 1966). If the works began after December 5, 1968, they must not alter the building by providing additional space below the ground (an amendment introduced by the 1968 Act).

The provision of this subsection requires some explanation. Any work which does not affect the external appearance of the building does not concern the planning authority, as such work does not affect the environment of the land in question. But three exceptions should be noted: the conversion of a house into separate flats requires permission, because from the point of view of planning (density of population, traffic, etc.) such a change is material; secondly, the planning authority requires full control over making good war damage, as it may be in the interests of planning that the house should not be rebuilt to its pre-war style, but that the war damage should create an opportunity to develop the land according to modern ideas; thirdly, it is undesirable to allow the extension of a building underground without supervision, as this may weaken its foundation or the space may be required by the statutory undertakers. It may also be undesirable to use underground space for car parks, particularly in town centres.

(*b*) The carrying out by a local authority of any works required for the maintenance or improvement of a road on land within the boundaries of the road. Thus those works include any improvement of the road, but not its widening.

(*c*) The carrying out by a local authority or statutory undertakers of any works for the purpose of inspecting, repairing or renewing any sewers, mains, pipes, cables or other apparatus, including the breaking open of any street or other land for that purpose.

(*d*) The use of any building or other land within the curtilage of a dwelling-house for any purpose incidental to the enjoyment of the dwelling-house as such (this provision applies only to a change in the use and not to operation, i.e. does not include erection of any additional structure). There is no statutory definition of 'curtilage'; in the case *Sinclair-Lockhart's Trustees v. Central Land Board* (1950) the Court held: 'The ground which is used for the comfortable enjoyment of a house or other building may be regarded in law as being within the curtilage of that house or building.'

(*e*) The use of any land for the purpose of agriculture or forestry and the use for any of these purposes of any building occupied on land so used. As the use of any land (or building) has to be for agriculture or forestry, it does not include the changing of use from agricultural storage into a farm's labourer cottage (*McKeller v. Ministry of Housing and Local Government*, 1966). 'Agriculture' is very widely defined in s. 290, but does not include horse-breeding for show jumping, as these animals are not used in farming (*Belmont Farm Ltd v. Minister of Housing and Local Government*, 1962). The placing of an egg-vending machine by a roadside on a poultry farm was considered a material change of use (*Hidderley v. Warwickshire C.C.*, 1963).

(*f*) In the case of building or other land used for a purpose of any class specified in any order made by the Secretary of State under this Section, the use thereof for any other purpose of the same class. This means that any change of use within the same class specified by the order is allowed, even if it is a material change (Town and Country Planning (Use Classes) Order, 1972, S.I. 1972/1385). It should be noted, moreover, that a change from one class to another may be allowed if the change is not 'material', as only a material change of use constitute a development.

In order to understand the provisions of this Order, it is necessary first to become acquainted with some definitions contained in the Order:

(*a*) An **industrial building** is defined as a building (other than a building in or adjacent to and belonging to a quarry or mine and other than a shop) used for the carrying on of any process for, or incidental to, any of the following purposes, namely:

the making of any article, or part of any article; or
the altering, repairing, ornamenting, finishing, cleaning, washing, packing or canning, or adapting for sale, or breaking up for demolition of any article; or without prejudice to the foregoing paragraphs, the getting, dressing, or treatment of minerals.

Industrial buildings are divided into three categories: light industrial building, general industrial building and special industrial building. A light industrial building is one in which the processes carried out or the machinery installed are such as could be carried on or installed in any residential area without detriment to the amenity of that area by reason of noise, vibration, smell, fumes, smoke, soot, ash, dust or grit. A special industrial building means one used for the purposes specified in classes V–IX. Buildings in these classes include those which are offensive for the neighbourhood. A general industrial building is any industrial building which is neither light nor special.

(*b*) The word **office** includes a bank and premises occupied by an estate agency, building society or employment agency, or (for office purposes only) for the business of car hire or driving instruction, but does not include a post office or betting office.

(*c*) The word **shop** means a building used for the carrying on of any retail trade or retail business, wherein the primary purpose is the selling of goods by retail, and includes a ticket office or post office, or a building used for the purposes of a hairdresser, undertaker, travel agency, or for the reception of goods to be washed, cleaned or repaired, or for any other purpose appropriate to a shopping area, but does not include a building used as a funfair, amusement arcade, pin-table saloon, garage, laundrette, petrol filling station, office, betting office, hotel, restaurant, snack bar or cafe, or premises licensed for the sale of intoxicating liquors for consumption on the premises.

Of the 18 classes only the first four are of general application:

Class I. 'A change of use from one to another type of shop; but planning permission is required for a change into the following shops: hot food shop, a tripe shop, a shop for the sale of pet animals or birds, a cat's meat shop or shop for the sale of motor vehicles.'
Class II. 'A change of use from one type of office into another.'
Class III. 'A change of use of a light industrial building into another light industrial building.'
Class IV. 'A change of use of a general industrial building into another general industrial building.'

Other use classes are less important. For example, a hospital may become an institution for old people, or a mental hospital may become a house for epileptics; an exhibition hall may become a concert hall, a theatre may become a cinema, etc.

Even a change within a class requires planning permission if the local planning authority on granting a planning permission adds a condition that only a specified use is allowed.

28.5   Some Changes of Use which, although a Development, do not Require Planning Permission

A further qualification of the definition of development requiring planning permission is contained in s. 23, which states that six changes of use are developments, but do not require planning permission.

The first three changes of use are of lesser importance, as they preserve the right of persons 'caught' by the enactment of the 1947 Act which, for the first time, introduced the requirements of obtaining planning permission. For example, if on July 1, 1948, land was temporarily used differently from its normal use, the resumption of its normal use (if effected before December 5, 1968) was permitted without the necessity of obtaining planning permission. Thus the importance of these provisions is gradually diminishing in the course of time.

The next three changes of use which do not require planning permission have permanent application:

(*a*) If planning permission is granted for a limited period, the resumption of the previous use.

(*b*) Where planning permission has been granted subject to limitations by a development order, permission is not required for the normal use of that land apart from the use in accordance with that permission, provided that such use does not contravene the provisions of the Act.

(*c*) If an enforcement notice has been served in respect of the unauthorised use of land, planning permission is not required for the resumption of the previous legal use.

28.6   Some Developments Permitted by the General Development Order which do not Require Individual Planning Permission

The last qualification of the definition of a development requiring planning permission arises from s. 24, which instructs the Secretary of State to issue a 'Development Order' which provided for the granting of planning permission.

The General Development Order ('GDO'), amended on numerous occasions and reissued in 1977 (S.I. 1977/289) (see also Appendix 1),

itself grants planning permission for developments specified in the order;
provides for the local planning authorities to grant planning permission on an application by a person interested.

The general principle is that a person seeking permission for development should apply to the local planning authority, unless the GDO grants such permission generally for some classes of development called **classes of permitted development**.

The classes of permitted development are important, as they permit many types of development of a minor nature without the need for applying for permission. Two general limitations of permitted developments are stated; GDO does not authorise any development which:

(*a*) Requires or involves the formation, laying out or material widening of a means of access to an existing highway which is a trunk or classified road.

(*b*) Creates an obstruction to the view of persons using any highway used by vehicular traffic at or near any bend, corner, junction, or intersection so as to be likely to cause danger to such persons.

Schedule 1 to the order specifies permitted development. Of 23 classes, only Classes I–XI are of general interest and importance; the remainder concern development by public bodies, such as local authorities, the National Coal Board, etc.

The Classes I–X are given below; with regard to others the GDO should be consulted. The most important is Class I.

Class I. Development within the Curtilage of a Dwelling House

This class is divided into five parts:

(1) The enlargement, improvement or other alteration of a dwelling house, so long as:

(*a*) The cubic content of the original dwelling house (as ascertained by external measurement) is not exceeded by more than 50 cubic metres or one tenth, whichever is greater, subject to a maximum of 115 cubic metres ('original' means, in relation to a building existing on July 1, 1948, as existing on that date; in relation to a building built on or after July 1, 1948, as it was built).

(*b*) The height of the building as so enlarged does not exceed the height of the highest part of the roof of the original dwelling house. This is more flexible than the previous wording of the GDO 1963, which imposed the condition that the height after enlargement must not exceed 'the height of the original building'.

(*c*) No part of the building as so enlarged projects beyond the forwardmost part of any wall of the original dwelling-house which fronts on a highway.

The erection of a garage within the curtilage of the dwelling-house is treated as an enlargement, i.e. is counted towards the cubic contents allowed under (*a*).

(2) The erection of a porch outside the external door of a dwelling-house so long as:

(*a*) The floor area does not exceed two square metres.

(*b*) No part of the structure is more than 3 metres above the level of the ground.

(*c*) No part of the structure is less than two metres from any boundary of the curtilage which fronts on a highway.

The porch is not counted towards the enlargement allowed under Class I and may project beyond the forwardmost part of the building, as long as 2 metres of space to the pavement is preserved.

(3) The erection within the curtilage of a dwelling-house of any building or enclosure required for a purpose incidental to the enjoyment of a dwelling-house so long as:

(*a*) No part of such building or enclosure projects beyond the forwardmost part of any wall of the original dwelling-house which fronts on a highway.

(*b*) The height does not exceed, in the case of a building with a ridge roof, 4 metres or, in other case, 3 metres.

(*c*) The area of ground covered by buildings within the curtilage does not exceed one half of the total area of the curtilage, excluding the ground area of the original dwelling-house.

Curtilage has been judicially defined as the ground which is used for the comfortable enjoyment of the house (*Sinclair Lockhart's Trustees v. Central Land Board*, 1950).

(4) The construction within the curtilage of a dwelling-house of a hard-standing for vehicles for a purpose incidental to the enjoyment of the dwelling-house as such. This is a new and quite important concession. Apparently it has been decided that it is less detrimental to the environment to keep cars on a hard-stand in the front of a house than to congest the streets with parked cars.

(5) The erection within the curtilage of a dwelling-house of a tank for the storage of oil for domestic heating. There are three limitations: capacity 3500 litres, height 3 metres, not projecting beyond the wall of the dwelling-house fronting on the highway.

Class II. Sundry Minor Operations

(1) Erection of gates, fences, walls or other means of enclosure provided that they do not exceed 1 metre in height when abutting on a road used by vehicles, or 2 metres in other cases.

(2) Construction of means of access to a highway (not being a trunk or classified road) if required in connection with development permitted under this Order.

(3) The painting of the exterior of any building (other than advertisement).

Class III. Changes of Use

This class authorises a change of use of a building from a general industrial building to a light industrial building (although it is a change from one class of uses to another, it is beneficial from the point of view of planning). It also permits the change of use of any of the shops excluded from Class I of the Use Classes Order ('smelly shops') into a normal shop.

Class IV. Temporary Buildings and Uses

Under this class permission is given for the erection or construction on land of buildings, plant and machinery needed temporarily for the carrying out of authorised development. It also gives permission for the temporary use of land for any purpose for not more than 28 days in any calendar year, and permits the erection and placing of movable structures on the land for the purpose of that use. This permission is applicable to fairs, markets and camping (but not caravan sites).

However, not more than 14 days in total may be devoted to the use for the purpose of motorcar or motorcycle racing or for the purpose of holding markets.

Class V. Uses by Members of Recreational Organisations

Under this class land not within the curtilage of a dwelling-house may be used for recreation and instruction involving the use of tents (but not caravans) by members of recreational organisations which hold a certificate of exemption under s. 289 of the *Public Health Act, 1936* (e.g. the Boy Scouts Association).

Class VI. Agricultural Buildings, Works and Uses

This class authorises the carrying out on agricultural land of more than one acre and comprised in an agricultural unit of all the building and engineering operations likely to be undertaken on a normal farm. The provision and alteration of dwellings, however, are not included. Some conditions are attached regarding the size and height of the buildings, particularly in the vicinity of aerodromes.

Class VII. Forestry Buildings and Works

Similar permission to Class VI is given in respect of buildings and other operations required for forestry.

Class VIII. Development for Industrial Purposes

Permission is given for additions to industrial buildings (by extensions or new erections) not beyond one tenth of the cubic capacity of the original building. Permission is also given for various works and installations on industrial premises.

Class IX. Repairs to Unadopted Streets and Private Ways

Permission is given to the carrying out of works for the maintenance and improvement of an unadopted street carried out on land within the boundaries of the street or way.

Class X. Repairs to Services

Under this class, repairs of sewers, underground telephone cables, etc., are allowed.

Under Art. 4 of the General Development Order the Secretary of State or the local planning authority may withdraw the benefit of any permission granted either generally or in relation to a particular piece of land. In such case the developer has to apply for planning permission. The approval of the Secretary of State is necessary for such a direction if issued by the local planning authority, except in certain cases when the local planning authority may issue a direction which is valid for up to six months.

28.7 Section 53 Determinations

It will appear from the above discussion that the definition of development requiring planning permission is a complex one and problems may often arise in deciding whether any intended action (be it operation or change of use) constitutes a development requiring permission.

For this reason s. 53 provides that if any person who proposes to carry out any operation on land or to make any change of use of land wishes to have it determined beforehand whether this would constitute or involve development, or whether planning permission is required, he may apply to the local planning authority asking for the determination of that question. There is a right of appeal to the Secretary of State against the determination of the local planning authority and a further right of appeal to the High Court on limited grounds discussed later.

But any informal determination is of no value. Thus in one case (*Southend-on-Sea v. Hodgson* (*Wickford*) *Ltd*, 1961) the borough engineer, in reply to an inquiry wrote: '... the land has an existing user right as a builder's yard and no planning permission is, therefore, necessary'. The Company bought the land and were subsequently served with an enforcement notice requiring them to stop using the land as a builder's yard. The Divisional Court held that a public authority could not fetter themselves by estoppel in the exercise of their statutory discretion to serve an enforcement notice, and so allowed the Corporation's appeal against the quashing of the enforcement notice by the local Magistrates under the enforcement procedure then in force. The position would be different if the local authority's certificate had been obtained under the procedure of s. 53. Thus informal applications and informal replies are of no legal validity.

28.8 Agreements Regulating Development or Use of Land (s. 52)

There is a scheme which facilitates developments by private persons if the development is desirable, but for some reason (e.g. excessive costs) it is not suitable to be carried out by local authorities.

A local planning authority may enter into an agreement with any person interested in land in their area for the purpose of restricting or regulating the development of the land either permanently or during a period prescribed by the agreement. Any such agreement may contain such incidental and consequential provisions (including provisions of a financial character) as appear to the local authority to be necessary or expedient.

Since 1968 it has not been necessary to obtain the Secretary of State's approval for such an agreement, which was required under previous Acts.

The agreement may be enforced against the developer and his successors in title, like any restrictive covenant. S. 52(2) states that the agreement may be enforced by the local planning authority against persons deriving title, as if the local authority were possessed of adjacent land and as if the agreement had been expressed for the benefit of such land. It continues: 'Nothing in the agreement shall be constructed as restricting any power exercisable by any Minister or local authority under the Act as long as those powers were exercised in accordance with the provisions of the development plans.' Thus although it enables the Secretary of State or local planning authority to override the agreement, nevertheless it is a considerable restriction of powers, as otherwise they would be able to override the agreement without any qualifications. If the agreement is broken there is no right of the developer to claim any damages, as the statutory powers of authority cannot be restricted by agreement (*Ransom and Luck v. Surbiton Borough Council*, 1949, and *Stringer v. Ministry of Housing and L.G.*, 1970). The question of damages for breach cannot arise very often, as such an agreement is usually immediately followed by the granting of planning permission. However, before investing money in consequence of an agreement under s. 52 the developer is well advised also to obtain the relevant planning permission.

In some cases it seems that planning permission is granted as part of a bargain under which the developer voluntarily accepts conditions which would be quashed by the Court if imposed on the granting of planning permission (as happened in the case of *Hall & Co. v. Shoreham U.D.C.*, 1964, discussed in Chapter 29).

In practice, the total number of agreements has not been great. One of the more publicised agreements between a local planning authority and a developer was that between the Oldham Estates Company Ltd and the London County Council for the development of St Giles Circus. The Council was anxious to improve traffic flow in an area where Oldham Estates already had substantial freehold interests and were proposing to acquire further land to redevelop the whole area. Rather than work in opposition to each other, an agreement was made, whereby Oldham Estates acquired the land required by the Council for their road scheme and dedicated it to them. In exchange the Council granted planning permission for the Oldham Estates development on the site they retained with floor space appropriate to the whole area. The ultimate development, 'Centre Point', has been the subject of much press and political comment.

29

GENERAL PLANNING CONTROL

29.1 Applications for Planning Permission

Planning permission is required for the carrying out of any development on land, unless permission is granted in general terms by the Act itself or by the General Development Order (ss. 24–8). The GDO was consolidated in 1977 (S.I. 289). It prescribes the detailed procedure of application for planning permission and of dealing with it.

The application must be made on a form issued by the local planning authority. It must include such particulars as the application form requires and must be accompanied by a plan sufficient to identify the land together with any other plans and drawings necessary to describe the development. The local planning authority may require such further information as is requisite to enable them to determine the application.

The developer, either before buying the land or before incurring expense involved in the preparation of detailed plans, may apply for **outline planning permission**, which can be granted subject to any 'reserved matters', in respect of siting, design, external appearance, means of access and landscaping of the site. The local planning authority is then committed to granting planning permission in some form or another and further permission is required only for 'reserved matters'. If outline planning permission has been granted subject to reserved matters the local planning authority may not at a later stage refuse planning permission for reasons falling outside the reserved matters (*Hamilton v. Sussex C.C.*, 1958). Outline planning permission can be asked only if the intended development includes the erection of a building and does not refer exclusively to a change of use.

The applicant for planning permission need not have a legal interest in the land in question. The application may be made by a prospective purchaser or lessee. The applicant has to attach to the application one of the following four certificates (s. 27):

Certificate A. This certificate states that no person other than the applicant was 21 days before the date of application the owner of any of the land to which the application relates.

Certificate B. This states that the applicant has given notice to all persons who are now, or have been within the preceding 21 days, owners of the land. The names and addresses of these persons should be supplied.

Certificate C. This is submitted if some of the persons entitled to the notice cannot be found.

Certificate D. This states that none of the owners can be found.

In the last two cases a notice must be published in the local newspaper.

In addition, another certificate must be published, stating either that none of

143

the land constitutes an agricultural holding or that notice has been given to all tenants of agricultural holdings.

The above notices must be accurate, since a false notice may involve criminal proceedings with a penalty of up to £100. The Act does not state the effect of planning permission if a false or incorrect certificate has been attached to the application, but it is submitted that if the certificate is apparently in order any subsequent falsity which may emerge (although this may be a reason for prosecution) cannot affect the validity of the determination of the local planning authority. Otherwise the rights of the *bona fide* purchaser might be adversely affected.

S. 26 and the GDO prescribe that in nine classes of development, commonly called 'bad neighbour developments', publication of the application in a local newspaper and a site notice are necessary. These nine classes of development are:

(*a*) Construction of buildings as a public convenience.

(*b*) Construction of buildings or other operations or use of land for the purpose of retention, treatment or disposal of sewage, trade waste or sludge.

(*c*) Construction of buildings or other operations, or use of land for the disposal of waste material, or as a scrap-yard, or coal-yard, or for the winning or working of minerals.

(*d*) Construction of buildings to a height exceeding 20 metres.

(*e*) Construction of buildings or use of land for the purpose of a slaughter-house or knacker's yard, or for the killing or plucking of poultry.

(*f*) Construction or use of buildings as a casino, fun-fair, or a bingo hall, a skating rink, a swimming bath or gymnasium (not forming part of a school, college or university), or a Turkish or other vapour or foam bath.

(*g*) Construction or use of buildings or land as a zoo or for the business of boarding or breeding cats or dogs.

(*h*) Construction of buildings and use of land for motorcar or motorcycle racing.

(*i*) Use of land as a cemetery.

If any person makes a representation concerning any of the above classes of development, the local planning authority must consider the representation.

An applicant for a 'bad neighbour development' must post a notice on the land involved, stating that an application for planning permission is to be made. Such a notice must be displayed for not less than seven days and in such a manner as to be easily visible and legible by members of the public, but the applicant is not responsible if the notice is removed or obscured by third persons. Moreover (although there is no statutory requirement), the local authority is advised by the Secretary of State (Circular 71/73) to ask the applicant to put up a site notice whenever the development may affect a residential area by smell, noise, vibration, bringing crowds into the area, causing activity and noise at unseemly hours, or otherwise have an adverse effect on the general character of the area.

In considering an application for planning permission, the local planning authority must take into account representations from landowners (if different from the applicant), neighbours and the general public (who may acquire knowledge of the application from a site notice displayed).

S. 87 of the *Local Government, Planning and Land Act, 1980*, allows the Secretary of State to make by regulations arrangements for the payment of a fee of a prescribed amount to a local planning authority. Fees may be prescribed not only for an application for planning permission, but also for applications for any other permission, consent, approval, declaration or certificate. Such regulations must be approved by both Houses of Parliament.

29.2 Determination by the Local Planning Authority on Application for Planning Permission (ss. 29–35)

Upon the receipt of an application for planning permission the local planning authority must send a receipt to the applicant. The decision should be given to the applicant within eight weeks. Only by the written consent of the applicant may this period be extended. If the applicant does not receive the decision within the above period, he is entitled to appeal to the Secretary of State as if his application had been refused.

Every local planning authority should keep a register of applications for planning permission, including information about the manner in which such applications have been dealt with.

In dealing with an application the local planning authority has regard to the development plan and other material considerations, but it may grant planning permission which does not agree with the development plan within the authority given generally or specifically by the Secretary of State.

The local planning authority, after having considered the application, may:

(*a*) grant permission unconditionally;
(*b*) grant permission subject to conditions 'as it thinks fit';
(*c*) refuse permission.

As the decision of the local planning authority is a vital document defining the rights of the developer, it is important that the decision should be clear and free from any ambiguity. If a problem of interpretation arises, it has been decided by the Court of Appeal (*Slough Estate Ltd v. Slough B.C. and another*, 1969) that the grant of permission is the document issued by the authority and not the authority's resolution. In the same case the House of Lords stated that since the purported planning permission was not complete or self-contained on the face of it in that, among others, it incorporated by reference the plan attached to the application, it was proper to examine the correspondence leading up to the grant of planning permission, with a view to ascertaining what the terms of the application were, how the plan was submitted and what functions it was intended to perform.

Without prejudice to the general power given to the authority to impose on planning permission such conditions 'as they think fit', the authority is empowered by s. 30(1) to impose the following conditions:

(*a*) Regulating the development or use of any land under the control of the applicant (whether or not it is land for which the application was made), or requiring the carrying out of works on any such land, insofar as it appears to the local planning authority to be expedient for the purposes or in connection with the development authorised by the permission.

(*b*) For requiring the removal of any building or works authorised by the permission, or the discontinuance of any use of land so authorised, at the end of specified period, and the carrying out of any works required for the rein-statement of land at the end of that period. Such permissions granted for a limited period are known as 'limited permissions'.

Although the local planning authority may impose such conditions as they think fit, it has been decided by the Court that this power must be exercised only for the purpose of the Act and therefore:

(*a*) A condition must fairly and reasonably relate to the proposed operation (Lord Denning in the case *Pyx Granite Ltd v. Minister of Housing and L.G.*, 1958);

(*b*) A condition must be certain and reasonable.

A few examples will show how far the courts control the freedom of a local authority in this respect.

In the case of *Fawcett Properties Ltd v. Buckingham C.C.* (1961) the county council had granted planning permission for the building of two cottages in the green belt subject to the condition that 'the occupation of houses shall be limited to persons whose employment or latest employment is or was employ-ment in agriculture, as defined in s. 119 of the *Town and Country Planning Act, 1947* [now s. 290 of the 1971 Act], or in forestry, or in industry mainly dependent upon agriculture and including also dependants of such persons'. This condition was accepted by the House of Lords as relating to the permitted development.

In the case of *Hall & Co. Ltd v. Shoreham U.D.C.* (1964) the plaintiff applied for planning permission to develop some land for industrial purposes. The land adjoined a busy main road and in granting planning permission the council imposed a condition requiring the company to construct an ancillary road over their land and to give a right of passage to the public at large. The Court of Appeal considered that the condition was unreasonable, because it required the Company to construct a road and dedicate it to the public without being paid any compensation, whereas a more regular course was open to the council under the Highway Acts, whereby the council should acquire the land after paying proper compensation.

In the case of *R. v. London Borough of Hillingdon* ex Parte *Royco Homes Ltd* (1974) the local authority granted the applicant outline planning permission for the development of land for residential purposes. The permission was granted subject to various restrictive conditions, including a condition that the first occupiers of the proposed houses should be persons on the local authority's housing waiting list, and that the occupiers should have security of tenure for 10 years. On the applicant's appeal for an order of *certoriari* to quash the condi-tion on the grounds that the condition was *ultra vires*, the Court granted the order. The reason for rejecting this condition was that 'it would go beyond anything that Parliament could have intended since the condition in effect required the applicant to assume at their own expense a significant part of the duty of a local authority as a housing authority'.

In another case (*Clyde v. Secretary of State for the Environment*, 1977), the Secretary of State refused planning permission for changing the use of a dwelling-house into an office. The sole reason was that 'it is desirable to retain the present premises for housing purposes'. The Divisional Court decided that this was not a valid reason for refusing the planning permission; the Court of Appeal, however, reversing the decision of the High Court, stated that the need for housing is a planning problem and the refusal was, therefore, concerning a 'material consideration'.

Lastly, in the case of *Kingsway Investment (Kent) Ltd v. Kent C.C.*, (1969) the Court of Appeal considered the following condition attached to an outline planning permission: 'permission shall cease to have effect after the expiration of three years, unless within that time approval of the reserved matters has been notified to the developers'. This condition was held by the Court of Appeal to be unreasonable and invalid, because the timing of the approval and notification would be outside the control of the developer. The House of Lords, however, on appeal accepted the condition as valid. They judged that when the outline permission was granted under Para. 5 of the General Development Order, the grantee would know that he should submit details two or three months before the end of the three years' period specified in the condition, allowing two months for the authority to give or fail to give their decision and a month in which to appeal to the Minister—a matter entirely within the grantee's control. Their Lordships construed the condition as including a case where the Secretary of State on appeal holds that the reserved matters should have been approved within the time limit. Thus as long as the developer submits his details in good time the clock is effectively stopped. This case, showing a divergence of opinion between the Court of Appeal and the House of Lords, illustrates the difficulties which may arise in the interpretation of planning permission.

Permission may also restrict the use of a building or limit the period of permission. Even if a development is permitted by the General Development Order or Use Classes Order, or even if the change of use would not in fact be a development (being not material), a condition attached to the permission may prohibit such a change (*City of London Corporation v. Secretary of State for the Environment*, 1971).

If a condition is declared invalid by the Court, the difficult problem arises whether the whole permission is quashed, or whether the permission should stand without the condition. This decision depends on the Court's view in each individual case, but the principle enunciated in the Kingsway Investment case, quoted above, seems to clarify the position. The permission remains in force, in spite of the quashing of a condition, if the condition relates not to development itself but to a matter preparatory or introductory to the permission, or, in short, not important to the development itself. But this opinion should be treated with some caution, since the House of Lords indicated in the same case that in their opinion a 'time' condition was fundamental, and even if it had been void it could not have been deleted so as to leave the permission subsisting.

The local planning authority dealing with applications for planning permission is usually the district authority. Only applications in respect of 'county matters' are to be dealt with by the county planning authorities (see Chapter 36).

The Secretary of State may direct that an application for planning permission be referred to him, instead of being dealt with by the district council (s. 35).

29.3 Appeals against Planning Decisions

If an application is made to a local planning authority to develop land, or for any approval required by the General Development Order, and the permission or approval is refused or granted subject to conditions, the aggrieved applicant may appeal to the Secretary of State. A right of appeal exists also against many other decisions of a local planning authority, which will be mentioned in the appropriate places.

A notice of appeal should be served within the time and in the manner prescribed by the General Development Order—i.e. in respect of appeals against refusal of planning permission, within six months. Appeals should be prepared on the form supplied on request by the Department of the Environment.

On appeal the Secretary of State (or inspector if the appeal is being considered by him) may allow or dismiss the appeal, or may reverse or vary any part of the local planning authority's decision even if it was not the subject of the appeal. Thus the applicant by his appeal puts the whole issue before the Secretary of State, whose decision may be even less favourable than that which was the subject of the appeal.

This is illustrated by the case of *Stringer v. Minister of Housing and L.G.* (1970), where the local planning authority and Manchester University signed an agreement under which the local planning authority (Cheshire County Council) undertook to discourage development within the limits of its powers within a specified area adjoining the Jodrell Bank radio-telescope. When a builder, Mr Stringer, applied for planning permission to erect 25 houses, the local planning authority refused permission on the grounds that the development would interfere with the efficient running of the telescope. The Minister dismissed the appeal on the same grounds. Dismissing the application for quashing the Minister's decision, the Court held that the agreement between the local authority and Manchester University was without legal effect, as its intention was to bind the local planning authority to disregard those considerations to which the authority was obliged to have regard under the Act. The local authority's determination was invalid because it intended to honour the agreement and this was the reason for the refusal of permission. Nevertheless, the Minister had powers to entertain the appeal *de novo* as he had not been influenced by the agreement. 'Material considerations' may, in a proper case, take into account private as well as public interests. The fact that the proposed development would interfere with the operation of the telescope was a material consideration.

Before deciding any appeal the Secretary of State must, on the request of either party, afford each of them an opportunity to be heard by an inspector, but he may, at his discretion (frequently exercised), order a public inquiry. If the problem is a legal one and no call of evidence is necessary, it is possible to dispense with the private hearing or inquiry; if, however, it is necessary to call some evidence to prove the appellant's ground of appeal, then a public inquiry should be asked for.

The Secretary of State may decline to determine an appeal if planning permission has not been granted (or granted on the condition complained against) in view of provisions:

(*a*) Relating to the Industrial Development Certificate (see Chapter 31).

(*b*) Relating to the conditions imposed by the General Development Order.

The decision of the Secretary of State or inspector is final and may be challenged in the High Court within six weeks on a point of law only.

The Secretary of State must give proper and adequate reasons for his decision, failing which his decision may be quashed by the Court (*Givaudan & Co. Ltd v. Minister of Housing and L.G.*, 1967).

29.4   Duration of Planning Permission (ss. 41–4)

There are two limitations in time as far as the duration of planning permission is concerned. The permitted development must start within the statutory time and, if the completion of the development is unduly delayed, the local authority may issue a completion notice (see below).

The general rule is that every permitted development must begin not later than within five years, or within such a shorter period as the local authority may impose as a condition in granting the permission. However, because this provision was introduced for the first time in the 1968 Act (which came into operation, as far as the relevant Part is concerned, on April 1, 1969), development permitted before that date should have begun within five years after April 1, 1969.

The development is deemed to begin if a **specified operation** has been carried out. Specified operation, which is widely defined, involves any of the following:

(*a*) Any work of construction in the course of erection of the building.

(*b*) The digging of a trench which is to contain the foundations or part of the foundations of the building.

(*c*) The laying of any underground main or pipe to the foundation or part of the foundations of the building.

(*d*) Any operation in the course of laying out or constructing a road or part of a road.

(*e*) Any change in the use of any land, where that change constitutes a material development.

For outline planning permission an application for the approval of reserved matters must be made within three years; the development itself must start either within five years from obtaining outline planning permission, or within two years of the approval of the reserved matters, which ever is the later.

It is possible, however, that the developer may start the development within the time prescribed by the Act or by the condition attached to the permission, but does not proceed with the works, leaving them unfinished for a considerable time. To avoid this unsatisfactory situation, s. 44 provides that if the local planning authority are of the opinion that the development will not be completed within a reasonable time, they may serve a notice—called a **completion notice**—stating that the permission will cease to have effect at the expiration of a further reasonable time, being not less than 12 months after the notice takes effect.

A completion notice should be served on the owner and other persons who may be affected by the notice. For its validity it requires confirmation by the Secretary of State, who may substitute a longer period for the completion of the works in question. After receiving a completion notice any person may require to be heard by a Department inspector and the Secretary of State has to arrange such a hearing before confirming the enforcement notice. If the completion notice is not complied with, the permission for development ceases to have effect. The local authority, however, is authorised to withdraw a completion notice even if it has been confirmed.

29.5   Revocation or Modification of Planning Permission (ss 45–6)

The local planning authority may at any time revoke or modify the planning permission granted by them, but such a revocation may be issued only before the operation permitted has been completed, or before the permitted change of use has taken place.

Such revocation or modification requires confirmation by the Secretary of State, unless the persons concerned agree in writing to the revocation and it appears to the authority that no claim for compensation is likely to arise. If the planning permission is revoked or modified, the local planning authority has a duty to pay compensation to any persons having interest in the land who had incurred expenditure in carrying out work rendered abortive by the revocation or modification, or who otherwise sustained loss or damage directly attributable to the revocation or modification (s. 164). For example, when planning permission for the building of Avongorge Hotel was revoked compensation amounting to £15 000 was paid.

29.6   Discontinuance of Use or Alteration or Removal of Buildings or Works (s. 51)

The planning authority has yet another power of control which is probably the most far-reaching. It can issue an order (which has to be approved by the Secretary of State) requiring the discontinuance of any use of land and building or removal or alteration of any building or works, even if the existing use or operation has been effected with full legality. In such cases, however, full compensation will be paid by the local planning authority issuing the order and it may be assumed therefore that this power will be used extremely cautiously.

30

ENFORCEMENT OF GENERAL PLANNING CONTROL

30.1 Introduction

When it appears to the local planning authority that there has been a breach of planning control which has taken place after 1963, then they may serve an **Enforcement Notice** requiring the breach to be remedied.

The local planning authority should not automatically serve an enforcement notice. It should first be satisfied that it is expedient to serve the notice, having regard to the development plan and to any other material consideration s. 87). It should consider whether planning permission would have been granted had the offender applied. Only if the view is taken that planning permission would have been refused should the enforcement notice be served.

A breach of planning control is not a criminal offence in itself, but failure to comply with a valid enforcement notice becomes an offence under s. 89, punishable by a fine.

30.2 The 'Four Years Rule'

The statutory provision that breaches of planning control which have occurred only after the end of 1963 may be the subject to an enforcement notice, can be understood only in the light of the history of planning control. When the *Town and Country Planning Act, 1947*, introduced for the first time a comprehensive control over development, an enforcement notice could be served only within four years after the breach had been committed. Thus, if somebody 'got away' with a breach for four years, he became immune from the enforcement procedure. Apparently it was considered that if a breach had not been noticed for four years, it was not sufficiently offensive to justify enforcement procedure. This provision became known as the 'four years rule' (it may conveniently be called 'four years privilege' as it benefits the offender if the development took place more than four years previously).

Experience showed, however, that the general application of the four years rule to all developments was too generous. Generally speaking, whereas developments consisting of *operations* were noticeable (and thus in these cases the four years rule was justified), developments consisting of *change of use* might not be readily noticed. For this reason the *Town and Country Planning Act, 1968*, retained the four years rule only in respect of developments consisting of *operations* (and exceptionally of one change of use: the conversion of a building into a *single* dwelling), but abolished the rule (or 'privilege') in all other *changes of use*.

However, the 1968 Act, which came into operation on January 1, 1968, changed the rule only for the future and did not affect those offenders who, at the time the Act came into operation, already enjoyed the immunity given to them by the original four years rule. Thus, although abolition of the rule

151

allows even very old changes of use to be challenged by the local authority, in no case can they go back further than 1964. Such uses are known as 'established uses' (see below), which do not apply to operations that still enjoy the four years privilege.

30.3 Established Use Certificate

The partial abolition of the four years rule means that developments affected before the end of 1963 were 'unimpeachable' at the time when the rule was abolished, whereas those which have been carried out on or after January 1, 1964, were caught by the abolition of the rule. For this reason it is essential to know whether the change of use in question took place before the end of 1963 or after, as only the latter can be challenged by the local planning authority.

If such a dispute arises, it may be extremely difficult, if not impossible, to decide whether the development had been carried out before or after the end of 1963 and therefore whether it is vulnerable or not. For this reason ss. 94 and 95 provide for a certificate of established use.

A use of land may, on application, be certified by a local planning authority as an established use, in which event the applicant is entitled to receive from the local planning authority an established use certificate. A use of land is established if:

(*a*) It was begun before the beginning of 1964 without planning permission and has continued since the end of 1964.

(*b*) It was begun before the beginning of 1964 under planning permission granted subject to conditions or limitations which have not been complied with since before the end of 1963.

(*c*) It was begun after the end of 1963 as a result of a change of use not requiring planning permission, and there has been no change of use requiring planning permission since the end of 1963 (a change of use of a building into a single dwelling-house does not require the certificate, as such a change is still subject to the four years rule).

An established use certificate may be granted either by a local planning authority or by the Secretary of State. It may be done either if he directs that a certificate should be issued by him ('called in application') or on an appeal against the local authority's decision refusing the issue of a certificate. If, on the application for a certificate, the local planning authority is satisfied that the claim has been made out, they must grant him the certificate; otherwise they must refuse it.

The detailed provisions about the method of applying for the certificate or appealing against the refusal and about the form of the certificate are given in Schedule 14.

An established use certificate is conclusive evidence in any appeal against an enforcement notice and it is, therefore, an important document. Any false or reckless statement made by the applicant in order to obtain a certificate is an offence punishable by a fine on summary conviction.

30.4 Enforcement Notices

An enforcement notice is served on the owner and on the occupier of the land

and on any other person having an interest which is in the opinion of the authority materially affected by the notice. It may be served not only when an unauthorised development has taken place, but also when a condition imposed by the planning permission has been broken.

An enforcement notice should specify:

(*a*) The matters alleged to constitute a breach of planning control.

(*b*) The steps required by the authority to remedy the breach.

(*c*) The period for compliance with the notice, i.e. the period (beginning with the date when the notice takes effect) within which those steps are requested to be taken.

An enforcement notice becomes operative at the date specified in the notice (which must be not less than 28 days after the service of the notice). However, if there is an appeal against the enforcement notice, the day of its effectiveness is postponed until the appeal is finally disposed of. Therefore, as the date when the notice will eventually become effective is not known, the period when the notice should be complied with is expressed not by a date (which is uncertain), but by a period of weeks or months starting from the moment the notice becomes effective.

An enforcement notice which does not comply with the above requirements is invalid. Thus if it does not clearly specify two periods, or if it is ambiguous and uncertain in its allegations and in indicating the steps required to be taken by the applicant, it will be null and void (*Burgess v. Jarvis and Sevenoaks R.D.C.*, 1952). In this case the local planning authority served an enforcement notice requiring the demolition of 16 houses 'within five years after the date of the service of this notice'. The notice was invalid as it did not indicate when it was to take effect.

The local planning authority may withdraw the enforcement notice at any time before it takes effect.

30.5 Appeals Against Enforcement Notices

Persons on whom the enforcement notice has been served, or any other interested person, may appeal to the Secretary of State within the period specified in the enforcement notice as the period at the end of which it is to take effect. Many of these appeals, of course, are dealt with by the inspector, as explained on page 185. The appeal may be made on any of the following grounds:

(*a*) That planning permission ought to be granted for the development in question or that the condition imposed ought to be disregarded.

(*b*) That the matters alleged in the notice do not constitute a breach of planning control.

(*c*) That the four years rule should have been applied and the notice has been served after the development became unassailable.

(*d*) That the development in question was carried out before the beginning of 1964.

(*e*) That the enforcement notice was not served as required by the Act.

(*f*) That the steps required to be taken by the enforcement notice exceeded those necessary to remedy the breach of planning control.

(*g*) That the period specified for compliance with the enforcement notice is too short.

An appeal should indicate the grounds for the appeal and the facts on which it is based. On any such appeal the Secretary of State shall, if either the appellant or the local planning authority so desire, afford to each of them an opportunity of appearing before an inspector nominated by the Secretary of State.

The enforcement notice does not take effect until the final determination of the appeal and the period given for compliance with the notice starts to run only when the notice becomes thus operative.

The Secretary of State, on receiving an appeal, may:

(*a*) Correct any informality, defect or error in the enforcement notice if he is satisfied that it is not material.

(*b*) If the ground of an appeal is the fact that the notice was not served on a person, he may disregard it if neither the appellant nor that person have been substantially prejudiced by this error.

If the appeal concerns only the above problems, it does not require to be determined.

On the determination of an appeal the Secretary of State shall, in addition to deciding the appeal, issue directions for giving effect to his decision, either by quashing the enforcement notice or by varying its terms. He may also:

(*a*) Grant planning permission for the development to which the enforcement notice refers, or discharge any conditions.

(*b*) Determine any purpose for which the land may be lawfully used, having regard to any past use and to planning permission relating to the land.

In considering whether to grant planning permission, the Secretary of State (or inspector) must pay attention to the provisions of the development plan and to any other material consideration. Any planning permission granted as a result of an appeal against an enforcement notice (since this appeal is treated also as an application for planning permission for the development which is the subject of the enforcement notice), may be granted subject to conditions. If the Secretary of State (or inspector) on appeal discharges a condition or limitation, he may substitute another condition or limitation, whether less or more onerous.

Any decision issued in respect of an appeal against an enforcement notice is final; however, the appellant, the local planning authority, or any other person on whom the enforcement notice has been served may either appeal against the decision to the High Court on a point of law, or require the Secretary of State or inspector to state a case for the opinion of the High Court (which, of course, would be binding on the Secretary of State).

If an enforcement notice is alleged to be not only 'invalid', but 'null and void' (*Ultra vires*—in excess of jurisdiction), the appellant instead of exercising his right of appeal to the Secretary of State may proceed in the Court for a declaratory judgment. It was by this procedure that many leading cases (e.g. *Pyx Granite*, 1959, and *Fawcett Properties Ltd*, 1960) about the conditions attached to the planning permission were decided.

30.6 Penalties for Non-compliance with Enforcement Notices

Under s. 89 any person who, at the time notice was served on him, was the owner of the land to which it relates and who has taken no steps required by the notice (other than discontinuance of a use of land) within the period allowed for compliance, shall be liable to a fine. A fine on summary conviction shall not exceed £400 but on conviction on indictment it may be of an unlimited amount.

Where an enforcement notice requires the discontinuance of the use of land, then if any person uses the land in contravention of the notice he will be liable to similar fines as above, but in addition he may be subject to a daily penalty of £50 on summary conviction or an unlimited fine on conviction on indictment.

If a person convicted for non-compliance with an enforcement notice fails to do everything in his power to comply with the notice as soon as practicable, he is liable to a further daily penalty of £50 on summary conviction or of an unlimited amount on conviction on indictment.

30.7 Stop Notice and its Consequences (s. 90)

The enforcement notice becomes operative only if the appeal and other legal proceedings challenging it have been disposed of. This means that the person on whom an enforcement notice has been served could (until 1968) protract an unauthorised development by vexatious appeals. The 1968 Act introduced a new device—the 'stop notice'—the effect of which is to stop the carrying out of development almost immediately. These provisions have been amended and the scope of the stop notice was extended by the *Town and Country Planning (Amendment) Act, 1977.*

When in respect of any land the local planning authority have served an enforcement notice requiring a breach of planning control to be remedied and they consider it expedient to prevent the carrying on of any activity, they may issue a stop notice forbidding any further activity.

The stop notice may be issued in respect of all activities with the following exceptions:

(*a*) The use of any building as a dwelling-house.

(*b*) The use of any land as a caravan site if it is occupied by any person as his only or main residence.

(*c*) The compliance with the enforcement notice.

There is a further condition: if the enforcement notice is issued in respect of any operation (or one change of use—deposit of waste material) then it may be issued at any time. If, however, the stop notice refers to a development consisting of a change of use it may be issued only within 12 months since the breach. Apparently if the change of use was tolerated for 12 months it is not considered offensive to such an extent that urgent cessation of the relevant activity is necessary.

The stop notice must refer to the enforcement notice and the enforcement notice must be attached to the stop notice.

A stop notice may be served on any person who appears to the local authority to have an interest in the land, to occupy it, or to be concerned with the carrying out of any operation on the land. Thus it may be served on a contractor carrying out the operation subject to the stop notice.

The stop notice prohibits any person on whom it is served from carrying out or even continuing any specific operation on the land to which the enforcement notice relates, which is either covered by the enforcement notice as being in breach of planning control or is an operation so closely associated as to constitute substantially the same operation.

A stop notice:

(*a*) Must specify the date on which it is to take effect and this may be not earlier than three and not later than 28 days from the date on which it is first served on any person. In addition, the local authority may put an appropriate notice on the land affected by the stop notice.

(*b*) In relation to any person served it will take effect on the date specified, but not earlier than three days from the date of serving.

(*c*) Is related to the enforcement notice and ceases to have effect when the enforcement notice is withdrawn or quashed.

It is also revoked automatically when the enforcement notice takes effect, as the stop notice is then no longer necessary.

There is no appeal against the stop notice. Failure to comply involves the same penalties as failure to comply with the enforcement notice.

The stop notice can have serious consequences for the person affected; in building contracts it may involve heavy losses for the contractor. Since there is no defence against a stop notice, compensation may be due (see Chapter 34).

31

ADDITIONAL CONTROL IN SPECIAL CASES

31.1 Buildings of Special Architectural or Historic Interest ('Listed Buildings')—(ss. 54–8)

In order to assist local planning authorities in considering buildings of special architectural or historic interest, the Secretary of State compiles a list of such buildings. In listing the buildings the Secretary of State takes into account not only the building itself, but also questions of its contribution to the historic or architectural interest of any group of buildings or its curtilage. A copy of the list is supplied to district councils and the owners and occupiers are notified. The listing is also noted in the local land charges register.

Listed buildings are registered as one of two grades. Only buildings of exceptional importance are placed in **Grade I**. The overwhelming majority of listed building are in **Grade II**. Some buildings which are very valuable but not good enough to be in Grade I are 'starred' to distinguish them from ordinary Grade II buildings.

Even if a building is not listed, the local planning authority may issue a **building preservation notice**, which is valid for six months and has the same effect as if the building had been listed. The Secretary of State may list such a building within six months, but if it is not listed within that period the building preservation notice becomes ineffective.

The legal consequences of listing are of far-reaching importance. Any act causing damage to a listed building is an offence punishable by a fine.

It is also an offence to demolish, alter, or extend listed buildings without obtaining a **listed building consent**. This should be distinguished from the normal planning permission which may not be necessary according to the provisions of Part III of the Act (general control). Thus a listed building consent may be needed even for internal alterations which do not affect the external appearance of the building and the conditions imposed on listed building consent may be wider than in a normal planning permission.

In considering whether to grant planning permission for development which affects a listed building or its setting, the authority granting the permission must have special regards to the desirability of preserving the building or its setting.

Contraventions of the provisions for control over listed buildings may be subject to a **listed building enforcement notice**. This notice is subject to an appeal to the Secretary of State, and the grounds of appeal are similar to those in the normal enforcement procedure, with the additional grounds that the building is not of special architectural or historic interest although listed, or that the works were urgently necessary in the interest of safety or health or the preservation of the building.

In the event of non-compliance with the notice the local planning authority may recover penalties from the person in default, and may themselves take steps to implement the enforcement notice. The costs of these steps may be recovered from the offender.

Although so far as general planning control is concerned it is an open question whether the demolition of a building constitutes a development, the demolition of a listed building requires listed building consent.

Ancient monuments and churches (but not parsonage houses) are exempted from the provisions of these Sections of the Act.

If a listed building has become incapable of reasonably beneficial use in its existing state and listed building consent is refused, the owner may serve on the local authority a **listed building purchase notice**, requiring the local authority to buy the building.

The local authority or the Secretary of State may acquire compulsorily any listed building which is not being properly preserved, but this may be done only after a repair notice has been ineffective for at least one month. The compensation paid is assessed according to normal rules of compensation (see Chapter 38), but recognises the fact that demolition is forbidden, thereby reducing the sum to be paid. This amendment was introduced by the *Town and Country Amenities Act*, 1974. If it is established that the building has been deliberately allowed to fall into disrepair, then 'minimum compensation' is payable, which excludes any profit that may arise from the possibility of the development of the site.

Schedule 19 provides for the procedure on application for the listed building purchase notice. The procedure in dealing with listed buildings is governed by the Town and Country Planning (Listed Buildings and Buildings in Conservation Areas) Regulations, 1977 (S.I. 228), which revoked and re-enacted with amendments previous Regulations (S.I. 1972/1362). The Regulations prescribe the manner in which applications for listed building consent are to be made and advertised, and the manner in which appeals may be made by persons aggrieved by decisions of local planning authorities; they prescribe the manner in which claims are to be made for compensation arising from the application of listed buildings control, the serving of listed building purchase notice, the advertising of unopposed orders revoking or modifying listed building consents and the execution of works under listed building enforcement procedure; they also prescribe the form of notices to owners and occupiers of buildings which become listed or which have ceased to be listed.

Thus it appears that listing a building has far-reaching consequences for the owner and may affect his future plans for the building. For this reason the *Local Government, Planning and Land Act, 1980*, introduced a new Section 54A to the 1971 Act. If on application for planning permission for any development involving a building, such a planning permission is granted, the developer may apply to the Secretary of State for a certificate stating that the Secretary of State does not intend to list the building. If the Secretary of State issues such a certificate, it is valid for five years and during this time the building cannot be listed and the local planning authority cannot issue a building preservation notice.

31.2 Special Provisions in Conservation Areas

Until the *Civic Amenities Act, 1967*, only individual buildings had been subject to preservation, but that Act created the new concept of **Conservation Areas**.

The provisions concerning town and country planning were incorporated into the *Town and Country Planning Act, 1971*, and have been amended extensively by the *Town and Country Amenities Act, 1974*. Thus under s. 277 (as amended) 'every local planning authority shall from time to time determine which part of their areas are areas of special architectural or historic interest the character of which it is desirable to preserve or enhance, and shall designate such areas as Consevation Areas'. The Secretary of State may also determine that a part of the authority's area should be designated as a Conservation Area.

There is a number of special provisions in respect of Conservation Areas, the most important being:

(*a*) The Secretary of State is empowered to make Regulations protecting Conservation Areas from advertising.

(*b*) Any application for development which in the opinion of the local planning authority would affect the character or appearance of a Conservation Area must be published by a notice advertised in a local newspaper and displayed on the site, and members of the public may raise objections to the application.

(*c*) The Secretary of State is authorised to give direction to local planning authorities as to the matters which they must consider when dealing with applications for development and as to the consultation with persons or bodies which ought to take place before a decision is made.

(*d*) The local planning authority can execute urgent work to preserve any unoccupied building and they can do so to preserve a listed building (in both cases seven days' notice must be given to the owner).

(*e*) S. 277A states that a building in a Conservation Area shall not be demolished without the consent of the appropriate authority, unless some classes of building are exempted by the Secretary of State.

Detailed provisions on control over buildings in Conservation areas are contained in the Town and Country Planning (Listed Buildings and Buildings in Conservation Areas) Regulations, 1977 (S.I. 1977/228).

31.3 Trees (ss. 59–62)

In granting planning permission, the local planning authority must ensure, whenever it is practicable, that a condition for the preservation or planting of trees is made. In addition, the authority has a duty to issue a **tree preservation order** if it is in the interests of the amenity to preserve a single tree, a group of trees, or a woodland. Such an order may make provisions for:

(*a*) The prohibition of the cutting down, topping, lopping, uprooting, wilful destruction or damaging of trees except with the consent of the local authority.

(*b*) The securing of re-planting of trees.

It is permitted to fell trees which are subject to an order if they are dead, dying or dangerous, or insofar as they are a nuisance. In the case of nuisance, the applicant must prove not merely inconvenience, but inevitable and imminent damage to premises (*Edgeborough Building Co. v. Woking U.D.C.*, 1966).

An application to a local authority for any consent in respect of tree preservation follows the procedure for usual planning applications with a few exceptions—for example, there is no necessity to give publicity to the application. A purchase notice may be served in respect of land subject to a tree preservation order in similar circumstances as in other planning decisions.

If a local planning authority intends to make a tree preservation order, it must serve a copy of the order upon the owners and occupiers of the land affected. The persons interested may submit objections within 28 days, and these are sent to the Secretary of State. If no objections are made, the local authority may confirm the order.

If any person, in contravention of a tree preservation order, cuts down or wilfully destroys a tree, or tops or lops a tree, he is liable to a fine, and a further daily fine for continuing the offence after the conviction.

In addition, the local planning authority may, within four years from the failure to comply with the tree preservation order, serve the owner of the land a notice requiring him to replant a tree or trees of such size and species as may be specified, within the stated period. There is a right of appeal to the Secretary of State against a notice demanding the replacement of trees. If the notice is not complied with the local planning authority may do the work themselves and recover the cost from the offender.

Ss. 8–10 of the *Town and Country Amenities Act, 1974*, protect the trees in Conservation Areas in a similar way to trees subject to a tree preservation order; the applicant may inform the local planning authority of his intentions affecting the tree. If the applicant does receive a consent, or receives no reply within six weeks, he can proceed with his plans within two years. The Secretary of State may make regulations restricting the protection of trees in Conservation Areas. Regulations have been issued dealing with details of this protection and its restrictions (Town and Country (Tree Preservation Order) Regulations, 1969, S.I. 1969/17, and Town and Country Planning (Tree Preservation Order (Amendment) and Trees in Conservation Areas (Exempted Cases) Regulations, 1975, S.I. 1975/148).

31.4 Advertisements

S. 290 defines advertisements very widely as 'any word, letter, model, sign, placard, board, notice, device or representation, whether illuminated or not, in the nature of, and employed wholly or partly for the purpose of advertisement, announcement or direction, and (without prejudice to the preceding provisions of the definition) include any hoarding or similar structure used, or adapted for use, for the display of advertisements, and reference to the display of advertisements shall be construed accordingly'.

Regulations issued under s. 63 restrict and regulate the display of advertisements (Town and Country Planning (Control of Advertisement) Regulations, 1969 (S.I. 1532), as amended in 1972 (S.I. 489), 1974 (S.I. 185) and 1975 (S.I. 898)). Some advertisements, however, are excluded from the operation of the Regulations and are, therefore, not subject to any control:

(*a*) On land enclosed by a hedge, fence, wall or similar screen or structure, where the advertisements are not readily visible from outside the enclosure.

(*b*) Inside a building and not visible from the outside.

(*c*) On or in a moving vehicle.

(*d*) Incorporated in and forming part of the fabric of a building, but an advertisement does not become part of the fabric of the building by merely being affixed or painted on.

(*e*) Displayed on an article for sale or on its packet or container.

Regulation 9 also allows the following three types of advertisements ('deemed consent'):

(*a*) Pending parliamentary or local government election (also pending referenda or election to the European Parliament).

(*b*) Advertisements displayed under statutory obligations.

(*c*) Advertisements in the nature of traffic signs.

Six classes of advertisements enumerated in Regulation 14 may be displayed without obtaining express consent from the local planning authority, but the authority may serve a notice of discontinuance if it is considered to be expedient in the interest of amenity or public safety:

Class I. This comprises the functional advertisements of local authorities, statutory undertakers and public transport undertakers. Examples of these advertisements are bus stop signs, signs indicating the way to railway stations, etc.

Class II. This includes miscellaneous advertisements relating to the premises on which they are displayed and includes, for example, advertisements for the purpose of identification, direction or warning, advertisements relating to a person or firm carrying on a profession, business or trade at the premises, etc.

Class III. This includes certain advertisements of a temporary nature—e.g. 'for sale', 'to let' boards, etc.

Class IV. This comprises advertisements displayed on business premises wholly with reference to the following matters: the business carried on, the goods or service provided, the name and qualification of the persons carrying on such business or activity or supplying such goods or services on those premises.

Class V. This comprises advertisements displayed on any forecourt of business premises with reference to the matters specified in Class IV.

Class VI. This comprises advertisements in the form of a flag attached to an upright flagstaff, fixed on the roof of the advertiser's building and bearing his name and device only.

All these advertisements are limited in their sizes and the limits are indicated separately for each class.

Advertisements which were displayed on August 1, 1948, are called 'existing advertisements' and are permitted without the necessity of obtaining express consent.

Even if the advertisement is not subject to consent, the local planning authority may 'challenge' it, which means that the authority may require that even such an advertisement shall be the subject to application and consent. The local planning authority must give full reasons why, in the interest of amenity, such consent is required. The challenging procedure is not allowed for advertisements permitted by Regulation 9, as those are displayed in the public interest.

S. 63 allows the Regulations to define 'areas of special control', being either rural or other areas requiring special provisions in order to preserve amenity. In such areas advertisements may be either completely disallowed, or allowed within special limits imposed by the Regulations. Under the *Town and Country Amenities Act, 1974* (which amended s. 63), the Secretary of State is empowered to make Regulations protecting Conservation Areas from advertising.

An application for express consent should be made in London to the London boroughs, elsewhere to the district planning authority. The authority may either grant consent or refuse it. Every grant must be for a fixed term, which may exceed five years only with the consent of the Secretary of State.

An applicant for express consent who is aggrieved by the decision of the local planning authority may appeal to the Secretary of State within one month from the receipt of notification. The decision of the Secretary of State is final, but may be challenged in the High Court within six weeks on a point of law only.

Any person displaying an advertisement so as to contravene the Regulations is liable to a fine, and if the offence continues after conviction to a further daily fine.

31.5   Waste Land (s. 65)

If it appears to a local planning authority that the amenity of its area is seriously injured by the condition of any garden, vacant site or other open land, then it may serve on the owner and occupier of the land a notice requiring the abatement of the injury within a specified period.

If the requirement is not complied with, an enforcement notice may be served by the local planning authority as in cases of other contraventions of planning control. The local planning authority may also enter the land and take the necessary steps, recovering the costs from the offender.

31.6   Industrial Development (ss. 66–72)

Industrial building is widely defined (see Chapter 28).

With some exceptions mentioned in s. 67(5) and in s. 68, any application to the local planning authority for permission to develop land by the erection of an industrial building shall be of no effect unless an **Industrial Development Certificate** is issued by the Secretary of State. Such a Certificate must state that the development is consistant with the proper distribution of industry and a particular regard should be paid to the need for providing appropriate employment in development areas. An Industrial Development Certificate is not required:

(*a*) For an extension of an industrial building if the extension taken by itself would not be an industrial building.

(*b*) For the retention of a building or the continuance of the use of land after the end of any period specified only in planning permission and not in the Industrial Development Certificate.

(*c*) S. 68 exempts from the necessity of obtaining an Industrial Development Certificate if industrial floor space does not exceed 5000 square feet, but Regulations issued by the Secretary of State under s. 69 have altered this limit in the following manner:

(*i*) In some areas (roughly corresponding to 'development areas') no

Industrial Development Certificate is required for any industrial development (Town and Country Planning (Industrial Development Certificates) Regulations, 1979, S.I. 1979/838).

(ii) In some areas (generally speaking in Greater London and the Home Counties) the limit now amounts to 50 000 square feet (Town and Country Planning (Industrial Development Certificates: Exemption) Order, 1979 (S.I. 1979/839).

(iii) In other areas of the country the limit is 15 000 square feet.

These limits, however, are flexible and are changed by the Secretary of State from time to time.

An Industrial Development Certificate may impose conditions which the Secretary of State considers appropriate having regard to the proper distribution of industry. The scope of these conditions is much more extensive than the scope of planning conditions and in particular they may:

(*a*) Require the removal of any building or the discontinuance of any use of land at the end of specified period.

(*b*) Restrict the amount of office floor space in any building to which the certificate relates.

Although the local planning authority cannot consider an application for industrial development which is not supported by an Industrial Development Certificate, they must consider whether they would have given permission if the Certificate had been obtained. If they would not have given permission they must notify the applicant accordingly and in such case the absence of the Industrial Development Certificate will not prevent the applicant from obtaining compensation for refusal of planning permission or a serving of a purchase notice.

31.7   Office Development (ss. 73–86)

These provisions were originally valid until August 5, 1972, as they were enacted for seven years by the *Control of Office and Industrial Development Act, 1965*, and were incorporated into the 1971 Act. They have been extended for further periods and were due to expire on August 6, 1982, but Control of Office Development (Cessation) Order, 1979 (S.I. 1979/908), provided for termination of the control of office development in England and Wales on August 6, 1979.

31.8   Caravans

Use of land as a caravan site is of considerable importance from the point of view of planning, because these sites, if not properly established and maintained, may become detrimental to the amenity of the neighbourhood. For this reason caravan sites are subject to dual control. In the first instance the developer must obtain planning permission for the establishment of a site for caravans (it will usually be a development involving a material change of use in the land) but, in addition, he is required afterwards to obtain a **site licence** under the *Caravan Sites and Control of Development Act, 1960*. Contravention of this requirement is an offence punishable by a fine.

The local authorities responsible for the issue of the site licence are housing authorities, i.e. district councils. If planning permission has been granted for the use of land as a caravan site, the local authority must issue a site licence; thus the real significance of the site licence is not whether it would be granted or not—as it must be granted if planning permission has been given—but the possibility of imposing conditions far more severe than those allowed under the planning law. These conditions must be such as the local authority considers necessary or desirable to impose in the interest of:

(*a*) Caravan dwellers of the site itself.

(*b*) Any class of persons (e.g. neighbours).

(*c*) The public at large (s. 5(1) of the *Caravan Sites and Control of Development Act, 1960*).

Apart from any conditions the local authority may impose, the Act specifically authorises the imposition of the following conditions:

(*a*) For restricting the occasions on which caravans may be stationed on land for human habitation, or the total number of caravans which may be so stationed at any one time.

(*b*) For controlling the types of caravans which may be stationed on the land.

(*c*) For regulating the position in which the caravans may be stationed on land for human habitation and for prohibiting, restricting or otherwise regulating the placing or erection on such land, at any time when caravans are so stationed, of structures and vehicles of any description whatsoever and of tents.

(*d*) For securing the amenity of land, including the planting of trees and bushes.

(*e*) For securing fire precautions.

(*f*) For securing that adequate sanitary facilities and other facilities are provided for the use of persons dwelling in caravans.

If the developer is aggrieved by the conditions attached to the site licence, he may appeal to the Magistrates' Court within 28 days.

There are some minor exceptions from the requirements to obtain a site licence (s. 2 of the 1960 Act and Schedule 1). The most important are:

(*a*) The use of land within a curtilage of a dwelling-house as a caravan site, such use being incidental to the enjoyment of the house.

(*b*) The use of any land as a site for a caravan for a period including not more than two nights by a person travelling with the caravan.

(*c*) The use of agricultural or other land as a caravan site for seasonal accommodation of agricultural or forestry workers employed on the land.

(*d*) The use as a caravan site for the accommodation of persons employed in connection with building or engineering operations on the same or adjoining land.

(*e*) The use as a caravan site by a travelling showman (recognised by a certificate of the Secretary of State).

32

PLANNING INQUIRIES

32.1 Introduction

It has been noted that where the action of a local planning authority is challenged, the aggrieved person is often entitled, before the final decision is taken, to ask for a hearing before a person nominated by the Secretary of State. It is within the discretion of the Secretary of State to order a public inquiry instead of granting a hearing. This discretion is freely exercised, particularly if the person aggrieved asks for an inquiry. A public inquiry may take place if objections are made against a local development plan (objections against structure plans are dealt with under a different procedure mentioned in Chapter 27), if an appeal is lodged against a decision of a local planning authority refusing permission for development or granting it subject to conditions or limitations, if a local planning authority issues an enforcement notice and in deciding other appeals allowed under the *Town and Country Planning Act, 1971*.

32.2 Procedure

The procedure for the planning inquiry in respect of appeals is now governed by two statutory instruments: when the issue being the subject of the inquiry is to be determined by the Secretary of State himself, it is governed by the Rules issued in 1969 and now consolidated in the new Rules of 1974 (Town and Country Planning (Inquiries Prodecure) Rules, 1974 (S.I. 419)); where the appeal is to be determined by an inspector, the Town and Country Planning Appeals (Determination by Appointed Persons) (Inquiries Procedure) Rules, 1974 (S.I. 420), govern the procedure. The procedures are similar in either case up to the close of the inquiry.

Not later than 28 days before the inquiry the local planning authority must send a written statement outlining its case to the appellant and to every 'Section 29 party'. Section 29 parties are persons who, being estate owners, have been notified about the application according to s. 27, who have made representations in the case where the application was advertised in the local newspaper, e.g. in case of 'bad neighbour developments', who are agricultural tenants or who made representations regarding an application for the development in a conservation area or in respect of listed buildings.

The statement of the local planning authority must contain the following:

(*a*) The statement of the submission which the authority proposes to put forward at the inquiry.

(*b*) A list of all documents to which the authority intends to refer at the inquiry. All interested parties must be allowed to examine these documents.

(*c*) Any relevant direction given by the Secretary of State or the Minister of Transport and a copy of the direction with the reasons given for its making.

(*d*) Any expression of views given by any other Department on which the authority proposes to rely.

The local planning authority must not depart from their statement without the leave of the inspector conducting the inquiry.

The inspector may also require the appellant to supply a written statement of the submissions which he proposes to put forward to the inquiry and a list of documents. Here again the appellant must obtain the leave of the inspector if he wishes to depart from his statement. Thus a statement by the local authority is obligatory, whereas the appellant has to submit his statement only if instructed to do so by the inspector.

A 42 days' notice about the date and place of the inquiry should be given to all interested parties.

The procedure at the inquiry is as follows: The inspector opens the proceedings by stating the purpose of the inquiry. The appellant and the local authority 'enter their appearance' either personally or by an advocate (solicitor, barrister, or other professional representative).

It is usually the appellant who opens the case and calls the witnesses. Although witnesses may be required to make their depositions on oath, in practice this is done only in appeals against enforcement notices and rarely in other cases. The rules of evidence are much less strictly applied than in a court of law. Even hearsay evidence may be allowed, although the inspector may disregard it. Each witness of the appellant may expect to be cross-examined by the representative of the local planning authority or by any Section 29 party. Other interested persons may ask questions by the leave of the inspector.

The appellant may also produce letters or other documents.

Afterwards the local planning authority puts its case in a similar manner, and the same right to ask questions is available to Section 29 parties.

The appellant makes his final speech and the inspector then usually visits the site in the company of both parties or their representatives.

If the case is to be decided by the inspector, he notifies his decision, with reasons, to the appellant, local planning authority and Section 29 parties. If he intends to take new evidence not revealed during the inquiry, he must notify the parties, who are entitled to make further representations within 21 days.

If the decision lies with the Secretary of State, the inspector submits his report with his conclusions. Usually he makes recommendations, but he may refrain from doing so, giving reasons. The Secretary of State may disagree with the inspector on findings of fact and then no additional inquiry is ordered, but the applicant, the local authority and the Section 29 parties are notified about the Secretary of State's views and may submit written observations. If, however, the Secretary of State receives new evidence or intends to base his decision on new facts not raised at the inquiry, he must notify the parties who are entitled to make representations within 21 days and then the Secretary of State must re-open the inquiry. The Secretary is not bound by the inspector's recommendation and may issue a decision against his recommendation.

Sometimes there arise quite complicated questions as to what is the inspector's recommendation (which may be disregarded by the Secretary of State without consulting the parties) and what are his findings of fact (in which case, if the Secretary of State does not agree with the inspector, he has to give the parties an opportunity of submitting observations). An example of this is the case of *Lord Luke of Pavenham v. Minister of Housing and L.G.* (1968). The inspector reported that building even a well designed house would affect the amenity of the country, but the Minister rejected this recommendation without notifying the parties. The local authority appealed to the Divisional Court, claiming that this was not a 'recommendation' but a finding of fact and that they should be given an opportunity to submit their observations. The Divisional Court accepted this as a finding of fact and quashed the planning permission granted by the Secretary of State, but the Court of Appeal accepted it as a recommendation and found no fault with the Minister's decision.

When the Secretary of State decides the case, he usually encloses with his decision a copy of the inspector's report. If either party requests it, the Secretary of State has to supply the inspector's report for the information of the party concerned.

32.3 Planning Inquiry Commission

The Secretary of State has power to constitute a Planning Inquiry Commission. Such a Commission consists of a chairman and between two and four members.

Matters may be referred to the Planning Inquiry Commission if they are considered of national or regional importance, or if technical or scientific aspects of the proposed development are of so unfamiliar a character as to prejudice a proper determination in the absence of a special inquiry for the purpose.

The following four matters may be referred to the Planning Inquiry Commission:

(*a*) Any application for planning permission which the Secretary of State has called in for decision by himself.

(*b*) Any appeal against a planning decision.

(*c*) Any proposal under s. 40 in respect of some developments by statutory undertakers (i.e. if planning permission is 'deemed' to be granted to them).

(*d*) Any proposals that the development should be carried out by or on behalf of a Government department.

The duties of the Planning Inquiry Commission fall under the following three headings:

(*a*) To identify and investigate the technical or scientific problems relevant to the question whether the proposed development should be permitted.

(*b*) To afford interested persons (and the local authority) an opportunity to appear before one or more members of the Commission.

(*c*) To report to the responsible Minister on the matter referred to them.

Thus the Planning Inquiry Commission acts exclusively in an advisory capacity and has no authority to decide the issue.

33

POSITIVE PLANNING AND BETTERMENT

33.1 Introduction

Since the inception of town and country planning law, two problems have remained outstanding and their treatment by the two main political parties has always been different.

Labour's idea of securing 'positive planning' is to introduce the concept of public ownership of the development land; the Conservatives' is by creating an atmosphere in which private enterprise would pay. However, besides the need to secure positive planning, the nation has to deal with another problem, that of land prices and betterment. As early as in 1909 Lloyd George stated the problem succinctly: 'The growth in value, more especially of urban sites, is due to no expenditure of capital or thought on the part of ground owner, but entirely owing to the energy and enterprise of the community.... It is undoubtedly one of the worst evils of our present system of land tenure that instead of reaping the benefit of the common endeavour of its citizens, a community has always to pay a heavy penalty to its ground landlords for putting up the value of their land.'

Even before town and country planning law dealt comprehensively with the problem of betterment, there were several attempts at securing for the community the profit resulting from increased land values due to public work. Three methods may be discerned: direct levy, set-off and recoupment.

Endeavours to introduce a **direct levy** in the nineteenth century were ineffective. In the context of Victorian society the idea was too radical and contrary to the tenet of *laissez faire*.

Set-off means that if an acquiring authority purchases only a part of land belonging to a person, and if as the result of this acquisition the remaining land increases in the value, the acquiring authority is entitled to deduct from the purchase price the amount by which the remaining land has increased in value. In the event of subsequent acquisition of the remaining land the owner will be entitled to this higher price. The principle of set-off, although still being applied (s. 7 of the *Land Compensation Act, 1961*), is very limited in its scope, as it has its efficacy only in purchasing a part of land belonging to a person.

Recoupment is less restricted in its scope. It depends on the acquisition by a public authority of land part of which is used for a project and the remainder sold with the profit which arises due to the project carried out.

In 1942 a Committee under the chairmanship of Lord Justice Uthwatt published a Report on compensation and betterment. Betterment was defined as 'any increase in the value of land arising from central or local government action'. The Report, in support of Lord George's views, recommended that betterment should be appropriated by the community and suggested a rather complicated procedure to achieve this end.

33.2   Problem of Betterment after the Second World War

The *Town and Country Planning Act, 1947*, drew substantially on the Uthwatt Report's work. The statutory provisions are complicated, but in a nutshell they provided for the betterment value to accrue to the State by the imposition of a development charge, which was payable to a Central Land Board before the permitted development commenced.

The provisions of the 1947 Act in respect of this problem are dealt with more fully in the next chapter.

On coming into power in 1951, the Conservatives abolished the development charge. This no doubt encouraged the development of land but, on the other hand, it caused rising land prices and gains realised by developers.

When Labour won the election in 1964, they set up a Land Commission as a central body to acquire land suitable for development. Development gains on land were subject to a special flat rate tax, the **betterment levy**, set at 40 per cent. Like the 1947 Act, the *Land Commission Act, 1968*, was repealed following another change of Government in 1970.

After coming into power again, the Labour Government made another attempt to secure the betterment to the community, by passing two Acts: the *Community Land Act, 1975*, which visualised that at some future date virtually all development land would pass through public ownership, and the *Development Land Tax Act, 1976*, which imposed a new tax on development profit (amounting, after some deductions to 80 per cent of the gain). Before the election in 1979 the Conservative party committed themselves to the abolition of both these Acts. In partial fulfilment of this promise it repealed the *Community Land Act, 1975*, and considerably lowered the development land tax.

Without becoming involved in the political philosophy of either party's attempts at a solution, it seems clear that the greatest problem stems not so much from which philosophy is current, but from the fact that, as the developer plans for many years to come, he must be sure there will be no changes in the following years which would frustrate his calculations. Thus the greatest evil is the constant changing of policy. When the Conservatives are in power the developer does not invest boldly for fear of future changes. When Labour runs the country, the developer again refrains from investing in the hope of a change to a better climate for him.

It seems that the only proper solution would be a nationally agreed policy which would be constant for many years, but in view of the opposing ideologies of the two parties this seems an unlikely goal.

34

COMPENSATION FOR ADVERSE PLANNING DECISIONS

34.1 Introduction

Planning control creates a problem arising from the fact that planning decisions very often result in losses for the owner of the land.

If land is compulsorily purchased, i.e. if the owner is deprived of the property in the land, the principle is that property shall not be acquired without full compensation. This principle was judicially recognised in the leading case of *Attorney General v. De Keyser's Royal Hotel Ltd* (1920), where it was said: 'It is a well established principle that unless no other interpretation is possible, justice requires that statutes should not be construed to enable the land of a particular individual to be confiscated without payment.' There is no legislation in the present system of English law which enables the Government to confiscate property without compensation assessed according to existing statutory rules.

On the other hand, there is another general principle that compensation is not payable for any restriction in the use of the property, unless an Act of Parliament expressly so provides. In many instances (in Public Health Acts, Landlord and Tenant or Rent Acts and Housing Acts) use of land by the owner is restricted without any compensation. But, as decisions under the Town and Country Planning Acts restrict the use of land much more than other legislation, they amount to a partial confiscation, if not of the property itself, then at least of some rights of use over it. It is recognised that many planning restrictions are in effect confiscatory and for this reason compensation is provided by legislation concerning some restrictions.

Two Parts of the 1971 Act deal with compensation for planning restrictions. Part VII deals with compensation for planning decisions restricting 'new development' (paid by the Secretary of State); Part VIII deals with compensation for other planning restrictions (paid by the local planning authority).

S. 22, after giving the general definition of development, divides it into **new development** and **'existing use development'**, the former being any development other than that specified in Parts I and II of Schedule 8 to the Act. In order to explain the reasons for dividing developments into these two categories, it is necessary to consider the Government's policy behind the *Town and Country Planning Act, 1947*, which created this distinction.

The 1947 Act did not nationalise land itself, as advised by the Uthwatt Report ('Report of the Committee on Compensation and Betterment', 1942, Cmnd 6386), but, without using this expression, virtually nationalised future development values which would accrue after July 1, 1948, i.e. after the 1947 Act came into operation. It was considered that existing development values should not be nationalised, as this would mean confiscation of valuable existing assets without compensation.

Since it was realised that it might be difficult to decide in the future which development value accrued after July 1, 1948 (and, therefore belonged to the state), and which accrued before that date (and so had not been expropriated), it was decided to 'nationalise' all development values—whether existing on July 1, 1948, or accruing later—and to pay compensation for the rights existing on July 1, 1948.

A sum of £300 million was earmarked as compensation for the rights existing on July 1, 1948 (mostly suburban land, as neither land in towns, already expensive, nor land in remote rural areas without hope of development had any significant 'development value'). The owners of the land were invited to submit claims within 12 months. The claims actually submitted amounted to somewhat more than £300 million and, after allocating the full amount claimed for some 'near ripe' developments, the balance was applied to other claims which were not met in full (80 new pence for each pound claimed). The money itself was not paid, but the claims were noted in a special register with the intention to pay this compensation within seven years.

The result of the implementation of this policy was that when planning permission was granted, the developer would pay a development charge representing the development value of the land accrued after July 1, 1948. No compensation was due if planning permission was refused (because although the owner admittedly could not realise the development value, it was not his, but the Government's property).

In 1953 the Conservative Government abandoned the idea that the development value of the land (accrued after July 1, 1948) should become 'nationalised'. The development charge was abandoned and developers could develop their land without any payment if they obtained planning permission. As a result of this, no payments were made towards the claims registered under the 1947 Act for development value accrued before July 1, 1948.

The logical consequence of the Government's policy of 1953 should be that if planning permission was refused, and if the developer was deprived of realising his development value, full compensation should be paid to him for his loss, i.e. amounting to the full development value which had not been realised. However, payment of such claims would be too expensive and the Government, somewhat illogically, used the registered claims to the £300 million as the basis for payment of compensation for the refusal of planning permission. These claims (after some adjustments) have become known as 'unexpended balance of established development value'.

Developments enumerated in Schedule 8 to the 1971 act (previously Schedule 3 of the 1947 and 1962 Acts) were exempted from the 'nationalisation' scheme. They were developments consistent with or required for the existing use of the land or buildings in question. These developments may be called **existing use developments**. As no claims were made, the deprivation of full compensation for refusal of these developments would amount to the confiscation of valuable assets without compensation, which would be contrary to the basic principles of English law. Consequently the value of the existing use development is treated differently from the value of the new developments as regards compensation for restricting planning decisions.

34.2 Compensation for Planning Decisions Restricting New Developments

Part VII of the Act deals with compensation for 'new development' i.e. development outside the scope of Schedule 8.

In order to obtain compensation if planning permission is refused or subjected to conditions, it must be shown in the first instance that the land in question has an unexpended balance of established development value. Any compensation paid under this Part of the Act will be deducted from the unexpended balance, and if the compensation as assessed exceeds the amount of the unexpected balance, only the balance will be paid. This means that compensation amounts either to the depreciation of the value in the land due to refusal or due to the conditions attached to the decision of the local planning authority, or to the unexpected balance of established development value, whichever is the less. Consequently, if at a later date development is permitted, then the compensation paid to the owner has to be repaid by him.

However, a number of planning decisions do not rank for compensation, even if there is an unexpended balance attached to the land. Compensation shall not be payable (ss. 146–149):

(*a*) For the refusal of planning permission for any development which consists of or includes the making of any material change in the use of any building or other land. As the majority of planning permissions in build-up areas are for changes of use, it follows that in quite a number of cases compensation is not payable.

The reason for this exclusion seems to be that although the intended change of use might enhance the value of the land, nevertheless the existing use of the land established for many years has, apparently, been reasonably profitable to the developer, as otherwise he would not have kept the land in such use.

(*b*) On the refusal of planning permission for the display of advertisements or on the grant of it subject to conditions. Apparently, as the advertisement may be offensive to the environment, the Government wants to retain the right to refuse permission without being called upon to pay compensation.

(*c*) On imposing conditions relating to:

the number or disposition of buildings on any land;
the dimensions, design, structure or external appearance of any building, or material to be used in its construction;
the manner in which any land is to be laid out for the purposes of the development, including provisions for parking, loading, unloading or fuelling of vehicles on the land;
the use of building or other land;
the location or design of any means of access to a highway, or the material to be used in the construction.

Thus the Government reserves for itself a free hand in the matters above and is not obliged to pay compensation for imposing conditions pertaining to them.

(*d*) On imposing conditions on the duration of planning permission, reserved matters in outline planning permission, or conditions imposed by the Industrial Development Certificate.

(*e*) If the reason for the refusal is that the development will be premature due to:

the order of priority indicated in the development plan for the areas in which the land is situated for the development of that area;
any existing deficiency in the provision of water supplies or sewerage services

and the period within which any such deficiency may reasonably be made good. However, in the case of premature application delay in providing the services cannot be longer than seven years and if the applicant makes another application after the expiration of seven years and the permission is still considered premature, compensation will be paid.

(*f*) If the reason for the refusal is that the land is unsuitable for the proposed development because of its liability to flooding or subsidence. It may be assumed that such applications are made in bad faith and only in order to obtain compensation after the expected refusal.

(*g*) If, notwithstanding the refusal, permission for an alternative development may be granted. This provision applies to any development of residential, commercial or industrial character that consists wholly or mainly of the construction of houses, flats, shops or office premises, or industrial buildings. The reason for this provision is that, provided some reasonably remunerative development is allowed, the owner is not entitled to compensation only because he envisaged a more profitable development.

(*h*) If the Secretary of State issues a direction under s. 38. This Section allows him to review a planning decision issued by the local planning authority which would involve the payment of compensation and subsequent variation of it in favour of the applicant so as to avoid the payment of compensation. Before the Secretary of State interferes with the decision of the local authority, he must give notice to the applicant and to the local planning authority and, on the request of either of them, must afford each an opportunity to be heard by an inspector.

If an owner who intends to apply for permission for development is unable to obtain an Industrial Development Certificate, he may nevertheless claim compensation if he obtains a notice under s. 72, which is issued by the local planning authority and states that the local authority would refuse permission even if a formal application, supported by an Industrial Development Certificate, were submitted to them (s. 151). In such a case it is shown that the refusal has been issued on planning and not other grounds.

Claims for compensation under this part of the Act must be submitted within six months of the relevant decision and must be sent to the local planning authority for transmission to the Secretary of State, together with any evidence and information supplied by the claimant and considered relevant by the authority or the Secretary of State. If it appears to the Secretary of State that the claim is not justified, he has to notify the claimant and invite him to withdraw the claim. If the claim is not withdrawn, the Secretary of State gives notice of his refusal to pay compensation to all persons having interest in the land (s. 154).

Questions as to whether the claim is justified, what should be the amount of compensation, and how it should be apportioned, are in disputed cases decided by the Lands Tribunal (s. 156).

34.3 Compensation for Planning Decisions Restricting Developments other than New Development

'Existing use developments' are listed in Schedule 8. The Schedule specifies eight classes of development, some involving operations, some changes of use. The Schedule does not give permission for any of those forms of development, but it has an important bearing on the rights of the owner if the land is compulsorily purchased, as in this case the compensation paid to the owner assumes that planning permission would be granted for any class of development specified.

The Schedule divides the existing use developments into two categories. Part I of the Schedule describes developments which do not rank for compensation under s. 160 for refusal of permission to carry them out, or for attaching conditions for planning permission. Part II describes developments which do rank for compensation on refusal of permission.

The following developments, given in Part I, do not rank for compensation:

(*a*) The *rebuilding* of any building existing on July 1, 1948, or any building destroyed or demolished between January 7, 1937, and July 1, 1948, or any building existing at a 'material date' (i.e. the date of the relevant planning decision, which means the date of the decision which may give the right for compensation). Rebuilding includes the making good of any war damage and also the carrying out of works for the *maintenance*, improvement or other *alternations* of any building which affects only its interior or does not materially affect its external appearance and which is *work for making good war damage*. In these cases the cubic content of the original building should not exceed:

in the case of a dwelling-house, more than one tenth of the volume or 1750 cubic feet, whichever is greater; and
in any other case by more than one tenth of the volume of the building.

(*b*) The conversion of any building which on July 1, 1948, was used as a single dwelling-house into two or more separate dwellings.

These developments do not rank for compensation because in war-damaged buildings 'war damage' was paid and, if the development was not permitted, the owner could have served a purchase notice on the local authority asking it to buy the land if it was not capable of reasonable beneficial use. In other buildings that have been destroyed after the war it is assumed that insurance was paid and the claimant has not suffered undue loss. In all these cases it may be in the interests of the community that the building should not necessarily be rebuilt in the same manner as it previously existed and that some other development may be more suitable. For this reason the local planning authority should have a free hand to refuse the development without being hampered by any financial considerations—i.e. the possibility of payment of compensation.

Part II of the Schedule 8 lists six developments (some of them being operations, some changes of use) which do rank for compensation if permission in respect of them is refused (or granted subject to conditions):

(*c*) The enlargement, improvement or other alteration of any building which is in any of the categories listed above under point (*a*), if the enlargement is within the limits given in Part I of the Schedule (i.e. one tenth of the cubic content of 1750 cubic feet). The difference between (*a*)—not ranking for compensation—and (*c*)—ranking for compensation—is that the former is work for making good war damage and the latter is not. The original wording of the Schedule 8 was amended in 1963 by providing that not only the cubic space, but also the floor space should not be exceeded by more than 10 per cent. The reason for this is that in the alteration of a building it is possible to extend the useful floor space extensively up to 40 per cent by lowering the ceiling height, still keeping the increase of cubic content within 10 per cent. The amendment became necessary because some developers, particularly in the city of London, did just this. Thus Schedule 8 was supplemented by the 1963 Act, now consolidated in Schedule 18 to the *Town and Country Planning Act, 1971.*

(*d*) The carrying out on land used for agriculture or forestry of any building or other operations required for that use. The erection, enlargement or improvement of the following buildings are excluded: dwelling-houses, buildings used as market gardens, or buildings used for purposes not connected with farming or forestry operations.

(*e*) The winning and working on land held for agriculture purposes of any minerals required for that use.

(*f*) Any change of use within Use Classes Order. It should be explained that the 'Use Classes Order for the Purpose of the Third Schedule' (now the Eighth Schedule) was originally identical to the Use Classes Order prescribing the permitted changes of use; at that time any change within the first order was permitted by the second order and the problem of compensation did not arise. Now, however, there are small differences and some changes within the first order are *not* within the second order and planning permission is therefore necessary. On refusal of planning permission in this situation compensation is payable.

(*g*) Where only a part of a building (erected before July 1, 1948) or other land is used for a particular purpose, the use for that purpose of any additional part of that land or building not exceeding one tenth of the part used for the original purpose.

(*h*) The deposit of waste material or refuse in connection with mineral working on a site used for that purpose.

The conditions for obtaining compensation for the refusal of permission in respect of Schedule 8, Part II, developments, may be summarised as follows:

(*a*) Planning permission must have been refused by the Secretary of State, which means that if the decision is taken by a local planning authority, an appeal to the Secretary of State is imperative.

(*b*) There must be a diminution in the value of the interest as a result of the Secretary of State's decision.

(*c*) The claim must be submitted within six months to the local authority. This period may be extended by the Secretary of State.

34.4 Compensation for Other Planning Restrictions

Compensation is also due for a variety of other planning restrictions which impose undue loss on the claimant.

Compensation for Revocation or Modification of Planning Permission (ss. 164–168)

S. 45 allows the local planning authority to revoke or modify permission to develop land at any time before the operation in question has been completed or a change of use has taken place. Unopposed revocation or modification may be issued by the local planning authority itself but, if it is opposed by the claimant, it requires confirmation by the Secretary of State.

If the order is opposed and confirmed by the Secretary of State, compensation is payable by the local planning authority for the expenditure in carrying out work which has been rendered abortive or for loss which is directly attributable to the revocation or modification. Preparatory work (e.g. the drawing of the plans) may be included in the claim. Even if the permission which has been revoked or modified had been granted not by express permission of the local planning authority, but by the General Development Order, compensation may be claimed.

The Town and Country Planning General Regulations, 1976 (1419), prescribe the detailed procedure for claiming compensation. Compensation must be claimed from the local planning authority within six months. Any compensation exceeding £20 is apportioned among the various parts of the land and registered as local land charges, as it will be recoverable by the local planning authority on subsequent permission to carry on any 'new development'.

Compensation for Orders under s. 51 (*Requiring Discontinuance of Use or Alteration or Removal of Buildings or Works*) (*s. 170*)

Proper planning may require the removal of a building or the prohibition of a use undertaken with due planning permission. Such orders entitle any person suffering loss to apply for compensation. The compensation is equivalent to the depreciation of the value of land and expenses reasonably incurred in carrying out any works in compliance with the order.

Compensation for Listed Buildings (*ss. 171–712*)

There are three types of compensation with listed buildings.

The first is due when an application for consent to alter a listed building is refused, and such an alteration does not constitute a development, or is a development allowed by the GDO. In such circumstances it is clear that the owner suffers loss for the sole reason that the building is listed, as otherwise he would be able to carry out the work. A condition of this type of compensation is that the application must have been refused by the Secretary of State, and not by the local planning authority only. Thus if the refusal is given by the local planning authority, the applicant must in the first instance appeal against the decision. The extent of compensation is the amount by which the value of the buildings has been reduced by the refusal of the alteration or extension. S. 6 of the *Town and Country Amenities Act, 1974*, puts a limitation on the amount of compensation. Refusal of alteration or extension is taken into account, but not the fact that demolition is forbidden.

The second type of compensation is due where the listed building consent has been revoked or modified. If a person has incurred expenditure in carrying out works which were rendered abortive or has otherwise sustained loss or damage directly attributable to the revocation or modification, the authority has to pay compensation.

The third type of compensation refers to the loss or damage attributable directly to the issue of a building preservation notice. If the building to which a building preservation notice refers is not in fact listed, the building preservation notice ceases to have effect. Compensation is then due to cover any expenditure, damage or loss sustained by the fact that the abortive building preservation notice had been served.

Compensation for Tree Preservation (ss. 174–175)

Compensation is due for loss or damage cause in consequence of the refusal of any consent required under the tree preservation order, or if consent is granted subject to conditions. If in pursuance of the provisions in the order, a direction is given for securing the replanting of trees which have been felled in the course of an operation permitted under the order, compensation is due. The compensation is conditional on a certificate of the Forestry Commission that they will not pay a grant, which may be due under s. 4 of the *Forestry Act, 1967*. This condition is imposed in order to avoid the payment of double compensation.

Compensation for Restriction of Advertisements (s. 176)

If a person is compelled to remove an advertisement which has been displayed since August 1, 1948, or to discontinue the use of a site for the purpose of advertising which was so used on that date, he is entitled to recover compensation for any expenses reasonably incurred by him on that behalf, as before August 1, 1948, no permission was required for displaying advertisements.

Compensation for Loss due to Stop Notices (s. 177)

Where a stop notice (page 155) ceases to have effect, a person who at the time when it was served had an interest in the land may be entitled to compensation. S. 2 of the *Town and Country Planning (Amendment) Act, 1977*, enlarged the scope of persons entitled to compensation, including also the other occupiers of the land.

It will be remembered that the stop notice's validity depends on the existence of an enforcement notice. If, therefore, the enforcement notice is quashed on appeal or is withdrawn, then the stop notice also ceases to have effect. Appeals against enforcement notices may be made only on seven specified grounds which have been outlined in Chapter 30. The grounds of appeal given in (*b*) to (*g*) (see page 153) allege fault on the part of local authority, because in these four cases the enforcement notice should not have been issued in the first place. But if the appeal succeeds on the grounds enumerated under (*a*), it is not because the enforcement notice should not have been issued, but because a discretionary consideration has been given to the problem and it has been decided to take a more lenient view of the breach. In these cases the local planning authority was fully justified in issuing an enforcement notice. For these reasons compensation is payable for loss attributable to a stop notice in the following circumstances:

(*a*) If the enforcement notice has been quashed on the grounds of s. 68(1), Paragraphs (b), (c), (d), (e), (f) or (g).

(*b*) If the allegation in the enforcement notice on which the prohibition in the stop notice is dependent is not upheld for the reason that the enforcement notice has been varied on one of those grounds.

(*c*) If the enforcement notice is withdrawn (otherwise than as a result of the granting of belated planning permission).

(*d*) If the stop notice itself is withdrawn.

An application for compensation should be submitted to the local planning authority within six months.

Compensation is payable only to a person having an interest in the land or occupying it, so that presumably the contractor who complies with a stop notice served on him has no direct claim against the local authority, but can claim damages from his employer for breach of contract. The employer can include in his claim damages paid to the contractor for the breach of contract.

All compensation paid under this Part of the Act is assessed under the provisions of the *Land Compensation Act, 1961*, and the amount of compensation in case of dispute is decided by the Lands Tribunal.

Claims for compensation should be made to and paid by the local planning authority which took the action through which the claim arose. The detailed provisions are in Paragraphs 34–36 of the Schedule 16 to the *Local Government Act, 1972*.

35

PURCHASE NOTICE BY OWNERS—
PLANNING BLIGHT AND HIGHWAYS

35.1 Introduction

Many planning decisions do not allow the owner to use land in the most profitable manner and, as has been seen, he can under certain circumstances obtain compensation for his loss.

In some cases, however, because of planning restrictions the land is of no value for the owner or, in the words of the statute, 'is not capable of reasonably beneficial use in the existing state'. In these circumstances it is equitable that the owner should have the right to ask the local authority to purchase his interest in the land. Other occasions when the owner of an interest in land may suffer severe financial loss by its depreciation in value occur when a development plan 'blights' some areas, i.e. allocates them in such a manner as to depreciate the value of the land. Here it is also equitable that the local authority, under some conditions, should be obliged to acquire the land.

Thus a purchase notice may be served by the owner on the local authority in some cases of:

(*a*) Adverse planning decisions.
(*b*) Adverse planning proposals ('planning blight').

35.2 Interests Affected by Adverse Planning Decisions (ss. 180–191)

If an application for planning permission is refused, or granted subject to conditions, the owner of the interest in land may, within six months, serve on the local planning authority a notice requiring that the authority purchase the land if he claims:

(*a*) That the land has become incapable of reasonably beneficial use in the existing state.
(*b*) In a case where planning permission was granted subject to conditions such that the land cannot be rendered capable of reasonably beneficial use by carrying out the permitted development.
(*c*) In any of these cases that land cannot be rendered capable of reasonably beneficial use by the carrying out of any other development for which planning permission has been granted or for which the local planning authority or the Secretary of State has undertaken to grant planning permission.

In determining what would be a reasonably beneficial use, no account is to be taken of the possibility of any 'new development' (i.e. outside the scope of Schedule 8— see page 171). Thus it is not open to the owner to show that the existing use of the land is substantially less profitable than it would have been if a new development were permitted. In addition, the purchase notice cannot be served if the intended development would contravene the conditions set out in Schedule 18 (see page 175).

The fact, however, that no Industrial Development Certificate has been refused does not affect the possibility of a claim.

The local authority on which the owner has served the purchase notice can comply and agree to buy the land in question, or can find another local authority or statutory undertaker which is willing to acquire the land, but if neither of these eventualities can materialise, it must submit the purchase notice to the Secretary of State, who has to approve it before it becomes operative.

The Secretary of State may either confirm the purchase notice or he may grant permission for the development sought by the owner, or he may direct that planning permission for another development should be granted in the event of an application for that development being submitted. The Secretary of State must give notice to persons affected by the proposed action and the persons concerned must be given an opportunity of being heard by the inspector in order to claim, for instance, that this other development would not render the land capable of reasonable beneficial use.

It frequently happens that when an application is submitted for planning permission to develop a housing estate, open space as 'amenity land' is left out and sometimes the authority imposes a condition requiring the preservation of some areas as 'amenity land'. S. 184 enables the Secretary of State to refuse to confirm the purchase notice if he is satisfied that the land ought to remain in its existing state as 'amenity land' for the benefit of the development authorised in the earlier permission.

The Secretary of State's decision whether to confirm the purchase notice, or to refuse to confirm it, or to grant permission for other development, may be challenged in the High Court on a point of law within six weeks.

If the Secretary of State does not issue any decision:

(*a*) Within nine months of the service of the purchase notice by the owner or

(*b*) Within six months of the submission of the copy of the purchase notice to the Secretary of State (whichever period expires earlier)

then the notice is deemed to be confirmed.

A purchase notice may be served by the owner not only if permission to develop the land is refused, but also on the revocation or modification of planning permission, or if the local planning authority issues an order requiring the discontinuance of use or alteration or removal of buildings or works. A purchase notice can also be served if listed building consent is refused, if consent in respect of a tree preservation order is refused, or if permission to display advertisements is denied (and the land, of course, cannot be rendered capable of reasonably beneficial use in the existing state).

The conditions and procedure for the service of a purchase notice in these special cases are broadly similar to those for refusal of planning permission to develop the land.

35.3 Interests of Owner–Occupiers Affected by Planning Proposals ('Planning Blight') (ss. 192–207)

In some cases planning proposals affect the interests of the owner–occupier of land to such an extent that it is equitable to enable him to serve a purchase notice, called a **blight notice** in the Act.

S. 192 enumerates 10 circumstances in which a planning blight notice may be served. The more important of these may be summarised as follows:

(*a*) The land is indicated in a structure or local plan as required by a Government department, local government, statutory undertakers or the National Coal Board, or is included in an action area.

(*b*) It is land on which a highway is proposed to be constructed.

(*c*) It is indicated as land which the local authority proposes to acquire to be included in the general improvement area under s. 31 of the *Housing Act, 1969* (now ss. 50 and 51 of the *Housing Act, 1974*).

(*d*) It is land for which a compulsory purchase order is in force, but notice to treat has not yet been served. (This means that the authority in question has acquired power to purchase the land compulsorily, but has not yet undertaken any steps to exercise that power.)

The *Land Compensation Act, 1973*, in Part V extended the blight categories. Generally speaking, if the blight affects owner–occupiers of houses, small business or agricultural interests, the blight notice may be served somewhat earlier than under the *Town and Country Planning Act, 1971*. This extension covers land affected:

(*e*) By proposals in a structure plan which has been submitted to the Secretary of State even if it has not yet come into force.

(*f*) By modifications proposed to be made by the Secretary of State in a structure plan submitted to him for approval.

(*g*) By proposals in a draft local plan made available for inspection by the public at large.

(*h*) By other similar plans, proposals and resolutions enumerated in s. 68 of the *Land Compensation Act, 1973*.

Thus a blight notice refers exclusively to cases where the land may be compulsorily purchased in the future. The need for the notice comes from the fact that the projects affect the value of the land and may even make it unsaleable.

The blight notice may be served by a resident owner–occupier of a dwelling-house irrespective of its rateable value, but an owner–occupier of any other type of land (i.e. not a dwelling-house) may serve a blight notice only if the annual value of the hereditaments in question does not exceed £2250 (Town and Country Planning (Limit of Annual Value) Order, 1973, S.I. 1973/425). Special consideration is given to the owner–occupier of agricultural units, as he is entitled to serve a blight notice irrespective of the annual value of the unit if the land is not only wholly, but even partially, contained in a blight area. The term owner–occupier includes a freeholder or a leaseholder with at least three years to run; in addition, a mortgagee affected by the blight (as his security could be threatened) may serve a blight notice.

A person who intends to serve a blight notice must claim that:

(*a*) He is entitled to an interest in the hereditament or unit.

(*b*) The interest is one which qualifies for protection under the provisions of the Act.

(*c*) Since the relevant date he has made reasonable endeavours to sell that interest. With reference to this point, the *Land Compensation Act, 1973*, simplified the procedure to some extent. At present, any person who has tried to sell the land on the open market but has been unsuccessful because of the threat of blight, does not have to try again after his land became formally blighted in order to be able to serve a blight notice.

(*d*) He has been unable to sell it, except at a price substantially lower than that which he might reasonably have expected if no part of the hereditament or unit had been blighted.

The blight notice can be served in respect of the whole land blighted or in respect of any part of the land which is affected by the blight.

The local authority may, within two months after receiving the blight notice, serve on the claimant an objection to the notice. This must be based on one of the eight grounds specified in s. 194. Generally speaking, it may be based on the fact that the conditions of serving the notice were not satisfied. One reason for objecting is worthy of attention: if the land is blighted due to its inclusion for a specified purpose in a development plan, the local authority may avoid buying the land by issuing a certificate that the land will not be required in the course of the next 15 years.

When a notice of objection has been served, the owner-occupier may within two months require the matter to be referred for decision to the Lands Tribunal. The onus of proof that the notice of objection is not well founded is on the owner-occupier.

If the local authority does not serve a notice of objection, or if it is not upheld by the Lands Tribunal, the local authority is deemed to be authorised to acquire the land in question, and to have served a notice to treat. Thus the local authority is not only authorised, but also obliged to acquire the land.

The compensation is the price of the land in its unblighted condition and may include compensation for disturbance and injurious affection (see Chapter 38).

It is the district planning authority which pays compensation when a purchase notice has been served by the owner of the land.

35.4 Local Authority Powers in respect of Highways

A highway is defined as land over which the public at large has a right to pass and re-pass. Although the Common Law rule is 'once a highway, always a highway', a number of Acts, and in particular the *Town and Country Planning Act, 1971*, give the authorities large powers in respect of highways (ss. 209–221).

The Secretary of State may by order authorise the stopping up or diversion of any highway if he is satisfied that it is necessary to do so in order to enable a development to be carried out in accordance with the planning permission, or to be carried out by a Government department.

Footpaths and bridleways may be stopped or diverted by the 'competent authority' that is, the local planning authority or the authority to which the planning authority has delegated its powers.

A highway which is not a trunk or special road may be converted into a footpath or bridleway by an order issued by the Secretary of State. If, due to the issue of such an order, somebody's land depreciates in value by the deprivation of access to a road, the person affected may claim compensation.

The Secretary of State may by order extinguish a public right of way over land being subject to development, provided that he is satisfied that an alternative right of way is or will be provided.

The Secretary of State or a local planning authority may be authorised to acquire land compulsorily for the purposes of providing or improving any highway or for providing any right of way, if it is done for the purpose of realising planning proposals.

The Act provides a detailed procedure for putting these orders into effect.

36

JURISDICTION

36.1 Jurisdiction of County and District Planning Authorities in Planning Control

The *Local Government Act, 1972*, as amended by s. 86 of the *Local Government, Planning and Land Act, 1980*, allocates the responsibility for planning control to both county and district councils.

Until the allocation of jurisdiction was amended in 1980 it was not easy to decide whether a particular problem was a 'county matter' (belonging, as such, to the county's jurisdiction), or not (belonging to the district's jurisdiction). As a judge complained in the case of *Attorney General at the Relation of Co-operative Retail Services Ltd v. Taff-Ely B.C. and others* (1976): 'County matters are difficult for anybody to understand: it requires inspection of documents, development plans and statements of policy.'

The 1980 amendment simplified the problem. Now every application for planning permission (including listed building consent), for determination under s. 53 (i.e. whether an application for planning permission is required) or for established use certificate should be made to the district planning authority. The applications so submitted are in one of the following three categories:

(*a*) 'County matters'; copies of these applications should be sent to the county authority within seven days for the county to deal with them. County matters are the following:

the winning and working of minerals, erection of buildings or use of land in this connection. This includes also the use of land or the erection of buildings for the carrying out of any process for the preparation or adaptation for sale of any mineral or manufacture of any articles from a mineral;
searches and tests for mineral deposits;
the disposal of mineral waste; also the use of land or the erection of buildings in connection with the extraction or transfer of sand, gravel, crushed rock, cement, etc.;
any development affecting National Parks;
any development or class of developments prescribed by the Secretary of State as being a county matter (so far this has not been done).

If a county planning authority is determining an application for planning permission, it should afford the district planning authority an opportunity to make representations.

(*b*) The second group of applications are those in which the district authority should consult the county before making the appropriate decision. There are a number of those applications enumerated in Para. 19 of Schedule 16 to the *Local Government Act, 1972*, as amended. Generally speaking, these are applications which conflict with the structure or local plans, which are of major importance

184

for the implementation of a structure plan, or are other applications 'called in' by the county.

(*c*) Other applications are decided by the district authority without the necessity of consulting the county.

In taking some decisions, there is concurrent jurisdiction of both county and district (but in all cases, if the district council takes a decision, it should consult the county). Thus concurrent jurisdiction exists in the following cases:

(*a*) The revocation or modification of planning permission.
(*b*) The issuing of an order requiring a discontinuance of use.
(*c*) The imposing of conditions on the continuance of use.
(*d*) The requiring of alterations or removal of buildings.
(*e*) The serving of enforcement notices or stop notices.

The following matters are within the exclusive jurisdiction of district council:

(*a*) To maintain a register of planning applications and decisions.
(*b*) To deal with listed buildings, including enforcement procedure, to issue building preservation notices, and to be concerned with the control of advertisements.

If the Secretary of State so directs, the planning authority dealing with these two problems has to obtain specialist advice in connection with the exercise of these functions.

Other functions are, generally speaking, within the jurisdiction of both county and district authorities. Detailed allocation is given in Schedule 16 to the *Local Government Act, 1972.*

It is not difficult to see that the division of jurisdiction is so complex that disputes between the two tiers of the local authorities are inevitable. One such example is the case quoted above, where the Court of Appeal took a different view from that of the High Court.

It should be noted that a local highway authority can impose restrictions on the granting by the local planning authority of planning permission for means of access to a classified road, and also where the development in question appears to increase the volume of traffic (Para. 17 of Schedule 16).

Sensibly, under Para. 51 of Schedule 16 the validity of any determination could not be called into question on the ground that it should have been made by some other planning authority than that authorised by the Schedule.

36.2 Determination of Appeals by the Inspector Nominated by the Secretary of State

Under Schedule 9 some appeals of prescribed classes are determined not by the Secretary of State, but by 'a person nominated by him' (i.e. by an inspector).

The inspector (unless the Secretary of State by a direction limits the inspector's powers) determines appeals in the following matters:

(*a*) Appeals against the decision of a planning authority refusing permission for development or granting it under conditions.
(*b*) Appeals against an enforcement notice.
(*c*) Appeals against a refusal to issue an established use certificate.
(*d*) Appeals against listed building enforcement notice.

(*e*) Appeals against a refusal of permission or against an enforcement notice in respect of tree preservation.

(*f*) Appeals against a rejection of an application for listing a building as being of special historic or architectural interest.

The Secretary of State has on several occasions issued Regulations setting out the appeals which might be determined by the inspector. The latest were issued in 1972 (Town and Country Planning (Determination of Appeals by Appointed Persons) (Prescribed Classes) Regulations, 1972, S.I. 1652) and amended twice in 1977 (S.I. 1977/477 and S.I. 1977/1939). The following appeals may be decided by an inspector:

(*a*) The erection, enlargement or other alteration of a building or buildings for use as not more than 60 dwelling-houses.

(*b*) The development for residential purposes of land not exceeding 2 hectares in area, where the application for planning permission does not specify the number of dwelling-houses to which it relates.

(*c*) The erection, enlargement or other alteration of buildings for or in connection with any of the following purposes: a shop, an office, a repository or warehouse, a hotel, boarding house, residential club, lodging house, a petrol filling station, the repair of motor vehicles or the garaging of private motorcars, religious worship or instruction, or the breeding, training or keeping of dogs, cats or horses—if the aggregate floor space created by the development does not exceed 500 square metres and the area of land to which the application relates does not exceed 8000 square metres.

(*d*) The formation, laying out or widening of a means of access.

(*e*) The carrying out of building, engineering or other operations on land for a purpose ancillary or incidental to an existing or proposed development of any kind specified in the foregoing or following classes.

(*f*) The change in the use of a building or buildings to use as not more than 60 dwelling-houses.

(*g*) The change in the use of a building or buildings to use for or in connection with any purpose specified in class (*c*) above, if the aggregate floor space used for such purpose does not exceed 1500 square metres and the area of land to which the application relates does not exceed 8000 square metres.

Appeals in the following categories will, however, be decided by the Secretary of State:

(*a*) If the application has been the subject of a direction by the Secretary of State.

(*b*) If the appeal has been made by a local authority or a statutory undertaker.

(*c*) If the local planning authority refused permission or imposed conditions because of the views expressed by a Government department or a new town corporation.

(*d*) If another appeal or application relating to the same development is concurrently being considered by the Secretary of State.

(*e*) If another appeal or application not within the classes entrusted to the inspector, but relating to the same land, is concurrently considered by the Secretary of State.

Any inspector who becomes empowered to determine an appeal is afforded the same powers and duties as the Secretary of State. The parties should be asked by the inspector whether they wish to be heard and, if they do, they must be afforded at least a private hearing. The inspector may hold a public inquiry before he decides the appeal and must do so if instructed by the Secretary of State. When the appeal is decided by the inspector his decision is equivalent to that of the Secretary of State.

The Secretary of State has power to substitute one inspector for another or to restore the responsibility for individual decisions to himself. The substituted inspector must begin his consideration afresh, but it is not necessary for him to give any person the opportunity either of making fresh representations or of modifying or withdrawing representations already made.

36.3   Planning Control in Greater London

The special provisions of town and country planning law for Greater London are contained in:

(*a*) Schedule 3 to the *Town and Country Planning Act, 1971*, as amended by s. 86 of the *Local Government, Planning and Land Act, 1980*, which designated local planning authorities for Greater London.

(*b*) Schedule 1 to the *Town and Country Planning (Amendment) Act, 1972*, which replaced Schedule 4 to the *Town and Country Planning Act, 1971*, and deals with surveys and development plans for Greater London.

(*c*) Part II of Schedule 5 to the *Town and Country Planning Act, 1971*, which contains transitional provisions for Greater London due to the existence of old and new styles of the development plans.

(*d*) Para. 39 of Schedule 16 to the *Local Government Act, 1972*, which deals with the stopping and diversion of highways.

(*e*) Town and Country Planning (Local Planning Authorities in Greater London) Regulations, 1980 (S.I. 1980/443), which prescribe the manner in which applications for planning permission for development of land in Greater London are to be dealt with. These Regulations re-enact those of 1978 (S.I. 1978/602), which consolidated with amendments the Town and Country Planning (Local Planning Authorities in Greater London) Regulations, 1965 to 1974 (S.I. 1965/679, S.I. 1966/48, S.I. 1968/815 and others).

The control of development is divided between the Greater London and London boroughs. London boroughs deal with any planning applications for development subject to general planning control. With respect to control in special cases, only applications for listed building consent are within the jurisdiction of London boroughs. All other special cases (tree, advertisements, waste land and industrial development) are dealt with by the Great London Council. A copy of a planning decision issued by a London borough council is usually sent to the Greater London Council for information.

This general rule, is, however, subject to some exceptions. Thus a statutory instrument may prescribe some classes of development or development in some areas of Greater London which should be dealt with by the Greater London Council, although under the general provisions they belong to the jurisdiction of the London boroughs. This exclusion, however, does not apply to the issue of established use certificates.

On the other hand, the Greater London Council may in a particular case which would normally belong to its jurisdiction, entrust the London borough with the carrying out of the enforcement procedure, including compensation for loss due to the issue of a stop notice. The Greater London Council may, with the consent of the Secretary of State, delegate to the council of a London borough any of those functions which are within the jurisdiction of the Greater London Council, and these functions will be performed by the borough council on behalf of the Greater London Council.

37

COMPULSORY PURCHASE OF LAND BY PUBLIC AUTHORITIES

37.1   Introduction

The compulsory acquisition of land for public purposes is necessary in modern society. Governments in many countries have the power to confiscate land for various purposes with or without compensation. However, in the United Kingdom compulsory acquisition can only be carried out if there is a power of acquisition granted by law, and the law invariably provides for compensation, which does not depend on the discretion of the acquiring authority but must be effected according to the existing legal provisions.

If land is compulsorily acquired—for whatever purpose—the following four stages have to be considered:

(*a*) There must be an Act of Parliament authorising the authority to purchase the land compulsorily for the stated purpose.

(*b*) The acquiring authority, having the power to acquire land, has to select the land which it intends to purchase and has to obtain power to acquire that piece of land.

(*c*) When the acquiring authority has obtained power to purchase the selected land compulsorily, it must exercise this power and obtain ownership by the prescribed procedure.

(*d*) Compensation should be assessed and paid by the acquiring authority.

The first stage is best explained by reference to the history of compulsory purchase.

It was in the closing years of the eighteenth and the first half of the nineteenth century that, for the first time, powers for the compulsory purchase of land were given on a large scale to commercial undertakings such as canal and railway companies. Those undertakings, while sanctioned by Parliament in the interests of the community, were primarily intended to be a source of profit to their promoters.

During those times the recognised method of obtaining compulsory purchasing powers was by means of a Private Bill which might be opposed by interested parties during the Committee stages in either House before it became a Private Act.

Each Private Act prescribed its own procedure for the whole process of compulsory acquisition of land. Although these provisions were naturally similar in most cases, they could nevertheless be contested on each occasion by opponents and the result was much unnecessary expense and a great waste of Parliament's time. For this reason the *Land Clauses Consolidation Act, 1845*, was passed, which provided a remedy by incorporating in one Act the type of provisions formerly inserted in each separate Act, thus giving a complete code of law covering all questions pertaining to the exercise of the power, once it was granted by the Private Act. The provisions covered 'Notice to Treat', assessment and payment of compensation, right of entry on the land acquired, etc. The Act dealt not only with a host of provisions covering the problem of purchase itself, but also with the principles of compensation. Its purpose was, in the words of the preamble, 'to consolidate in one Act certain provisions usually inserted in the Acts authorising the taking of land for undertakings of a public nature'.

In the middle of the nineteenth century the urgent sanitary problems resulting from the rapid urban expansion after the Industrial Revolution necessitated the compulsory purchase of land by public authorities for numerous public health purposes, both under individual Town Improvement Acts and later under the *Public Health Act, 1875*. From that time onwards powers of compulsory purchase have been given for many other purposes: slum clearance, building of schools, new towns, atomic energy stations, etc. As a consequence of these developments, the acquiring bodies are at present Government departments, local authorities and public corporations (British Rail, National Coal Board, British Broadcasting Corporation, etc).

The procedure of Private Acts of Parliament is not appropriate for the host of compulsory purchases effected today and powers of compulsory purchase are now given in general terms to certain classes of public bodies—for example, to local authorities—under general Acts applying to the whole country.

The second stage of the procedure—the selection of land to be compulsorily acquired and the obtaining of the power to acquire that land—was, and still usually is, exercised by the acquiring body making an order (a **Compulsory Purchase Order**) applying the compulsory purchase power conferred by the Act to the particular piece of land. The Order usually requires confirmation by an appropriate Government department.

At one time each public general Act prescribed its own procedure for the making and confirmation of the compulsory purchase order. Now uniformity of procedure has been achieved under the *Acquisition of Land (Authorisation Procedure) Act, 1946*.

In one case, however, that Act provides that the compulsory purchase order should be subject to the Special Parliamentary Procedure (Part III of Schedule 1). This means that such an order shall be of no effect until laid before the Parliament in accordance with the provisions of the *Statutory Orders (Special Procedure) Acts, 1945* and *1965*. Generally speaking, it means that Parliament may annul the Order by a resolution of either House. It is mainly in respect of land held by the National Trust that this Special Parliamentary Procedure is required. Other categories of land which had been subject to this procedure are now freed from it by s. 41 of the *Community Land Act, 1975* (not repealed).

The third stage of the procedure—**acquisition** itself—was originally governed by the *Land Clauses Consolidation Act, 1845*, which has now been replaced, with some amendments, by the *Compulsory Purchase Act, 1965*. The provisions of that Act are substantially similar to those of the 1845 Act, which still has application to some compulsory purchases carried out under some older Acts.

The fourth stage is the **assessment and payment of compensation.** Here again the *Land Clauses Consolidation Act, 1845*, was replaced by the *Acquisition of Land (Assessment of Compensation) Act, 1919*, which was afterwards repealed and replaced by the following two Acts:

(a) The *Lands Tribunal Act, 1949*, which created a Tribunal with a wide jurisdiction covering among others the question of assessment of compensation when a dispute arises over the amount of compensation for the land acquired.

(*b*) The *Land Compensation Act, 1961*, which is the present legal basis for the assessment of compensation.

Thus at present the law covering compulsory purchase may be summarised as follows:

(*a*) There must be an Act of Parliament granting the powers to purchase land compulsorily for stated purpose (e.g. the *Town and Country Planning Act, 1971*, grants extensive powers to local authorities and Government departments).

(*b*) These powers (in almost all cases with some insignificant exceptions) are obtained in respect of individual pieces of land under the *Acquisition of Land (Authorisation Procedure) Act, 1946*.

(*c*) Once the powers have been obtained they are usually exercised under the *Compulsory Purchase Act, 1965* (with a few exceptions where the *Land Clauses Consolidation Act, 1845*, still applies).

(*d*) The problem of compensation is dealt with under the *Land Compensation Act, 1961* (in respect of some houses unfit for human habitation assessment is made under *Housing Act, 1957*, as amended by the *Housing Act, 1969*).

37.2 First Stage: Obtaining of Compulsory Purchase Powers

The most important Act of Parliament granting local authorities power to acquire land compulsorily is the *Town and Country Planning Act, 1971*, as amended by the *Local Government, Planning and Land Act, 1980*. It gives wide powers to local planning authorities for the acquisition of land for development and other planning purposes. These provisions are consolidated in Part VI of that Act.

The compulsory acquisition of land by local authorities requires the approval of the Secretary of State.

A local planning authority has power (on being authorised to do so by the Secretary of State) to acquire compulsorily any land which is in their area and which is:

(*a*) Required in order to secure development, redevelopment or improvement.

(*b*) Required for the proper planning of an area in which the land is situated.

A local planning authority may also, with the authority of the Secretary of State, acquire compulsorily:

(*a*) Any land adjoining the land required as above.

(*b*) If compulsory purchase includes a common, open space, or fuel or garden allotment, any land required for exchange for that land.

In the last two cases the land to be compulsorily acquired need not be within the area of the local authority concerned.

After consulting with the interested authorities the Secretary of State may authorise the acquisition of land situated within the area of another local authority. In addition, he may acquire compulsorily any land necessary for public purposes or acquire an easement or other right over land.

These powers of compulsory purchase are very far reaching and in the opinion of the Conservative Government they are sufficient for the proper use of land in this country, as their policy is to leave as much initiative to private enterprise as possible.

The Labour Party, however, considers that these powers are not sufficiently comprehensive and for this reason the *Community Land Act, 1975*, enacted that any 'development land' (as defined by the Act, with some 'exemptions' and 'exceptions') would pass through the local authorities' ownership (being afterwards either developed by the local authority itself, or sold to the developers). This Act, has now been repealed by the present Conservative Government (see Appendix 1).

37.3   Compulsory Acquisition of Listed Buildings (ss. 114–117)

There are special provisions for the acquisition of listed buildings, i.e. buildings of a special architectural or historic interest.

If such a building is not properly maintained, the Secretary of State may himself compulsorily acquire the land, or authorise the local planning authority to take this action. However, before a compulsory purchase order is issued, a notice must be sent to the owner, specifying the works which are considered reasonably necessary for the proper preservation of the building and explaining the Secretary of State's or the local authority's power of compulsory purchase. Only if the notice is not complied with within two months, may the acquisition be effected.

The *Acquisition of Land* (*Authorisation Procedure*) *Act, 1946*, applies to this type of compulsory acquisition. The Secretary of State confirms the compulsory purchase order only if he is satisfied that it is expedient to make provisions for the preservation of the building by compulsory acquisition for that purpose.

Any person having an interest in the listed building which is subject to a compulsory purchase order may apply to the Magistrates' Court for an order staying further proceedings on the order, and if the court is satisfied that reasonable steps have been taken in the preservation of the building, the Court may make an order accordingly. An appeal is allowed to the Crown Court against the decision of the Magistrates' Court.

The measure of compensation for the compulsory acquisition of a listed building has been reduced by the *Town and Country Amenities Act, 1974*. Previously compensation ignored the restrictions on altering, extending or demolishing the building and was paid on the fiction that listed building consent would be granted to permit these changes. Now, however, compensation does not take into account the possibility of obtaining listed building consent, thus reducing the sum to be paid. Only 'existing use developments' (see Chapter 34) are taken into account.

If it has been established that the building has been allowed to fall into disrepair deliberately for the purpose of justifying the redevelopment of the site, the compulsory purchase order may include a direction that the assessment of compensation shall be subject to 'minimum compensation'. This means that the compensation will be a sum which disregards any profit that may have accrued from the redevelopment of the site. There is a right of appeal against a direction for minimum compensation to the Magistrates' Court with a further appeal to the Crown Court.

37.4   Acquisition of Land by Agreement (s. 119)

A local planning authority may acquire by agreement:

(*a*) Any land they require for any purpose for which a local authority may be authorised to acquire land compulsorily under the *Town and Country Planning Act, 1971.*

(*b*) Any building appearing to them to be of a special architectural or historic interest.

(*c*) Any building contiguous or adjacent to such a building which appears to the Secretary of State to be required for preserving the building or its amenities or for affording access to it or for its proper control or management.

Land may also be acquired for the purpose of exchanging it for land required for planning purposes or for the green belt around London. The consent of the Secretary of State is required unless the land is immediately required by the council for the purpose for which it is to be acquired, or is land within the area of the council acquiring the land. Thus, in effect, the permission of the Secretary of State will seldom be required.

Where a local authority has acquired land for planning purposes it may, instead of developing it themselves, dispose of it to such persons, in such a manner and subject to such conditions as may appear to it to be expedient. Sometimes the consent of the Secretary of State is required for disposal, namely:

(*a*) By any authority other than a county or district.

(*b*) Of land acquired for planning purposes in connection with development, redevelopment or improvement.

(*c*) Of land which is part of a common.

Thus the land may be disposed (i.e. sold or leased) to a developer who has no powers of compulsory purchase, but who is prepared to develop the land. Much land after the war has been developed in this manner. The Secretary of State may require a local planning authority to dispose of it to a specified person, but only for the best price reasonably obtainable. Such disposal has to secure, as far as practicable, that persons formerly living or carrying on business on such land may be able to get accommodation there at a suitable price.

37.5   Second Stage: Obtaining Compulsory Purchase Powers

In the vast majority of cases the procedure of obtaining compulsory purchase powers for a particular piece of land is governed by the *Acquisition of Land (Authorisation Procedure) Act, 1946.* This Act covers almost all compulsory purchase with the following more important exceptions:

(*a*) Purchases for the purpose of the *New Towns Act, 1965* (Schedules 3 and 4 of that Act).

(*b*) Purchases under Part III of the *Housing Act, 1957* (clearance areas— Schedule 3 of that Act).

The procedure under the 1946 Act may be summarised as follows:

The acquiring authority prepares a compulsory purchase order for submission to the 'confirming authority'. The form of the order is prescribed by the Compulsory Purchase of Land Regulations, 1976 (S.I. 300). The order must identify the land to which it applies by a map. Before submitting the order to the confirming authority the acquiring authority must publish a notice about the order for two consecutive weeks in at least one local newspaper. The notice must conform with the above Regulations and must state that the order may be inspected and that objections may be made within a specified period of not less than 28 days. In addition, a notice must be served on every owner, lessee and occupier of the land affected, except tenants for a month or shorter periods. If the acquiring authority cannot serve the notice on some persons (e.g. if the address is unknown), the confirming authority may allow the notice to be affixed to a conspicuous object on the land. Where the land is an ecclesiastical property owned by the Church of England, notice must be served on the Church Commissioners.

If no objections are raised, or if all are withdrawn, the confirming authority, if satisfied that proper notice has been served and published, may confirm the order with or without modifications, but the area of land cannot be increased without the consent of all interested parties. If objections are made, the confirming authority must either hold an inquiry or at least give the objectors an opportunity of being heard by a person nominated by the confirming authority. The objector may be asked to state the grounds of his objections in writing and the confirming authority may ignore the objections if they relate exclusively to matters which can be dealt with by the Lands Tribunal, which assesses the compensation. Objections are not restricted to legal matters; problems of policy, suitability of land for the intended purposes and other reasons may be raised by the objectors.

After considering the report of the inspector who held the local inquiry or private hearing, the confirming authority (in most cases the Secretary of State for the Environment) may confirm the order with or without modifications, or may refuse to confirm. The confirming authority may be required to furnish reasons for his decision, but he may refuse to do so on grounds of national security. Confirmation of the order must be advertised in the form prescribed by the Regulations and notice must be served on those persons who were notified previously of the preparation of the draft order. The notice describes the land covered by the order and indicates where the order may be inspected.

A compulsory purchase order becomes operative from the date when notice of its confirmation is first published. Any person aggrieved may challenge its validity by an application to the High Court within six weeks of that date, on the grounds either:

(*a*) That the order is *ultra vires* (in excess of jurisdiction) of the Act; or

(*b*) That some essential requirements of the Act or of the Regulations made under it have not been complied with and that in consequence the challenger's interests have been substantially prejudiced. Under s. 64 of the *Land Compensation Act, 1973*, these requirements include references to any requirements of the *Tribunal and Inquiries Act,1971*, or any Rules under that Act.

Unless an application is made to the Court within the prescribed period, the order cannot be questioned in any legal proceedings (by the prerogative order of *certiorari*), not even if the order was made in bad faith (*Smith v. East Elloe R.D.C.*, 1956). Some doubt has been expressed whether the East Elloe case is good law in view of a later decision of the House of Lords which enlarged the scope of judicial control over administrative powers (*Anisminic Ltd v. Foreign Compensation Commission*, 1969), but in a subsequent case (*Regina v. Secretary of State for the Environment* ex parte *Ostler*, 1977) the Court of Appeal accepted the East Elloe case as good law.

37.6   Third Stage: Acquisition of Land

(a) Definition of Land

Both the *Land Clauses Consolidation Act, 1845*, and the *Compulsory Purchase Act, 1965* define land rather widely: it includes fixtures, (e.g. buildings), rents, commons and profits *à prendre*. It also includes future real property rights, e.g. options.

With regard to easements it has been held by the Court that an owner cannot be compelled to grant an easement over his land, unless the authorising Act clearly so provided (as it has done in s. 113 of the *Town and Country Planning Act, 1971*). The owner may grant it voluntarily, or, if an easement is required by the acquiring authority, it has to purchase the land it would like to burden with an easement (*Pinchin v. London and Blackwall Rail Co.*, 1854). On the other hand, if the acquired land is a dominant tenement enjoying an easement, then the easement is included in the purchase.

If the acquired land is a servient tenement, the easement over the land compulsorily acquired is not extinguished, and if the acquiring authority consequently interferes with it then full compensation must be paid for the damage caused to the dominant land.

(b) The Purpose for which Land may be Acquired

The purpose for which land may be acquired is defined in the special or general Act granting the power to acquire land. The land may be acquired under the existing power, but also for other, secondary purposes, provided that they are closely connected with the main purpose (e.g. power to purchase land for railway purposes includes sidings and car parks at the stations, but not a sand pit to extract the sand required for building the track—*Galloway v. City of London*, 1865).

(c) Acquisition of Part of the Property

It often happens that only a part of a property is required by the acquiring authority. In this case the taking of a part may so alter the character of the remainder as to make it of very little value to the owner.

Section 92 of the *Land Clauses Consolidation Act, 1845*, gave some protection; this has also been provided by s. 8(1) of the *Compulsory Purchase Act, 1965*, which decrees that no person shall be required to sell any part of any 'house, building or factory' if it cannot be taken without material detriment to the land. In the case of a park or a garden it is sufficient that taking a part would affect the amenity or convenience of the house. Under ss. 53–57 of the *Land Compensation Act, 1973*, an owner or tenant of agricultural land, part of which has been compulsorily acquired, may serve a notice upon the acquiring authority requiring them to acquire the whole of his land if the remaining part is not reasonably capable of being farmed. Disputes are determined by the Lands Tribunal. If the Tribunal determines that the part of land may be acquired, then it awards compensation for any loss due to the severance of that part, in addition to the value of the land acquired. This additional compensation for **injurious affection** is discussed in Chapter 41.

(d) Mines and Minerals under the Land Acquired

When land is acquired compulsorily, any coalmine in the land is excluded from the sale, with the obvious exception of any coal which it is necessary to dig out in the course of the operations for which the land was acquired. All other minerals (except gold and silver, which are Crown property under Common Law) would be included in the conveyance and have to be the subject of compensation by the acquiring authority. The *Railway Clauses Consolidation Act, 1845*, in ss. 77–85 introduced provisions whereby the acquiring authority may be relieved of this additional burden of compensation and the owner may be free to continue to work the minerals. These provisions, known as the **mining code**, are now of general application if incorporated in the compulsory purchase order.

The main provisions of the mining code are:

(*a*) The acquiring authority will not be entitled to any mines of ironstone, slate or other materials.

(*b*) The authority may purchase them if they wish.

(*c*) If not purchased they can be worked by the owner (after giving 30 days' notice to the authority). There is a possibility of a counternotice, in which case compensation will be paid.

(*d*) Even later the acquiring authority is entitled to serve a notice stopping work carried out by the previous owner. But if a notice is not served, the owner is entitled to carry on the extraction of the minerals.

(e) Purchase of Land by Agreement

In many cases, in practice, land is acquired for statutory purposes by agreement between the parties and, if so, the acquiring authority does not resort to compulsory powers. In such cases conveyance is effected in the same way as between private persons.

37.7 Compulsory Purchase: Procedure

The acquiring authority must exercise its power within three years after the compulsory purchase becomes operative, unless a special Act gives more time.

There are two alternative procedures of acquiring the land: 'Notice to Treat', which is in more general use, but this may be replaced by the more speedy procedure of serving a 'General Vesting Declaration'.

37.8 Notice to Treat Procedure (s. 5 of the *Compulsory Purchase Act, 1965*)

The Notice to Treat is the notification of the acquiring authority's intention to purchase the owner's interest in a particular piece of land and of its willingness to pay compensation for the loss arising from that acquisition.

The Notice to Treat should be served on all persons interested in, or having powers to sell and convey or release the land, so far as they are known to the acquiring authority after making diligent inquiries. It must be served on the owners of freehold, leaseholders (with the important exception of tenants having no greater interest than for a year or from year to year—statutory tenants protected under the *Rent Act, 1977*, belong to this category), mortgagees, but not beneficiaries of restrictive covenants or easement over the land, as they are not expropriated.

The exact form and wording of the Notice is immaterial, but s. 5(2) provides that the Notice shall:

(*a*) Give particulars of the land to which the Notice relates.

(*b*) Demand particulars of the owner's interest and of his claim.

(*c*) State that the acquiring authority is willing to treat for the purchase of the land and for the compensation to be paid for damage due to the execution of the works (in order that the details of the owner's interest may be obtained in a concise form, it is usual for the acquiring authority to enclose a special form of claim with the Notice to Treat showing clearly the particulars required by the acquiring authority).

The legal consequences which follow the service of a valid Notice to Treat are:

(*a*) The owner may be forced to sell and the authority may be forced to purchase the land in question. Only in special circumstances, explained below, may the Notice to Treat be withdrawn. If no agreement is reached as to the compensation, either party may ask for an assessment by the Lands Tribunal. The assessment of compensation, together with the Notice to Treat, will then constitute a binding and enforceable contract, which may be the subject of specific performance by the Court.

(*b*) The Notice to Treat fixes the nature of the interest to be acquired. Thus the owner cannot by any subsequent action (e.g. by granting a lease or option) increase the burden of compensation to be borne by the acquiring authority (*Re Marylebone* (*Stingo Lane*) *Improvement Act*, ex Parte *Edwards*, 1871).

It is neither a contract for sale, nor a step putting in force the compulsory power. It is a neutral act, which may be followed either by an agreement on the price, or by an assessment by the Lands Tribunal (*Holloway and Another v. Dover Corporation*, 1960).

Until a few years ago, the date of the Notice to Treat also fixed the amount of compensation. However, since the case of *West Midland Baptist* (*Trust*) *Association v. Birmingham Corporation* (1969) this is not so. This important case and its implication will be considered in the next chapter, when the amount of compensation will be discussed.

As a general rule, a Notice to Treat once issued cannot be withdrawn by the acquiring authority without the consent of the owner, except in the following circumstances:

(*a*) The Notice to Treat refers to a part of the land belonging to the owner and he insists on selling the whole (s. 8(1) of the *Compulsory Purchase Act, 1965*).

(*b*) It may be withdrawn within six weeks after the service of the claim by the owner (s. 31(1) of the *Land Compensation Act, 1961*).

(*c*) If a statement of claim is not submitted and the Lands Tribunal assesses the compensation, the authority may withdraw the Notice to Treat within six weeks (s. 31(2) of the *Land Compensation Act, 1961*).

In all these cases it appears that the acquiring authority may withdraw the Notice after learning for the first time that the price is too high. In the first two cases the acquiring authority has to pay compensation for any loss or expenses resulting from the issue and withdrawal of the Notice.

If both parties fail to act after the Notice to Treat has been issued, the result is that the Notice may become ineffective. The principles covering this situation were judicially enunciated in the leading case of *Simpson Motor Sales* (*London*) *Ltd. v. Hendon Corporation* (1963):

(*a*) It is the duty of the acquiring authority to proceed within a reasonable time (although in the West Midland case mentioned above the 'reasonable time', with the agreement of both parties, lasted some 16 years).

(*b*) The acquiring authority may display an intention to abandon the purchase; delay in action may be an evidence of this.

(*c*) The Notice to Treat may be illegal and therefore not proceeded with.

(*d*) If there is inequitable conduct on the side of either party the Court may refuse to grant specific performance.

Although the acquiring authority usually obtains possession of the land after compensation has been assessed and paid, s. 11 of the *Compulsory Purchase Act, 1965*, allows the acquiring authority to obtain possession earlier. Provided that the Notice to Treat has been served and a 14 days' notice has been given to all interested parties, the acquiring authority may enter upon the land. Compensation, which is either agreed between the parties or assessed by the Lands Tribunal, will be paid with interest from the date of entry.

37.9 General Vesting Declaration Procedure

In addition to the usual procedure of acquiring land by using the Notice to Treat procedure, more recent legislation has introduced another procedure which enables the acquiring authority to obtain ownership and possession of the land much more quickly.

S. 30 of the *Town and Country Planning Act, 1968* (not repealed by the consolidating Act of 1971), and Schedules 3 and 3A are the statutory basis for the General Vesting Declaration procedure.

The more salient points of this procedure may be summarised as follows. If the acquiring authority decides to use this procedure they must include a notice about it in the notification that the compulsory purchase order has been confirmed, or later, but only if no Notice to Treat has been issued. The notice sent to the owners specifies the earliest date at which the General Vesting Declaration can be executed, which cannot be earlier than in two months' time. The notice is registered in the local land charges register.

After the General Vesting Declaration has been executed, the acquiring authority must serve on all interested persons (with the exception of occupiers holding under 'minor tenancies' or under 'tenancies about to expire') a notice in the prescribed form, specifying the land and explaining the effect of the Declaration. The General Vesting Declaration will take effect at the date stated, which cannot be earlier than 28 days from the service of the notice.

As from the date on which the General Vesting Declaration takes effect, the land specified will vest in the acquiring authority, which is then entitled to take possession. Tenancies under minor tenancies or tenancies about to expire are entitled to 14 days' notice before the possession is taken.

Compensation is either agreed between the parties or assessed by the Lands

Tribunal, and is paid with interest from the Vesting Declaration date. The rate of interest is established by a statutory instrument and usually follows closely the Bank of England minimum lending rate. Moreover, under s. 52 of the *Land Compensation Act, 1973*, where an authority has taken possession of any land the claimant has a right to an advance payment of 90 per cent of the compensation agreed or estimated by the authority.

The detailed procedure relating to the issue of a General Vesting Declaration is contained in the Compulsory Purchase of Land Regulations, 1976 (S.I. 1976/300).

Once the General Vesting Declaration has been executed, it has similar effects as if a Notice to Treat has been served. Possibilities of withdrawal of the Declaration are narrower than in the Notice to Treat procedure. The acquiring authority cannot withdraw the General Vesting Declaration solely because the assessment of compensation is higher than was anticipated. They can do so, however, if the owner objects to the severance of his property and his claim is sustained by the Lands Tribunal.

As the acquiring authority is committed to pay any price assessed by the Lands Tribunal, this procedure has, so far, been used sparingly by the acquiring authorities, mostly in cases where acquisition is urgent (for example, motorways).

38

COMPENSATION FOR COMPULSORY PURCHASE OF LAND

38.1 Historical Background

When an owner is deprived of his interest in land under statutory powers, he is entitled to compensation for his loss as a matter of right, unless Parliament expressly deprives him of that right (*Attorney General v. De Keysers Royal Hotel Ltd*, 1920).

The measure of compensation for land compulsorily acquired has been affected by the provisions of the following Acts, which together cover a period of over 120 years.

The Land Clauses Consolidation Act, 1845

Until 1947 everybody, with a few exceptions, was able to develop land without any interference by the authorities and it was therefore not a very difficult task to assess the value of land, taking into account not only the value in its existing use, but also the value by which it might be increased by the possibility of developing it (for example, by building houses or factories).

The *Land Clauses Consolidation Act, 1845*, was for years incorporated into every Act which gave any public authority compulsory purchase powers, except where its provisions were expressly modified or excluded. The compensation provisions of this Act were peculiarly vague, but certain principles were established in the course of their interpretation by the Courts and these may be summarised as follows:

(*a*) Compensation for land should include compensation for disturbance and other loss suffered by the owner in consequence of its acquisition.

(*b*) Service of a Notice to Treat determines the property, the nature of the interest to be taken and the date of valuation. This last principle has been abandoned by the judgment of the House of Lords in the case of *West Midland Baptist (Trust) Association v. Birmingham Corporation* (1969), discussed later.

(*c*) The burden of compensation cannot be increased after the Notice to Treat has been served.

(*d*) The value to be assessed is the value to the owner and not to the acquiring authority.

Acquisition of Land (Assessment of Compensation) Act, 1919

This Act prescribes that the general basis of compensation should be the price which land may be expected to realise if sold in the open market by a willing seller. This is known as the **open market value** (as opposed to the 'existing use' value) and it includes the development value which the land may possess (i.e. the difference between the existing use value and the market value).

The Town and Country Planning Acts, 1947 and 1954

The Acts enacted since 1947 created difficulty in assessing the compensation for the land acquired, as each piece of land may be considered as having a dual value: first the 'existing use value', which is the value of the land in its present use, and secondly the 'market value', which is very often considerably higher if planning permission is either already granted, or where there is every expectation that it would be granted. Thus the problem since 1947 has been: should the compensation be assessed on the assumption that any planning permission will be granted?

These two Acts applied to compensation payable under Notices to Treat issued between 1948 and 1958. The general basis of compensation was 'existing use value', assessed on the assumption that planning permission would be granted only for the very limited forms of development specified in Schedule 3 to the 1947 Act—now Schedule 8 to the 1971 Act (see Chapter 36).

The Town and Country Planning Act, 1959

This Act restored 'open market value' as a general principle, but with certain prescribed 'assumptions' in respect of planning permissions, which considerably lowered the full market value.

The Land Compensation Act, 1961

As from August 1, 1961, this Act applies to all cases where land is authorised to be acquired compulsorily. It enacts the general principles of the 1919 Act and the compensation provisions of the 1959 Act.

38.2 Compensation under the *Land Compensation Act, 1961*

This Act does not affect the owner's general right to compensation enunciated in 1845 and 1919 Acts, but it enacts principles governing assessment of compensation.

S. 5 of the Act lays down six basic rules for assessing compensation for the land acquired. Five of these concern the value of the land itself; the sixth affirms the right of the owner to obtain further compensation for 'disturbance and other matters not directly based on the valuation of land' (injurious affection).

In addition, ss. 14–22 contain certain planning assumptions which affect the assessment of compensation.

Rule 1

'No allowance shall be made on account of the acquisition being compulsory.'

When the value of land was assessed under the *Land Clauses Consolidation Act, 1845*, it became customary for the referees assessing the value to add 10 per cent as additional compensation for the forced sale. This custom has now been expressly excluded.

Rule 2

'The value of land shall, subject as hereinafter provided, be taken to be the amount which the land, if sold on the open market by a willing seller, might be expected to realise.'

Thus this rule accepts the principle of open market value. However, the fact that all land is now under strict planning control has given open market value a special meaning, different from that in 1919, when it was first clearly formulated. For, where the land is capable of development, 'the amount which the land might be expected to realise' depends on the kind of development for which (having regard to the development plan for the area) planning permission is likely to be obtained. The Act therefore provides for certain 'assumptions' as to the granting of planning permissions, which will be discussed later.

There is another important factor on which the value of the land depends—namely, the date at which the price is to be fixed. In the nineteenth century, when prices were relatively static, this problem was of no importance and the date of issue of the Notice to Treat was accepted as the convenient date governing the assessment of price. Nowadays, however, if some years elapse between the issue of the Notice to Treat and assessment of compensation, the owner may be detrimentally affected by being paid the price prevailing some years before. This problem came before the House of Lords and although it concerned the assessment under Rule 5, the House stated that the same rule should apply to the assessments of the price under Rule 2. The facts of the case (*West Midland Baptist Trust Association v. Birmingham Corporation* (1969) are as follows:

Birmingham Corporation, in carrying out a large improvement scheme in the centre of the city, acquired a Baptist Chapel compulsorily. The Notice to Treat was deemed to have been served on August 14, 1947 (its legality was not questioned), but the property was vested in the Corporation only in 1963. The point of issue was the date by reference to which the amount of compensation was to be fixed and it was agreed that compensation should be assessed on the basis of 'equivalent reinstatement' (Rule 5). If the relevant date was the date of Notice to Treat (1947) the compensation would amount to £50 000; if it was the date when reinstatement might reasonably begin (1961) then the compensation would amount to £90 000. The House of Lords unanimously decided that the later date should govern the assessment. Their Lordships stated that although in the nineteenth century the date was immaterial, as prices were static, and the date of Notice to Treat was a convenient one, nowadays, due to inflation it is essential that the date must be as late as reasonable. Thus in future the date of taking possession by the acquiring authority, or the date of assessment by the Lands Tribunal, whichever is the earlier, should govern the amount of compensation and this rule is now followed.

Rule 3

'The special suitability or adaptability of the land for any purpose should not be taken into account, if that purpose is a purpose to which it could be applied only in pursuance of statutory powers, or for which there is no market apart from the needs of a particular purchaser or the requirements of any authority possessing compulsory powers.'

This is simply an expression of the principle contained in the *Land Clauses Consolidation Act, 1845*, that the value to be assessed is the value to the owner and not to the acquiring authority. The authority may badly require a piece of land of negligible value for a specific purpose (say, for an atomic plant). Only this negligible value will be taken into account, as the project can be realised only 'in pursuance of statutory powers'.

Rule 4

'Where the value of the land is increased by reason of the use thereof or of any premises thereon in a manner which could be restrained by the Courts or is contrary to law, or is detrimental to the health of the inmates or to the public health, the amount of that increase would not be taken into account.'

This rule is self-explanatory.

Rule 5

'Where the land is, and but for the compulsory acquisition would continue to be, devoted to a purpose of such a nature, that there is no general demand or market for land for that purpose, the compensation may, if the Lands Tribunal is satisfied that reinstatement in some other place is *bona fide* intended, be assessed on the basis of the reasonable cost of equitable reinstatement.'

This rule applies to such buildings as chapels, schools, alms-houses and similar institutions.

Rule 6

'The provisions of Rule 2 shall not affect the assessment of compensation for disturbance or other matter not directly based on the valuation of land.'

This means compensation for disturbance and injurious affection, which will be dealt with later in this chapter.

Sections 6, 7 and 8 of the *Land Compensation Act, 1961*, contain three additional rules:

(*a*) No account should be taken of any increase or decrease in value due to the development under the acquiring body's scheme. The reason for this is that the development of the acquiring body could be of a large and special scale (e.g. a new town) such that they would not be carried out if the land could not be compulsorily acquired. This rule gives statutory validity to the principle formulated by the Privy Council in the leading case of *Pointe Gourde Quarrying and Transport Co. v. Sub-Intendent of Crown Lands* (1947). Hence it is called the 'Pointe Gourde' principle. In this case the land which was compulsorily acquired contained a stone quarry needed by the acquiring authority for building a port. However, as the stone could be profitably used only for the building of the port and not for any other purpose, the value of the quarry was disregarded.

(*b*) Any increase in the value of adjacent or contiguous land of the same owner shall be set off against the compensation payable for land taken from him. In any subsequent acquisition of this adjacent land the amount overpaid or underpaid will be set off. Any decrease in the value of land belonging to the person whose other adjacent land was purchased is compensated under the injurious affection rules.

(*c*) The loss of value due to the threat of compulsory acquisition should be ignored.

Although it is simple enough to say (as Rule 2 does) that 'compensation for the acquisition of land by public authorities will be the price which the property would obtain in the open market', a problem arises as to what this actually means, as the value of property cannot be considered without regard to planning permission, either granted or obtainable. Thus it is necessary to state some assumptions regarding planning permission, which are dealt with in ss. 14–22 of the *Land Compensation Act, 1961*.

S. 15 requires some general planning assumptions to be accepted in assessing the compensation:

(*a*) Where the authority's proposal involved the development of the land to be acquired, it shall be assumed that planning permission would be given to this development.

At first glance there seems to be some contradiction between Rule 3 and the Pointe Gourde principle on the one hand and this assumption on the other. The problem was neatly stated and resolved by Lord Denning in *Viscount Camrose v. Basingstoke Corporation* (1966). Basingstoke Corporation, requiring land for receiving an influx from London under the *Town Development Act, 1952*, acquired land belonging to the plaintiff. The problem was whether the value of the land should be assessed as agricultural land (as the land was required by Basingstoke Corporation and not by anybody else for building purposes)—this would be under Pointe Guarde or the Rule 3 principle— or whether the price would be as building sites within the Basingstoke town (s. 15 principle). Lord Denning stated that the price should be as for building sites, not within the limits of the enlarged Basingstoke town, but at such distance as it was before Basingstoke was enlarged.

(*b*) It shall be assumed that planning permission would be given to any form of development specified in the present Schedule 8 to the *Town and Country Planning Act, 1971*, i.e. to 'existing use' developments (see Chapter 34).

(*c*) It shall be assumed that planning permission would be granted for developments of any class specified in a 'certificate for appropriate development' issued under ss. 17–22 of the *Land Compensation Act, 1961*. In addition, if there is a development plan, the assumption is that planning permission would be granted in accordance with the development plan in existence.

Point (*c*) requires some explanation. Where the land acquired does not consist of an area defined in the development plan as an area of comprehensive development or clearly allocated for residential, commercial or industrial purposes, it may be difficult to decide what planning assumptions are appropriate. In such a situation either party may apply to the local planning authority for a certificate stating what development might reasonably have been expected to be permitted if the land had not been subject to compulsory purchase. When such a certificate is issued, planning permission for development will be assumed in assessing the value of the land. The party may appeal to the Secretary of State against refusal of the certificate or its contents, with a further appeal (on limited grounds) to the High Court. A statutory instrument (Land Compensation Development Order, 1974, S.I. 539) contains detailed provisions about the issue of the certificate and appeals.

In a case when there is a development plan covering the area there may still be problems as to how to apply its provisions to the possibilities of development of the land being acquired. S. 16 of the *Land Compensation Act, 1961*, contains detailed assumptions as to how the development plan should be applied to the land in question. For example, the developer may, within the provisions of the development plan, elect a more or less lucrative development. For this reason permission would be assumed only if it is development for which planning permission might reasonably be expected to be granted.

38.3   Compensation for Disturbance

Where the land is compulsorily acquired, the owner is entitled to compensation not only for the value of his interest in land, but also for the loss he has suffered from being disturbed in the enjoyment of it. This principle is recognised by Rule 6 of s. 5 of the *Land Compensation Act, 1961*, but was also pronounced clearly in the leading case of *Horn v. Sutherland Corporation* (1941), when it was stated: 'The owner has the right to receive money payment not less than the loss imposed on him in the public interest, but on the other hand no greater.'

Although the principle is clear, the precise operation is not easy to ascertain, but from the numerous cases decided it appears that the following losses have been recognised:

(*a*) The cost of removal with initial expenses (e.g. alterations of curtains and carpets), but not the higher rent paid in the new place, as it is assumed that the higher rent is due to better premises.

(*b*) Incidental expenses, e.g. the notification of change of address, the transfer of telephones, new stationery, etc.

(*c*) Depreciation of fixtures due to removal.

(*d*) Depreciation of stock.

(*e*) Diminution of value of goodwill, if any.

(*f*) The cost of the surveyor who examined the new premises, even if he advised against buying them and the transaction did not materialise.

The *Land Compensation Act, 1973*, improved further the position of owners whose land has been compulsorily acquired.

A disabled person whose house has been constructed or substantially modified to meet his special needs is entitled to the reasonable cost of equivalent reinstatement (s. 45).

The small businessman over 60 years of age whose premises' rateable value does not exceed £2250 and who does not wish to relocate his business is to be compensated on a total extinguishment basis, provided that he undertakes not to dispose of the goodwill or to re-engage in a similar business (s. 46).

Part III of the *Land Compensation Act, 1973*, provides benefits for persons displaced from land. The scope of this Part of the Act covers not only an owner whose land has been compulsorily acquired, but also other persons who are displaced.

The payments are as follows.

(*a*) Home Loss Payment (*ss. 29–33*)

This is quite separate from any right to compensation or disturbance payment. It is paid as recognition of the upset and distress of the displaced persons whenever the authority purchases the land either compulsorily, or even by agreement, but, in the last instance, only when having the powers to apply compulsion. It is also paid to persons who are displaced as a result of a 'housing order' (e.g. on condemning the house as unfit for human habitation). It amounts to a sum equivalent to three times the rateable value, subject to a minimum of £150 and maximum £1500. Caravan dwellers, if not provided with another site, are also entitled to this payment. Even furnished tenants and tenants under a contract of employment are so entitled. The home lost must have been the only or main residence of the claimant for the preceding five years.

(b) Farm Loss Payment (ss. 34–6)

This is not a compensation for the loss of a person's farm. It is a payment with the purpose of offsetting any temporary loss of profit when the person starts farming elsewhere on land unfamiliar to him. It applies only to owner-occupiers or leaseholders with at least a three years' outstanding lease. Year-to-year tenants are thus excluded, but they are covered by existing legislation—namely, the *Compulsory Purchase Act, 1965* (s. 20), and by the *Agriculture (Miscellaneous Provisions) Act, 1968*—under which they are entitled to a sum equal to four times the annual rent (ss. 9 and 12). The farm loss payment amounts to the average annual profit over the last three years in occupation.

Both payments—the home loss and the farm loss—cannot be claimed by persons who served a blight notice requiring acquisition of their interest.

S. 37 (of the 1973 Act) gives authorities a discretionary power to make a disturbance payment to persons displaced (apart from agricultural tenants) if they are not entitled to the home loss payment. This provision applies to licencees and to persons who do not fulfil the occupational qualifications. Payment amounts to removal expenses and, in the case of business, to compensation for loss of goodwill.

Finally, ss. 39–43 impose on the local authority a duty to rehouse the persons displaced in suitable accommodation if it is not otherwise available. Instead of rehousing, the local authority may grant a mortgage to any displaced person who intends to buy a house.

38.4 Compensation for Yearly Tenancies and Lesser Interests

Although these persons are not entitled to receive the Notice to Treat, they are entitled to some compensation under s. 20 of the *Compulsory Purchase Act, 1965*. Their compensation is limited to the value of their unexpired term and for any other injury or loss they may sustain. In the case of a tenancy for business premises the tenant is entitled to compensation assessed under either this heading or under the *Landlord and Tenant Act, 1954* (as amended by the *Law of Property Act, 1969*), whichever is the greater.

Under the *Land Compensation Act, 1961* (s. 10), the acquiring authority may pay such reasonable allowance as it thinks fit in respect of removal expenses or loss by disturbance of trade or business to persons displaced from any house or other building. This Section covers cases where there is no legal duty to pay compensation, but where the acquiring authority considers that some payment should reasonably be made to the persons displaced, and the Section gives the statutory power to make *ex gratia* payments. These provisions are similar to s. 37 of the *Land Compensation Act, 1973*, but the latter Act imposed on the local authority a duty (and not only powers) to make the payments, albeit within somewhat narrower limits.

38.5 Compensation for Injurious Affection

Compensation for injurious affection may be defined as compensation for owners whose land is injuriously affected by the undertaking for which compulsory purchase has been effected.

Until a few years ago compensation for injurious affection was generally considered inadequate and for this reason the *Land Compensation Act, 1973*, improved the position of persons injured. However, as the 1973 Act generally did not amend existing provisions but only added new headings for claims, it is appropriate to discuss first the compensation existing under earlier legislation and then to deal with additional compensation provided by the 1973 Act. In this connection two types of claim should be separately considered:

(*a*) Claims where the land affected is held by the same person as the land taken.

(*b*) Claims where the land affected is not held with the land taken.

In the first category it must be shown that the land was held with the land compulsorily acquired although it is not required that it should be contiguous. The test is whether the possession of both pieces enhances the value as a whole (*Cowper Essex v. Acton Local Board*, 1899).

Compensation is due under two headings: loss of the value due to severance of a part of the land and injurious affection in the stricter sense (due to dust, smell, noise, loss of privacy, etc). The measure of damages is the depreciation of the value of the land.

In the second category, claims where the land affected is not held with the land taken are dealt with by s. 10 of the *Compulsory Purchase Act, 1965*, and its judicial interpretation in the leading case of *Metropolitan Board of Works v. McCarthy* (1874). Here the possibility of obtaining compensation is very limited.

Compensation is given as a substitute for damages due for any tort committed by the acquiring authority which are denied to the injured person because the acquiring body was acting under statutory authority. This means that it is due only if damages would be recoverable under the law of tort. It is due only if there is a physical interference with any right, easement or natural rights of the fee simple owner. The McCarthy case formulated the following conditions for claiming compensation:

(*a*) The injury must result from some act which was made lawful under the statutory powers granted to the acquiring authority.

(*b*) The injury must be such that it would be actionable but for the statutory powers.

(*c*) It must be injury to land and not injury to person or trade (a very severe limitation!).

(*d*) It must flow from the execution of work and not from the subsequent use of the land acquired (again a very severe limitation as some owners of land adjoining motorways know).

On the other hand, if the land of a third person is increased in value due to the execution of the work, no payment may be required from the lucky owner for this betterment.

Public dissatisfaction with the principles of compensation for land compulsorily acquired, and particularly for loss of amenity and depreciation of value arising from the public work, has been rapidly and justifiably increasing in recent years. The general purpose of the *Land Compensation Act, 1973*, is to introduce improved arrangements for dealing with the impact of public works on their surroundings and to secure that where private rights or interests are affected, reasonable compensation will be provided. The 1973 Act provides compensation for depreciation caused by the use of public works only and not for their execution (this is provided under McCarthy's rules). For this reason, although it is not clearly stated, it seems that the compensation provided by the 1973 Act is in addition to compensation due under the previous legislation.

Part I of the Act provides compensation for depreciation caused by use of public works. Persons entitled to compensation are:

(*a*) Owners and owner–occupiers of residential property.
(*b*) Owner–occupiers of agricultural units.
(*c*) Owner–occupiers of other land if the rateable value of this other land does not exceed £2250.

Compensation amounts to the depreciation in the value of the interest caused by physical factors, i.e. noise, vibration, smell, fumes, smoke, artificial lighting, etc., arising from the use of highways, aerodromes, or other public works which have immunity from actions for nuisance. Claims must be submitted within a period of six years, starting one year after the start of use.

The compensation payable on any claim is assessed by reference to prices current on the first day of the claim period, i.e. 12 months after the 'relevant date' (this is the date of opening of the highway or in other public works the day on which they are first used). Assessment is made under s. 5 of the *Land Compensation Act, 1961*, but Rule 5 (equivalent reinstatement) is excluded.

In assessing the claim it is assumed that planning permission would be granted only for the development specified in Schedule 8 of the *Town and Country Planning Act, 1971* (existing use developments).

The source of the physical factors causing the injury must be situated on or in the public works, except in the case of aircraft arriving to or departing from an aerodrome.

Where land is acquired from a person for the purpose of works to be carried out partly on that person's land and partly elsewhere, compensation for injurious affection is to be assessed by reference to the whole of the works and not just the part situated on the land acquired from that person. This provision reverses the decision of the Court of Appeal in *Edwards v. Minister of Transport* (1964).

Once compensation has been paid, any extension or intensification of use does not give any right to further compensation.

Part II of the 1973 Act provides for three ways of reducing the deleterious effects of public works: insulation, land acquisition or remedial works.

Sound-proofing of dwellings affected by noise from aerodromes was already provided by way of grants in s. 15 of the *Airport Authority Act, 1965*. This section has now been extended to include other buildings in addition to dwellings. S. 19 of the 1973 Act allows the Secretary of State for the Environment to impose a duty on the responsible authorities to insulate buildings against noise created by public works or to make grants towards the costs of insulation.

S. 22 confers on highway authorities the power to acquire compulsorily or by agreement land outside the boundary of an existing or proposed highway in order to reduce the adverse effects of the use of the highway on its surroundings.

S. 23 enables highway authorities to carry out certain works on the land belonging to them, e.g. erection of walls, planting of trees or laying out an area as grassland, or to make arrangements with owners to allow trees to be planted and maintained. Such agreements may include financial provisions, i.e. payments to the owners.

If public works temporarily but severely affect occupiers of adjacent dwellings, the public authority may pay reasonable expenses incurred to the occupiers by taking alternative accommodation for the duration of the works.

38.6   Compensation for Houses Unfit for Human Habitation

Special rules apply if a house is unfit for human habitation (see page 6) and it is compulsorily purchased by the local authority. This applies both to the purchase of individual unfit houses and unfit houses within a clearance area.

S. 59(2) of the *Housing Act, 1957*, provides that the compensation for houses unfit for human habitation should be the 'value of the land as a site cleared of buildings and available for development'. As a cleared site may sometimes command a higher price than the market value of the land with an undemolished unfit house, s. 10 and Schedule 2 of the *Land Compensation Act, 1961*, provide that only the latter price should be paid if it is lower than the price of the site value. This severe rule, however, is mitigated by both the *Housing Act, 1957*, and subsequent legislation, and these mitigations may be summarised as follows:

(*a*) When the house, although unfit, has been 'well maintained', Schedule 2, Part I, of the *Land Compensation Act, 1961* (as amended by the *Housing Act, 1969*), provides that the additional payment for the well maintained house should be the rateable value of the house multiplied by eight (Housing, Payment for Well Maintained Houses Order, 1972, S.I. 1972/1792). But the payment must in no case exceed the market value of the land with the house. Even a tenant (and not only the freeholder) who maintained the house well is entitled to this payment, which may cover the whole or the part of the house (if only a part of the house had been well maintained).

(*b*) If the house is 'owner-occupied', then the payment for the house will be the full market value; if, however, only a part of the house is owner-occupied, the additional payment (the difference between the site value and the market value) will be paid only for the part occupied by the owner or his family.

(*c*) If the house is the property of a private person carrying on a business there for at least the preceding two years, he is entitled to an additional payment amounting to the difference between the market value and the site value.

39

LANDS TRIBUNAL

39.1   Constitution of the Lands Tribunal

S. 1 of the *Land Compensation Act, 1961*, provides that where land is compulsorily acquired, any question of disputed compensation shall be referred to the Lands Tribunal and determined by them.

The Lands Tribunal, set up by the *Lands Tribunal Act, 1949*, exercises its jurisdiction not only in regard to compensation for land compulsorily acquired, but also in many other problems where the valuation of land is involved. S. 1 of the 1949 Act specifies the Tribunal's jurisdiction.

The Lands Tribunal consists of a President, who must be a person who has held a judicial office or a barrister of at least seven years' standing, and of other members who are barristers, solicitors or valuers appointed by Lord Chancellor after consultation with the President of the Royal Institution of Chartered Surveyors. The jurisdiction of the Lands Tribunal may be exercised by any one or more members of the Tribunal.

Under s. 3(4) of the 1949 Act, a decision of the Tribunal shall be final, but any person aggrieved by the decision may appeal to the Court of Appeal on a point of law.

39.2   Procedure before the Lands Tribunal

Special procedural provisions have been enacted by the *Land Compensation Act, 1961* (s. 2), regarding any proceedings before the Tribunal dealing with compensation for land compulsorily acquired. Under these provisions:

(*a*) The Lands Tribunal must sit in public.

(*b*) Generally, no more than one expert witness on either side may be heard.

(*c*) A member of the Lands Tribunal is entitled to enter on and inspect any land which is subject to the proceedings.

(*d*) The Lands Tribunal must, on the application of either party, specify the amount awarded for any particular matter subject to an award.

The detailed provisions covering procedure at the Lands Tribunal are contained in the Lands Tribunal Rules, 1975 (S.I. 299). Proceedings start by a notice of reference on a prescribed form and in the manner stated. A copy of the Notice to Treat and the Notice of Claim must accompany the notice of reference. The main points of the procedure may be summarised as follows:

The Tribunal has power to make an order for discovery of documents, particulars and interrogatories. Notice must be given if a valuer is to be called; the expert witness's valuation must be sent to the Tribunal.

The proceedings are opened by the party claiming compensation. Evidence is usually given orally, but with the consent of the parties or by the decision of the Tribunal affidavits are allowed. Witnesses make their depositions under oath. Any party may appear and be heard either in person or by counsel or solicitor, or by any other person allowed by leave of the Tribunal to appear instead of the party.

The decision of the Lands Tribunal is final, but there is an appeal by way of case stated on a point of law to the Court of Appeal. A party may ask for a preliminary hearing on a point of law with a view to lodging an appeal. If the Tribunal so decides, it may give an alternative finding as to the amount which it would have awarded depending on the decision on the point of law. This saves time and costs. The famous West Midland Case (see page 202) has been decided by the House of Lords on further appeal from the Court of Appeal in this way.

The acquiring authority may make an unconditional offer of compensation; if it is accepted, it will constitute a binding contract for sale. If such an unconditional offer is not accepted and the question of compensation is referred to the Tribunal, the amount of the offer must not be disclosed to the Tribunal until the compensation had been decided, but a copy of the offer may be sent to the Registrar, and shall be opened by the Tribunal after the decision has been made. Under s. 4 of the *Lands Tribunal Act, 1961*, if the Tribunal's award does not exceed the offer, the Tribunal (if there are no exceptional circumstances) shall order the claimant to bear the costs of the proceedings.

SUMMARY OF AMENDMENTS TO THE GENERAL DEVELOPMENT ORDER, 1977

On February 27, 1981, the Secretary of State for the Environment laid before the Parliament two Statutory Instruments, amending the General Development Order, 1977 (see page 137). The first is the Town and Country Planning General Development (Amendment) Order, 1981 (S.I. 1981/245); the second is the Town and Country Planning (National Parks, Areas of Outstanding Natural Beauty and Conservation Areas) Special Development Order, 1981 (S.I. 1981/246). They came into operation on April 1, 1981.

The first Order enlarges the classes of development for which planning permission is granted by the Order (i.e. which do not require any application for planning permission).

In Class I.1., which is set out in Schedule 1 (enlargement, improvement or other alteration of a dwelling-house), the limits imposed on the amount of any increase in the size of the original dwelling-house are changed from 50 cubic metres, or one tenth, to 70 cubic metres, or 15 per cent; but the original maximum (115 cubic metres) remains unchanged. In respect of terrace houses, however, the previous limits are retained.

New limitations are added to Class I.1.: if an extension to the dwelling-house is within 2 metres of the perimeter of the premises, the height of the extension must not exceed 4 metres. This limitation, however, does not apply to the insertion of windows or alterations to the roof.

Until now the erection of garages or coachhouses was counted towards the limits imposed on the enlargement of the house. Now this limit applies only if the garage or the coachhouse is erected within 5 metres of the dwelling-house. Otherwise it is treated as any other building within the curtilage of the dwelling-house (i.e. it may cover 50 per cent of the area of the curtilage, excluding the area occupied by the house itself).

Class III (change of use) is amended by the addition of permission for changes of use from light industrial buildings, or general industrial buildings (Classes III and IV of the Use Classes Order—page 137), to wholesale warehouses or repositories (Class X of the Use Classes Order); and from use within Class X to use as a light industrial building (with the area used for these purposes limited to 235 square metres).

Class VIII (development for industrial purposes) is amended as follows: the permitted increase (in cubic content) is changed from one tenth to 20 per cent and (in aggregate floor space) from 500 to 750 square metres.

The second (Special Development) Order, has application to National Parks, Areas of Outstanding Natural Beauty and Conservation Areas. It leaves unchanged the limits of permitted development (which applied to the whole country until April 1, 1981). However, it imposes the limitation now introduced in the General Development Order—namely, that no part of the enlarged building which (as a result of the development) lies within 2 metres of any boundary of the curtilage of the dwelling-house may exceed 4 metres in height.

Appendix 2

REVISION QUESTIONS

Below are questions which could form the basis of a possible examination. They are not necessarily in examination form but should aid students with revision.

Chapter/question

2/1 In what circumstances is a house considered by the local housing authority to be unfit for human habitation?

2/2 What are the powers of the local authority in respect of a house unfit for human habitation?

2/3 Who is considered to be a person 'having control of a house'?

2/4 When is a closing order of a house unfit for human habitation more suitable than a demolition order?

2/5 Describe the remedies available against a local authority's decisions in respect of a house unfit for human habitation.

2/6 When may a house be accepted as being in 'multiple occupation'?

2/7 Summarise the powers of a local housing authority in respect of a house in multiple occupation.

3/1 What conditions must exist to enable a local authority to declare an area a 'clearance area'?

3/2 What are the powers of a local authority in respect of a house situated in a clearance area?

3/3 Describe the circumstances in which a housing action area may be created. Outline the procedure of creating such an area.

3/4 What are the main legal consequences of declaring an area to be a housing action area?

4/1 Outline the system of grants available under the *Housing Act, 1974*, in respect of a dwelling-house.

4/2 What are the purposes of improvement grants? What standard should the house attain after carrying out improvements for which the grant was given?

4/3 What are the conditions under which a local authority must give an intermediate grant? Explain what is meant by 'standard amenities'.

4/4 For what type of house may a special grant be given? Explain the purpose of the grant.

4/5 Explain the conditions under which a repair grant may be given.

4/6 The *Housing Act, 1974*, introduced the Concept of compulsion in the improvement of houses. Explain in what circumstances these compulsory powers may be exercised.

5/1 Outline the powers of local authorities in providing houses.

5/2 Describe in what circumstances a tenant in the public sector has a right to acquire the house which is let to him.

5/3 Explain the rules governing the acquisition price of a house let to a tenant in the public sector.

6/1 The Housing Corporation has been given extensive powers of control over housing

213

associations. Explain the scope of this control and the legal consequences of a housing association being registered by the corporation.

8/1 How far did the *Law of Property Act, 1925*, simplify real property law?

9/1 Why may it be said that a lease, once created, has two aspects? What is meant by recognising a lease not only as a contract between the parties but also creating an estate in land?

9/2 What is the legal difference between leases and licences? Why is it important to distinguish between them?

9/3 Explain what is meant by a tenancy 'at sufferance' and a tenancy 'at will'. Give an example of each of these tenancies.

9/4 Describe the legal status of squatters. If your house has been taken over by them, what remedies are available to you?

10/1 How may a lease be created by (*a*) statute and (*b*) estoppel? Illustrate your answer by examples.

10/2 Which leases may be created by informal agreement (without a deed) and under what conditions?

10/3 An agreement to create a lease in the future requires some form under s. 40 of the *Law of Property Act, 1925*. What formality is required to create such an agreement and how is this statutory provision interpreted by the Courts?

10/4 'Lack of formality required by s. 40 of the *Law of Property Act, 1925*, cannot be a vehicle of fraud.' Explain this statement by reference to the doctrine of part performance.

10/5 If a lease for a period of over three years, which requires a deed for its validity, is agreed between the parties in writing but not under seal, what are the legal consequences?

10/6 Why can it not be said that a written agreement for a lease is as good as a lease created by deed?

11/1 What do you understand by a 'covenant' in a lease? Why is it necessary to accept some covenants as implied by law?

11/2 Give examples of implied covenants which cannot be contracted out.

11/3 Explain the meaning of and illustrate by an example a covenant for quiet enjoyment.

11/4 A landlord 'having given a thing with one hand, is not to take away the means of enjoying it with the other'. Explain this statement in the light of an implied covenant. Which one?

11/5 What is a 'peppercorn rent'? Why is it advisable to reserve it on granting some leases?

12/1 Describe to what extent a tenant of a dwelling-house is responsible for maintenance and repairs if there is no express covenant in the lease. Illustrate your views with examples.

12/2 Outline the landlord's responsibility for the repair of dwelling-houses: (*a*) under the *Housing Act, 1957*; (*b*) under the *Housing Act, 1961*.

12/3 To what extent does an express covenant for repair impose on the tenant a duty to rebuild a destroyed house?

13/1 What is the difference between assignment and underletting?

13/2 Which covenants bind the assignee of a lease, and which do not?

13/3 If a lease contains a covenant that the tenant cannot assign the lease without the consent of the landlord, is the landlord permitted to refuse his consent without giving any reasons? If not, explain in what circumstances he is entitled to object to the assignment.

14/1 It is the traditional view that a lease cannot be terminated by frustration. Explain the reason for this view and illustrate your answer by examples.

15/1 Describe what is meant by a fixture. To what extent can the tenant at the end of the tenancy remove fixtures installed by him?

16/1 Explain what is meant by 'distress'. Is the landlord entitled to distrain all goods belonging to the tenant?

16/2 Is the proviso for forfeiture of the lease an implied covenant, or has it to be clearly reserved? What kind of relief may the tenant obtain if the landlord seeks forfeiture of the lease?

16/3 What are the remedies of the landlord if the tenant commits a breach of a repair covenant?

17/1 Why is it necessary to protect tenants in modern society?

17/2 Describe briefly how far Party politics have shaped the policy governing the protection of tenants since the Second World War.

17/3 What is meant by 'statutory tenancies'? How do such tenancies come into existence?

17/4 Outline the provisions of the *Housing Act, 1980*, in respect of assured tenancies. Consider what impact these tenancies may make on the supply of houses for letting.

17/5 What are 'restricted contracts' under the *Rent Act, 1977*? Do you agree with the changes in the protection of some tenants introduced by the *Rent Act, 1974*?

18/1 Is security of tenure under the *Rent Act, 1977*, absolute? If not, outline the most important situations in which the Court may or must grant possession to the landlord.

18/2 In which circumstances may the landlord creating a tenancy ensure that he will be able to obtain possession of the dwelling-house when he intends to terminate the tenancy?

18/3 'The *Rent Act, 1977*, has become obsolete in view of shorthold tenancies created by the *Housing Act, 1980*.' How far does this statement reflect the true situation?

18/4 Point out the main differences between security of tenure afforded to tenancies of dwelling-houses enjoying full protection and to restricted contracts. What is the rationale behind these differences?

19/1 Explain the significance of registration of rent by the rent officer. In what circumstances may the parties ask the rent officer to cancel the registration of rent in a particular case?

19/2 What is a 'certificate of fair rent'? Explain the usefulness of this concept.

21/1 What is meant by the 'prescribed information' which any notice to quit of dwelling-houses must contain? Do you agree that this information should be inserted and why?

22/1 If a tenant of a long lease intends to aquire the freehold of the house, what conditions must be fulfilled to enable him to do so?

22/2 Describe the two options available to the tenant of a long lease under the *Lease-hold Reform Act, 1967*.

22/3 What is the principle guiding the price of acquiring the freehold under the *Leasehold Reform Act, 1967*, as amended?

22/4 What is the 'scheme of management' allowed by s. 19 of the *Leasehold Reform Act, 1967*? Explain the reason for creating this concept.

23/1 Describe the three aspects of protection afforded to business tenancies.

23/2 Short tenancies are excluded from the scheme of protection of business tenancies. How is it ensured that protection cannot be avoided by creating a sequence of short tenancies?

23/3 The main purpose of the *Law of Property Act, 1969*, Part I, which amended the law pertaining to business tenancies, was to plug the holes in the previous Acts. Outline the provisions of the 1969 Act which tried to achieve this end.

23/4 What is meant by 'proper improvement'? In what circumstances and by what procedure may a tenant improve his business premises against the wishes of the landlord?

23/5 In what three ways may a business tenancy be terminated?

23/6 In what circumstances would you advise the tenant to ask for a new tenancy of business premises?

23/7 Outline the most important reasons for which the Court may refuse to grant a new tenancy to the tenant.

23/8 If the tenant has improved the premises, how and when are these improvements taken into account in assessing the rent for the new tenancy granted by the Court?

23/9 What is an 'interim rent'? Why has this concept been introduced by the *Law of Property Act, 1969*?

24/1 How far are agricultural workers protected in their possession of 'tied cottages'?

25/1 How has the principle of town and country planning been realised in the *Town and Country Planning Act, 1947*?

25/2 Explain why it appeared necessary to amend statutory planning law some 20 years after the 1947 Act was passed. What were the main deficiences of the law as it existed before these reforms?

26/1 Examine critically the powers of central Government in planning. Do you consider that control is inadequate, or excessive?

27/1 Explain the differences between the 'old' and 'new' style development plan. Do you consider that the new style is an improvement on the old style and, if so, why?

27/2 How is it ensured that public participation occurs in the preparation of structure and local plans?

27/3 Describe the remedies of a person dissatisfied with the provisions of the structure or local plan. How do the authorities deal with such objections?

27/4 What are 'development plan schemes'? Explain the rationale of these schemes.

28/1 Give the general definition of development under the *Town and Country Planning Act, 1971*. Outline any qualifications of the main definition.

28/2 To what extent is the 'planning unit' an important consideration in deciding whether change of use is material? Illustrate your answer by examples.

28/3 Do you require planning permission for the conversion of a building into two self-contained flats without changing its external appearance?

28/4 Explain the role of 'use classes'. Why was it advisable to introduce this concept?

28/5 The General Development Order permits some developments without the necessity of applying for individual planning permission. Outline the main categories of these 'permitted developments'.

28/6 What is 'Section 53 determination'? Explain the reason behind this provision.

28/7 Outline the powers of local authorities to acquire land compulsorily.

28/8 Under s. 52 of the *Town and County Planning Act, 1971*, local authorities may enter into an agreement with private persons for the purpose of regulating a development. Explain the possible scope of such agreements and illustrate it by an example.

29/1 What certificates should an applicant for planning permission enclose with his application? What is the reason for this requirement?

29/2 What are 'bad neighbour developments'? What special requirements has an applicant for planning permission to fulfil if he intends to carry out one of these developments?

29/3 A local planning authority granting planning permission may do so subject to such conditions 'as they think fit'. What limitations have been imposed by Courts in interpreting this provision?

29/4 Illustrate by an example the fact that the Secretary of State dealing with an appeal by the applicant against a refusal of planning permission (or a granting of it subject to conditions) looks at the whole problem anew.

29/5 If a planning permission is granted, for how long is it valid? How is it ensured that the developer carries out the development within a reasonable time?

29/6 What is the role of the Planning Inquiry Commission? Give the reasons for creating this body.

29/7 What are 'conservation areas'? Outline the legal consequences of planning law in these areas.

30/1 Write a short note on (*a*) the four years' rule, (*b*) the established use certificate and, (*c*) the stop notice.

30/2 What are the necessary statements which an enforcement notice must contain?

30/3 Outline the grounds on which an appeal against an enforcement notice may be lodged.

31/1 Outline the relevant provisions of planning law for buildings of special architectural or historical interest.

31/2 What additional control exists for industrial buildings? Give reasons for this control.

31/3 What permissions are necessary to develop land as a caravan site? What conditions may be imposed by the authorities?

33/1 Explain the meaning of 'betterment value' of the land and outline the history of endeavours to secure this value for the community.

34/1 In planning law developments are divided into 'new developments' and (so-called) 'existing use developments'. Explain the difference between these two types of development and the different ways in which they are treated as far as compensation for planning restrictions is concerned.

34/2 In what circumstances may a local authority refuse compensation for restricting planning permission for new developments? Give reasons for these provisions.

34/3 Schedule 8 developments ('existing use developments') are divided into two parts. Why do only developments of Part II attract compensation?

34/4 In what circumstances does a local authority pay compensation for planning restriction of listed buildings?

34/5 State when a local authority has to pay compensation after the issue of a stop notice.

35/1 What is a purchase notice? In what circumstances may an owner of land serve it?

35/2 If your land loses its value due to planning proposals, what remedies are available? Outline the procedure in these cases.

36/1 Day-to-day administration of planning problems is entrusted to districts. Some problems are reserved for counties. Outline the counties' jurisdiction in planning.

36/2 To what extent are some appeals entrusted to inspectors nominated by the Secretary of State for the Environment and which appeals are reserved for the Secretary of State himself?

37/1 It is possible to discern four stages in the procedure governing compulsory purchase of land for public purposes. Describe these stages.

37/2 Explain the role of the compulsory purchase order in the process of compulsory acquisition of land. If a person feels injured by his land being included in such an order, what steps can he take?

37/3 When can a private person object to the compulsory acquisition of part of his property? Are the rules identical in respect of buildings and other properties?

37/4 Describe two alternative procedures which an acquiring authority may use in obtaining land already included in a compulsory purchase order. What are the advantages and disadvantages of either of these procedures?

37/5 Explain the legal character of a notice to treat. In what circumstances may the acquiring authority withdraw its notice?

37/6 It has been stated that the general vesting declaration procedure is eminently suitable for the compulsory purchase of land for motorways. Why?

37/7 'Once a highway, always a highway' is the rule at Common Law. How far has this rule been undermined by planning legislation?

38/1 Rule 1 of the *Land Compensation Act, 1961* (s. 5), states: 'No allowance shall be made on account of the acquisition being compulsory. How far has this principle been eroded by the *Land Compensation Act, 1973*?

38/2 What do you understand by an 'equivalent reinstatement'? In what circumstances is this rule applied by the acquiring authority?

38/3 Explain the principle of 'planning assumptions' in assessing the compensation for land compulsorily acquired. What is the rationale of these assumptions?

38/4 How far is 'compensation for disturbance' recognised as a heading of claim? What changes have been introduced by the *Land Compensation Act, 1973*, in respect of a small business whose owner is approaching retirement age?

38/5 Describe the main principle of 'injurious affection'. What changes in this respect have been introduced by the *Land Compensation Act, 1973*? Do you consider that this Act does full justice to persons injured by public works?

39/1 Outline the jurisdiction of the Lands Tribunal. What is meant by a 'seal offer'? Explain how far this prevents vexatious claims of owners.

Table of Statutes

Table of Statutory Instruments

Table of Cases

Index